AFTER HEAVEN

After Heaven

Spirituality in America since the 1950s

ROBERT WUTHNOW

UNIVERSITY OF CALIFORNIA PRESS

Berkeley   Los Angeles   London

University of California Press
Berkeley and Los Angeles, California

University of California Press, Ltd.
London, England

© 1998 by
The Regents of the University of California

Library of Congress Cataloging-in-Publication Data

Wuthnow, Robert.

  After heaven: spirituality in America since the
1950s / Robert Wuthnow.
     p.   cm.—
  Includes bibliographical references and index.
  ISBN 0-520-21396-3 (cloth : alk. paper)
  ISBN 0-520-22228-8 (pbk. : alk. paper)
    1. United States—Religion—20th century.
  I. Title.
  BL2525.W85   1998
  2009.973909045—dc21   97-45121
                                      CIP

Printed in the United States of America
9 8 7 6 5 4 3 2

Contents

Preface

More than a decade ago, while writing *The Restructuring of American Religion* (part of a series concerned with the public side of religion in the United States), I became interested in how developments in public religion were accompanied by equally profound developments in the ways people express their personal relationships to the sacred—in spirituality. The present book is an effort to make sense of these developments and through them to understand some of the larger issues that have come to confront U.S. society during the second half of the twentieth century.

Writing about spirituality is more difficult (and more speculative) than describing developments in religious institutions, for spirituality is hidden from view except insofar as it is talked about or revealed through personal interviews or indirectly in public behavior. Especially in U.S. culture, faith is considered a private matter, and it is practiced mostly in the quiet recesses of personal life. But most people do take an interest in spirituality, and their interest is expressed in ways that often reflect the wider culture. Spirituality consists not only of implicit assumptions about life but also of the things people talk about and the things they do: the stories they construct about their spiritual journeys, the prayers they offer, the inspirational books they read, the time they spend meditating, their participation in retreats and at worship services, the conversations they have about it with their friends, and the energy they spend thinking about it.

At its core, spirituality consists of all the beliefs and activities by which individuals attempt to relate their lives to God or to a divine being or some other conception of a transcendent reality. In a society as complex as that of the United States, spirituality is expressed in many different ways. But spirituality is not just the creation of individuals; it is shaped by larger social circumstances and by the beliefs and values present in the wider culture. I am especially concerned with these larger meanings and influences.

The primary material for this book is of three kinds. My research team and I interviewed two hundred people who talked in detail—often for as long as five to seven hours—about their spirituality as part of a larger project on spiritual journeys and devotional practices. The people we interviewed are not a random cross-section of the population, but they encompass much of the diversity that characterizes our society. They range from men and women in their teens to those in their nineties, people with virtually no formal education and people with advanced academic degrees, people working in many different occupations, and people from a wide variety of religious, racial, and ethnic backgrounds. Second, I draw on existing research studies, influential scholarly interpretations of U.S. religion and culture that have been published over the past several decades, and popular books and articles about various facets of spirituality. Finally, I base my conclusions on several dozen large-scale opinion surveys.

The three kinds of evidence are complementary. The in-depth interviews provide illustrative material that helps make the discussion concrete and that shows how particular individuals make sense of spirituality in their lives. The published materials help to draw out the connections between themes in the lives of individuals and developments in the wider culture. The surveys permit statements to be made about trends in beliefs or about changes in other social conditions; they are also useful for pinning down statistical relationships among some of these changing beliefs and the social conditions that have influenced them. By bringing these kinds of evidence together, I try to suggest both how the meanings of spirituality have changed over the past half century and how these meanings have stayed the same.

This is a broadly interpretive book. It builds on a lifetime of reading and writing about religion in the United States, makes use of other studies that I have conducted, and brings together material from history, literature, philosophy, and theology. It is my attempt to make sense of the many scattered developments that have been changing U.S. spirituality by relating them to each other and to larger changes in society.

I am especially grateful to the people who participated in the interview phase of the research. They spoke candidly about their lives, and they tried to present the complexities and ambiguities with which they struggle as they attempt to practice spirituality. To protect their anonymity, I have altered names and places and withheld other identifying personal characteristics. But they are real people and their stories reflect the realities that many of us have experienced in our own spiritual journeys.

During the process of writing this book, many people made places available to me in which to discuss preliminary ideas and to receive constructive comments and criticism. I wish to thank Craig Dykstra for hosting a discussion of some of the ideas around which this book is organized in Indianapolis and Dorothy Bass, Jeanne Knoerle, Fred Hofheinz, and James Wind for taking part in that discussion. Fred Burnham at Trinity Institute in New York hosted a similar event that was also helpful in shaping some of the early ideas for the book. Special thanks go to the following for opportunities to present other parts of the argument as it began to take shape: Peter Berger and Robert Hefner at Boston University; Victor Furnish and William Babcock, who organized a colloquy on religion and spirituality at Southern Methodist University; John Mason, Stan Gaede, and Timothy Clydesdale, who organized a day of formal and informal discussion of these issues at Gordon College; Robert Royal at the Ethics and Public Policy Center in Washington, D.C.; and Kathleen Joyce, who gave me an opportunity to present some of this work at Duke University. Several other gatherings and conferences made it possible for me to receive feedback from clergy, seminary professors, and heads of denominations. The research itself was funded through a grant from the Lilly Endowment. I was ably assisted in the collection, transcription, and organization of the interview data by Natalie Searl, John Evans, Courtney Bender, Robin Rusciano, Wendy Young, and Diane Winston. Martha Sharp helped with library tasks, and Cindy Gibson provided administrative assistance. Jody Davie and David Hackett read parts of the manuscript and gave me valuable comments. Doug Arava at University of California Press provided extensive substantive comments and patiently shepherded the manuscript through several revisions.

As always, my deepest debt is to my wife, Sara, a true practitioner of spirituality and my closest companion in my own journey. Our children, Robyn, Brooke, and Joel, are explorers of spirituality in their own ways too. I have written this book with the special hope that it will be of value to them and to their generation as we enter the next millennium.

CHAPTER One

From Dwelling to Seeking

*J*udging from newspapers and television, Americans' fascination with spirituality has been escalating dramatically. Millions of people report miraculous interventions in their lives by such forces as guardian angels who help them avoid danger and spirit guides who comfort them in moments of despair. Faced with death, many people report seeing a brilliant tunnel of light that embraces them in its mysterious glory—and live to write best-selling books about these experiences. When pollsters ask, Americans overwhelmingly affirm their faith in God, claiming to pray often to that God, and testimonials of personal encounters with God enliven late-night radio programs and spark controversy on afternoon television.[1] Some observers proclaim that the dry spell of secularism is over; others wonder whether "spiritual" has become synonymous with "flaky."

To be sure, the character of spirituality appears to be changing. Despite evidence that churches and synagogues are, on the surface, faring well, the deeper meaning of spirituality seems to be moving in a new direction in response to changes in U.S. culture. Indeed, the foundations of religious tradition seem to be less secure than in the past. Insisting that old phrases are cant, many Americans struggle to invent new languages to describe their faith. As they do, their beliefs are becoming more eclectic, and their commitments are often becoming more private. Newscasters and talk-show hosts are eager to capitalize on this mood, offering simplistic views of where the United States is headed.

But there are deeper reasons for asking how spirituality is changing. Consider the fact that growing numbers of Americans say they are spiritual but not religious, or that many say their spirituality is growing but the impact of religion on their lives is diminishing.[2] How is this possible? Does it suggest that spirituality is becoming anything individuals want it to be? Or consider the fact that most Americans say their spirituality is private—that it must develop without the guidance of religious institutions. Does spirituality mean becoming more concerned with the quest for personal identity and less concerned with civic responsibilities? Are the clergy losing influence in relation to other sources of spiritual insight?

Historical perspective underscores the importance of these developments. At the start of the twentieth century, virtually all Americans practiced their faith within a Christian or Jewish framework.[3] They were cradle-to-grave members of their particular traditions, and their spirituality prompted them to attend services and to believe in the teachings of their churches and synagogues. Organized religion dominated their experience of spirituality, especially when it was reinforced by ethnic loyalties and when it was expressed in family rituals. Even at mid-century, when the religious revival of the 1950s brought millions of new members to local congregations, many of these patterns prevailed. Now, at the end of the twentieth century, growing numbers of Americans piece together their faith like a patchwork quilt. Spirituality has become a vastly complex quest in which each person seeks in his or her own way.

SEEKING THE LIGHT

In addition to their places of worship, many Americans now find inspiration at counseling centers and from popular authors and spiritual guides. Growing numbers of people shop for spirituality at New Age and recovery bookstores or pick up spiritual tips from films, talk shows, and news specials on television. Even those who are deeply involved in churches and synagogues have increasingly made difficult decisions about which congregation to join, how long to stay, and whether to supplement their participation with input from other sources. Many people take classes that expose them to science, secular philosophy, and the teachings of world religions. Large numbers of Americans participate in self-help groups, struggle with addictions, undergo therapy, and are exposed to endless sensationalism about spirituality in the media. Collectively, Americans have witnessed wars and genocide on a scale that raises fundamental spiritual questions. They have seen public figures murdered and watched as violence and drugs consumed their children. Many

Americans have experienced unparalleled affluence and many have attained advanced degrees. Yet they have found that their personal lives are filled with advertisements and anxiety.

These developments cannot have taken place without altering Americans' sense of the sacred, but observers have been slow in coming to terms with these changes. Activists have worried about the public role of religion, decrying its exclusion from schools, laws, and government, and fretting over infringements of church-state separation; and yet relatively little attention has been paid to what is happening in personal convictions about the sacred. Over a longer period, scholars have talked about the decline of the sacred, seeing it being replaced by secularity, but have failed to see fully how understandings of the sacred were changing.

Little wonder, then, that spirituality has become such a confusing topic. Journalists write about wiccans and gun-toting fundamentalists, but acknowledge privately that they are missing the bigger picture. Many people wonder whether the decline they see in their own congregations is indicative of something wider, whether the fringe groups they read about in the newspapers are characteristic of the majority, and whether young people are still searching for answers in the same places that their parents and grandparents did. Even social observers who have little personal interest in religion have been forced to consider the dramatic implications that a major transformation in spirituality could have for U.S. society.

The thesis of this book is that a profound change in our spiritual practices has indeed taken place during the last half of the twentieth century but not in the usual sense. My focus is not on laws against reading the Ten Commandments in classrooms or on how many people belong to religious organizations. I am interested in the more subtle reordering that has taken place in how Americans understand the sacred itself. In brief, I argue that a traditional spirituality of inhabiting sacred places has given way to a new spirituality of seeking—that people have been losing faith in a metaphysic that can make them feel at home in the universe and that they increasingly negotiate among competing glimpses of the sacred, seeking partial knowledge and practical wisdom. A consideration of these two kinds of spirituality, I want to suggest, also reveals their limitations and provides reason for serious consideration of a third alternative.

HABITATION AND NEGOTIATION

A spirituality of dwelling emphasizes *habitation:* God occupies a definite place in the universe and creates a sacred space in which humans too can dwell; to inhabit sacred space is to know its territory and to feel secure. A spirituality of seeking emphasizes *negotiation:* individuals search for sacred moments that reinforce their conviction that the divine exists, but these moments are fleeting; rather than knowing the territory, people explore new spiritual vistas, and they may have to negotiate among complex and confusing meanings of spirituality.

The one form of spirituality is not entirely new, nor is the other completely out of vogue. Indeed, the world's great religious traditions have been able to supply rich imagery that appeals to both kinds of spiritual interests. In settled times, people have been able to create a sacred habitat and to practice habitual forms of spirituality; in unsettled times, they have been forced to negotiate with themselves and with each other to find the sacred. Settled times have been conducive to an imagery of dwellings; unsettled times, to an imagery of journeys. In one, the sacred is fixed, and spirituality can be found within the gathered body of God's people; in the other, the sacred is fluid, portable, and spirituality must be pursued with a sense of God's people having been dispersed.

In Western religion, habitation spirituality is suggested in stories of the Garden of Eden and of the Promised Land; it consists of temple religion; and it occurs in the time of kings and of priests. A spirituality of seeking is tabernacle religion, the faith of pilgrims and sojourners; it clings to the Diaspora and to prophets and judges, rather than to priests and kings. The one inheres in the mighty fortress, the other in desert mystics and itinerant preachers. The one is symbolized by the secure life of the monastery, the cloister, the shtetl; the other by peregrination as a spiritual ideal. The difference is depicted lyrically in the story of the Shulamite woman who at first revels in the security of her spiritual home—"our bed is green/the beams of our houses are cedar/and the rafters of fir"—and who then wanders, seeking restlessly to find the warmth she has lost—"I will rise now . . . /and go about the city/in the streets and in the squares/I will seek the one I love."[4]

In social theory, a spirituality of dwelling is reminiscent of Aristotle's insistence that the patriarchal family supplies the fundamental model of social order and of Emile Durkheim's definition of religion as beliefs and practices that "unite into one single moral community" those who adhere to them. A spirituality of seeking is more akin to Plato's emphasis on the origins of society in the varied gifts of the individual and in Max Weber's metaphor of religion as a "switchman" guiding the ethical inclinations of individuals in their contemplative activities or in their worldly occupations. With Durkheim, a spirituality of dwelling pays considerable attention to ways of distinguishing sacred habitats from the profane world and to rituals that dramatize these differentiations. With Weber, a spirituality of seeking pays virtually no attention to the contrast between sacred and profane, or to the use of spatial metaphors, but concentrates on that mixture of spiritual and rational, ethical and soteriological, individual and collective activities whereby the person in modern societies seeks meaning in life and tries to be of service to others.[5]

A spirituality of dwelling requires sharp symbolic boundaries to protect sacred space from its surroundings; a spirituality of seeking draws fewer distinctions of such magnitude. Illustrating the difference, Max Lerner once wrote, "One might agree with Durkheim that 'the contrast between sacred and profane is the widest and deepest the human mind can make.' Yet for myself I find all sorts of things . . . to be sacred."[6] Rather than being in a place that is by definition spiritual, the sacred is found momentarily in experiences as different as mowing the lawn or viewing a full moon.

One form of spirituality seems more secure; the other appears to be less constraining. This difference does not make one more desirable than the other however. For instance, both types of spirituality offer freedom, but the meaning of freedom is quite different in the two. Places that are familiar offer the freedom of not having to worry about where one's next meal is coming from because caring people and known resources are always at one's disposal. A spirituality of dwelling can provide healing, even levity, because of the opportunity to share responsibilities with other inhabitants. Ann Truitt describes this experience as "the light-hearted feeling of being in a litter" of kittens.[7] Each occupant is, in a sense, inconsequential and thus able to relax, relieved of taking oneself too seriously or of striving too hard to be outstanding. In contrast, processes of seeking provide the kind of freedom that comes from not worrying about achieving any particular objective, of determining, as Thomas Merton wrote, not to be "bound by an inexorable result [but to be] like the birds or lilies . . . without care."[8]

The contrast between these two kinds of spirituality is profoundly evident in the sixth-century Rule of Saint Benedict, which asks monks to take vows of stability, *conversatio*, and obedience. Stability emphasizes settledness; *conversatio*, change; and obedience suggests a need for commitment to both. Some interpretations associate stability with the monastic family, with physical work within the monastery, and with a commitment to a local orientation that resists searching for greener pastures elsewhere. *Conversatio* is more difficult to interpret (and for this reason is often left untranslated). It connotes the changeable life of the

spirit, especially the ephemeral qualities of the Holy Spirit as opposed to
the enduring character of God the Father. *Conversatio* is a commitment
to live faithfully in unsettled times and to keep one's life sufficiently unsettled to respond to the changing voice of God. It emphasizes vulnerability as a basic fact of the human condition and mystery as a characteristic of the sacred. Whether one style is favored or the other, the Rule
of Saint Benedict encourages its followers to recognize that both styles
require humility as a condition for inward growth and dedication.[9]

The wisdom of Saint Benedict is that dwelling and seeking are both
part of what it means to be human. The desire for dwelling is evident in
the fact that many people associate God with churches and synagogues
and in the fact that humans build temples and construct altars as places
to worship. It is illustrated by the powerful feelings that are aroused by
memories of the homes in which people were raised and by the loss experienced when people are uprooted from their communities of origin.
For this reason a human habitat frequently takes on sacred meanings,
becoming a home that—in Mark Twain's words—has "a heart and a
soul," an abode that can be lived in with "grace and in the peace of its
benedictions."[10] As individuals journey through life, they continually
seek attachments to special locations, such as their places of birth, childhood haunts, colleges and universities, nation, a favorite vacation spot,
or a comfortable space in which to relax. Indeed, the experience of being "claimed by feelings" transforms these pieces of the environment into
"places." "We are homesick for places, we are reminded of places,"
writes Alan Gussow; "it is the sounds and smells and sights of places
which haunt us and against which we often measure our present."[11]
Equally strong is the human desire to be part of an unfolding process,
to negotiate, to be on the road, to experience novelty, and to grow. Places
become boringly the same, stifling imagination to the point that a person feels compelled to move on. Seeking is illustrated by people's insistence that the sacred cannot be known fully and by their knowledge that
they are mortals whose lives are constantly in transition.

Despite the fact that dwelling and seeking are familiar aspects of human life, the circumstances in which people live typically reinforce one
or the other of these orientations to a greater extent in different historical periods. With relative stability, a spirituality of dwelling can be a
compelling way of thinking about the universe, whereas times of uncertainty and change are more conducive to seeking. People who enjoy
the security of well-established homes and of enduring communities
and who live orderly lives with familiar routines and organized roles

can imagine that God is indeed in heaven and that the sacred may be worshiped within predefined spaces. People who are faced with a dizzying array of choices and who experience so much uncertainty and change that they must negotiate and renegotiate their relationships, if not their very identities, are likely to find it easier to imagine that the sacred manifests itself at odd times and in less predictable ways. At any historical moment, some people live more settled lives than others, yet it is not entirely the character of individual life that is at issue but the nature of institutions. In institutions the resources on which individuals rely for their ideas about the sacred are shaped. Paying attention to the relative emphasis on dwelling and on seeking, as well as to the social conditions that reinforce these orientations, is thus a way of clarifying how dominant understandings of spirituality have been changing.

There are many ways of experiencing the shift from dwelling to seeking. For some people, the shift is experienced as living no longer within a sacred space but between sacred spaces. At one time, people were residents of their communities; now they are commuters. Thus images of stable dwellings have increasingly been replaced by images of those who have left home: the migrant worker, the exile, the refugee, the drifter, the person who feels alienated or displaced, the person lost in the cosmos, the traveling salesman, the lonesome net surfer, the lonely face in the crowd, the marginal person, the vagrant, the dispossessed or homeless person. The same is true of spirituality. At one time, people identified their faith by membership; now they do so increasingly by the search for connections with various organizations, groups, and disciplines, all the while feeling marginal to any particular group or place. For some people, the shift is analogous to changes that have taken place in the economy. They no longer depend primarily on producing durable goods; instead, they produce services and information. In their faith, they once relied heavily on bricks and mortar, on altars, and on gods who were likened to physical beings and who called them to dwell eternally in sacred places. Now they concentrate on information flows—ideas that may help with the particular needs they have at the moment but that do not require permanent investments of resources. Other people experience change as a shift from spiritual production to spiritual consumption. They used to produce offspring for their churches and synagogues, send out missionaries and evangelists to convert others, and spend their time working for religious committees and guilds; they now let professional experts—writers, artists, therapists, spiritual guides—be the producers while they consume what they need in order to enrich themselves spiritually. In other ways, the shift from dwelling to seeking influences images of what it means to be spiritual. Faith is no longer something people inherit but something for which they strive. It provides security not by protecting them with high walls but by giving them resources, by plugging them into the right networks, and by instilling the confidence to bargain for what they need.

As Americans undergo this transition, they do not experience it as a linear shift but as a combination of past realities and present possibilities. Spirituality is an assortment of activities and interpretations that reflect the past, that include new ways of understanding the past, and that envision on the horizon something distinctly different from the past. If spirituality once provided people with a sacred home, they do not simply abandon the quest for such a home but rethink what a home may mean now that they feel spiritually homeless. They use the faith of their parents and grandparents as ways to identify their own, if only in contrast. The older generation could take their faith for granted, people tell themselves, but they have to work hard to maintain their own.

Although spirituality is always deeply personal rather than theoretical, the present shift implies a change that is sometimes expressed in abstract language about world-views and philosophies of life. A spirituality of inhabiting emphasizes an orderly, systematic understanding of life. Having a sheltering canopy that protects people from chaos is essential, and it is possible for those who live within a spiritual habitat to be relatively confident in their knowledge of the sacred. A spirituality of journeying is less likely to generate grand conceptions of the universe and more likely to invoke a pragmatic attitude that "advises us to try whatever promises to work and proves to be useful as the mind adjusts to the exigencies of events."[12] A negotiated spirituality offers fleeting encounters with the sacred—like a sustaining force behind an individual, felt momentarily as he or she teeters on a slippery rock in the river. Implicitly, this shift consists of movement away from a denial of doubt (shielding people from questions about the existence of God) to a redefinition of doubt as the essence of reality (uncertainty as a feature of the human condition). God's presence has to be verified with special appearances, such as near-death experiences and angels.

The shift from dwelling to seeking is also implied in changing understandings of institutions. The older pattern was tightly bounded and hierarchical, prescribing behavior through a formalized set of rules; individuals were expected to conform to these rules, indeed, to internalize them. Institutions were literally the building blocks of society, tightly cemented together and containing mass, like a brick. They provided the fortresses in which people needed to work in order to get anything done. Everything outside institutions was either strictly mental or of little consequence. The newer pattern emphasizes looser connections, diversity, and negotiation; practical activity takes precedence over organizational positions. Rather than rules, symbolic messages prevail. People do institutional work not simply by performing tasks but by engaging in performances. Display and image become increasingly important. Thus, instead of speaking about statuses and roles, people talk about making decisions, searching among options, and presenting themselves in the best light.[13]

Architecture and liturgy reflect these changes. In the past, places of worship were distinct buildings that drew people to leave the everyday world and enter a sacred space; now they are often nondescript, functional buildings that look like shopping malls and offices and that remind people of everyday life. Liturgy has shifted from providing a uniform experience (perhaps said in Latin or Hebrew) to providing a highly variable one that encourages shopping and comparisons. Previously, people participated as members, expecting to live nearby and contribute primarily to the support of the organization; now they are drawn by specific activities that they may support, such as a flower sale, the choir, or a marriage-encounter session.[14] In a dwelling-oriented spirituality, sacred space is set apart by formal dress; in seeker-oriented spirituality, casualness of dress blurs the boundaries between liturgy and everyday life. In the former, liturgy emphasizes texts and music in which "there is a kind of supernatural geography, a territory of faith, in which believers see themselves depicted as part of the great community of believers down the years all moving towards God's final sacred place"; in the latter, texts and music deal less with heaven as a place and more with momentary experiences of the divine.[15]

The newer understanding of institutions necessitates a shift in how individuals are viewed as well. In the older view people acquired social status in one of two ways: it was ascribed to them or they achieved it. Ascription meant being a member of a community, and identity was conferred by that community. Achievement meant expending effort to attain a position in an institution; the position was already there waiting to be claimed. In the newer view, status is attained through negotiation. A person does not have an ascribed identity or attain an achieved identity but creates an identity by negotiating among a wide range of materials. Each person's identity is thus understandable only through biography. The search that differentiates each individual is itself part of the distinct identity that person creates.

A spirituality of seeking is closely connected to the fact that people increasingly create a sense of personal identity through an active sequence of searching and selecting. In the older view, identity was manifested by the holding of predefined social positions within institutions. Moving up the ladder at work was a way of gaining a strong sense of who one was. Moreover, having multiple positions—in community organizations, at church or synagogue, within one's extended family—helped round out one's sense of identity. Private thoughts and feelings, doubts about who one was, or fantasies that one might be more than meets the eye were squeezed into the interstices of life at the margins of institutions. In the newer view, individuals are actively involved in creating and defining their jobs, in carving out spaces in which to work, and in securing resources from a variety of suppliers. Because their roles are not predefined, individuals have to worry about who they are, who they want to be, and how they want other people to perceive them. Self-definition is not necessarily more problematic, but it is understood to be more a matter of personal choice, more the result of an active process of searching, and more contingent on one's own thoughts and feelings than on the statuses that institutions confer. Questions about how much power individuals possess, the activities over which they have jurisdiction, and how they are going to package themselves become increasingly important.

As understandings of the sacred have changed, Americans have not lost interest in spirituality; if anything, interest in it has increased because its role in people's lives is more problematic. For many, the new understandings of spirituality nevertheless seem frightening and chaotic. When the sacred no longer has a single address, people worry that it may disappear entirely. Secularity seems on the verge of winning, for good or for ill. Many people remain convinced of God's existence but realize increasingly that the reality of their world is secular. Thus, they are constantly coming to terms with this secularity—and suffering the pangs of adjustment associated with acquiring any new status; like the newly arrived in a strange community, their spirituality has an arriviste or parvenu quality that gives it inconsistent and even bizarre formulations.

Much of Americans' current religious behavior can be understood as a result of this new confrontation with secularity. Some people revel in the fact that God is silent; some thrash about wildly in their attempt to rediscover the sacred; and some dig in their heels, arguing all the harder for the importance of older ways of understanding the sacred. In this respect, Americans are like people recently come into a great fortune. They do not know quite how to behave. They vacillate between the habits they have known and the new opportunities at their disposal. Compared with societies that have a longer history of secularity, the United States is in the throes of a major transition, and Americans are still experiencing all the turmoil of that transition. They are not marching steadfastly into a secular age but are reshaping deep religious traditions in ways that help make sense of the new realities of their lives.

THE SOCIAL FACTOR

If any single factor can be identified as the source of these changes, it is the increasingly complex social and cultural environment in which Americans live. As a people, Americans face conditions that are nearly out of control—environmental pollution, worldwide hunger and poverty, AIDS, crime, terrorism—and, as individuals, they know they can do little about these problems. Americans have created institutions to deal with the growing complexity of social life, but many of these institutions are now on overload; they have thrown the burden back on private individuals. In addition, in the United States, governing institutions have been reluctant to tell people what to think religiously or to limit the market of spiritual ideas; thus, there is profound confusion about how best to practice spirituality, especially because information now besieges people from all parts of the world, making particular religious traditions seem increasingly local and historically contingent. Thus, Americans are not simply people of faith who need to get religion back into the public life of their country; they are often confused individuals who are interested in spirituality but are unable to let organized religion solve all their problems and who therefore must work hard to figure out their own lives.

But broad uncertainties in the social environment are only part of the story. The religion industry is also responsible for the transformation that is taking place in spirituality. I use the word *industry* advisedly. Earlier in the century, scholars might have written about churches and religious leaders, congregations, denominations, and confessional traditions. Small gatherings of like-minded people who met for worship and prayer were the norm, and these gatherings often preserved the family and reinforced the neighborhood, even to the point of resisting pressures from the wider society. Religious leaders, however, were eager to make spirituality popular, to keep it relevant, and to adapt to changing times.

They became entrepreneurs, borrowing the tactics of bureaucrats and advertisers. They learned how to market religion, and they taught the faithful to become consumers.

For a time, the religion industry competed mainly with secular ideas and activities for the energy of consumers. In recent decades, however, the religion industry itself has experienced a significant expansion, and the boundaries between it and other industries have become blurred. Publishers, therapists, independent authors, and spiritual guides of all kinds have entered the marketplace. It is not surprising, therefore, that people shop for spirituality and that they do so in an increasing variety of ways.

Yet another factor that has contributed to changing conceptions of spirituality is what I call the conversation with our past. If Americans have been enticed toward new spiritual practices by social conditions and by religious leaders, they have conspired willingly in these developments. Each generation defines itself in comparison with previous generations by identifying with significant public events, such as a war, an assassination, or a protest movement, and letting these events become defining moments in their emerging conception of themselves. More important, people compare themselves with their parents, making assumptions about what their parents believed and defining themselves in relation to those assumptions. The present emphasis on seeking and negotiation is as much a reaction to how Americans perceive the past as it is an actual contrast to the past. If earlier generations found solace in a spirituality of inhabiting, people now take pride in the fact that they are seekers. These interpretations of who Americans are and of what they are doing serve reasonably well, but whether they will continue to serve well as new generations come to maturity is an open question.

The shift I describe in this book has not been automatic or inevitable but has been shaped by historical events. The story of America, Oscar Handlin observed, is a story of immigrants.[16] Until World War II, ethnic groups were still influenced predominantly by their immigrant experience. They came in search of a better life. Separately and collectively, they built institutions. They were in search of a home—physically and spiritually. In religion, they were not animists, but they did believe in creating sacred space within their families, in their congregations, and in their nation. The great age of empire building at the start of the century was put on hold only temporarily by the Depression and World War II. After the war, Americans returned feverishly to the task of building their various homes. If Levittown symbolized the new spate of homebuilding in the suburbs, the Cold War symbolized Americans' concern to have a safe nation in which to live, and the growth of churches and synagogues supplied a similar emphasis in spirituality. But the 1950s were to prove an exceptional decade, an ending as much as a beginning.

The 1960s forcefully created the realization that things were not so easily controlled. Race relations in the United States were out of control. The young president who dreamed of controlling the world was tragically slain—and people could not bring themselves to believe the tragedy was without larger significance. Increasingly, the offspring of those staid suburbs of the fifties were beyond the control of their parents. Institutions were being questioned, as was the identity of the nation. Religious leaders declared that God was dead. And new religious leaders rose up to take their place.

After a decade of questioning and unrest, many Americans were desperate to return to the past. As best they could, they rediscovered their conservative heritage and their evangelical Christian or orthodox Jewish roots. During the 1980s, many leaders talked heroically of family values, of the triumph of the democratic form of government and of capitalist economic organization, of a maturing of the American spirit, and of a calmer, more orderly, and more disciplined sense of spirituality. But increasingly people realized that returning to the past was impossible. Ronald Reagan was criticized as a president who lived more in a fictionalized past than in the present; the economic growth of the eighties was bought by mortgaging the future; and the business leaders who symbolized prosperity one year often faced grand juries the next.

Since the 1960s, a quieter change has also been taking place in matters of the heart, including the ways many Americans define themselves. Growing numbers of people have undergone therapy and participated in support groups that have encouraged them to rethink who they are. Terms such as *self-help* and *recovery* have taken on new meanings. Best-selling authors have counseled millions to look into their own souls and to get in touch with their inner selves. Ways to do this have proliferated. Religious leaders have run hard trying to keep up, often by bringing therapeutic motifs into their messages. A majority of the public has retained some loyalty to their churches and synagogues, yet their practice of spirituality from Monday to Friday often bears little resemblance to the preachments of religious leaders.

The full implications of this transformation are not yet clear. Like any such transition, however, this one has generated a great deal of collective anxiety. The newer understandings of spirituality are both liberating and frightening because they require people to do more of the work needed to understand spirituality and to put it into practice. As new-comers struggling to legitimate themselves in a new world, Americans often behave in ways that are as bizarre as they are hard to understand.

Certainly, however, the transformation of American spirituality poses new challenges for the public life of the nation as well as for individual lives. A great debate has erupted over the fate of religious values in our society. Some argue that religious values are being excluded vigorously, if inadvertently, from a growing number of institutions. Others deny the validity of this argument, pointing to the resurgence of religious groups in politics and to the vitality of standard religious indicators in the United States as compared with most other societies. Like many, I take comfort in the thought that the truth is somewhere in between. But the debate it-self is troubling. Behind the question of religion's influence is the issue of what religion is, not to mention the issue of what it should be. Do we cultivate spirituality in our personal lives? Does it shape the way we think and feel and behave? Are our children seeing how it influences us? Are we stronger, more virtuous, and of deeper character as a result?

Although the answers to these questions are up for grabs, I believe the United States is moving into an era of what might be termed a "thin consensus," in which relatively few values are held in common.[17] Most Americans may cherish democracy, fairness, and family, but they hold widely different views about what these terms mean. More important, the United States is entering a period in which it is becoming harder and harder to express personal convictions and to trust others who express theirs. Be-cause people have fluid identities as selves and as spiritual beings, they readily change their minds, but many also wonder how much they can trust themselves and their leaders if their minds are constantly in flux.

PRACTICES

If my analysis is correct, interest in spirituality will not wane as the United States enters the next century, but it will be increasingly difficult to determine precisely what spirituality means. Faced with growing un-certainties and with ample opportunities for choice, people will need to spend more time than ever before reflecting on the deep values that make life worth living and the sources of those values, including spirituality. If they are unable or unwilling to take their cues from a single member of the clergy or from a single congregation (or even from one religious tradition), they will nevertheless need to work hard at sifting through the many messages available about spirituality.

Dwelling-oriented spirituality is likely to remain an appealing alternative for many Americans, and religious leaders who promise secure spaces in which to worship God in familiar ways and to pursue personal happiness will be able to attract sizable audiences to these places. For them, the congregation's mission will be to provide a safe haven amidst the growing uncertainties of the world in which people live. Such leaders will need to draw distinctions between sacred space and the profane world, calling God's people to live apart from the world as a community, a family, a remnant. Within Christianity, denominations may be relatively unimportant compared with the warmth of the local church. But denominations may reinforce a dwelling-oriented spirituality by federating congregations, even by creating cartels that keep other people out or that preserve a kind of gentlemen's agreement about the sanctity of the United States as a nation.

But seeker-oriented spirituality will be more compatible than dweller-oriented spirituality with the changing lives that growing numbers of Americans are leading, offering them freedom to make their own choices about how to understand the sacred and exposing them to a variety of ways to worship. Many of these people will continue to find established religious organizations attractive, at least as one path for pursuing spirituality. For seeker-oriented spirituality, however, the congregation is less aptly characterized as a safe haven; rather, it functions as a supplier of spiritual goods and services. Large congregations offer a wide variety of goods and services, luring customers to come and to attend often in search of different gratifications—an Alcoholics Anonymous group, youth activities, a bowling league, book-discussion clubs. Smaller congregations function more as boutiques, competing by becoming very good at something special, such as a ministry to the homeless, music, or sponsorship of a peace coalition. In this mode, the congregation's mission is to expand its conception of itself, deploying the clergy as resources and developing networks that link together a wide variety of supportive organizations. Larger entities such as denominations will continue to be one of these networks. Their future may be that of the franchise chain, standardizing the product and enhancing customer satisfaction but mostly staying in the background, helping congregations to secure supplies and to compete with other franchises.

Yet neither of these styles is entirely satisfactory, nor is it enough to argue that individuals must simply find some way to combine both. Habitation spirituality encourages dependence on communities that are inherently undependable and fosters an idolization of particular places to the point that energies gravitate too much to those places rather than being deployed to the full round of human needs in a complex world. A spirituality of seeking, in contrast, is invariably too fluid to provide individuals with the social support they need or to encourage the stability and dedication required to grow spiritually and to mature in character. It was not without reason that the Rule of Saint Benedict emphasized obedience rather than stability or *conversatio* alone.

In my view, the ancient wisdom that emphasizes the idea of spiritual practices needs to be rediscovered; indeed, a practice-oriented spirituality should be considered seriously as an alternative both to dwelling and to seeking. Spiritual practices put responsibility squarely on individuals to spend time on a regular basis worshiping, communing with, listening to, and attempting to understand the ultimate source of sacredness in their lives. Spiritual practices can be performed in the company of others, and they are inevitably embedded in religious institutions, but they must also be performed individually if they are to be personally meaningful and enriching. Spiritual practices require individuals to engage reflectively in a conversation with their past, examining who they have been, how they have been shaped, and where they are headed. Spiritual practices have a moral dimension, for they instruct people in how they should behave toward themselves and with each other, but these practices are also an item of faith, encouraging people to walk each day with partial knowledge and in cautious hope.

Spiritual practices have been largely ignored in recent scholarship, especially in the social sciences, or they have been reduced to simplistic studies of prayer and of religious experience. As a result, some scholars have been tempted to think that religious communities are the answer to the problems of the United States; they have focused on congregations and religious membership, on the one hand, or on completely privatized, idiosyncratic, self-serving spirituality, on the other hand. Spiritual practice is a way of retrieving the neglected middle in our understandings of religion. People who engage seriously in these practices may be involved in religious communities, or they may be sojourners whose lives exist on the edges of these communities. But the quality of their faith is to be judged by the seriousness of time spent in worshipful communion with the divine and in the consequences of this time for the rest of their lives. Spiritual practices have been a vital part of all religious traditions. They should not be thought of as inward or mystical but as such an important aspect of spirituality that leaders as diverse as Augustine, Teresa of

Avila, Erasmus, Spinoza, John Wesley, Thomas Merton, and Abraham Heschel could all agree on their significance.

Practice-oriented spirituality preserves some of what has always attracted people to a spirituality of dwelling, for it too requires the setting aside of a space in which to meditate, to pray, and to worship, and in the confusion of everyday life such a space may be possible only by carefully demarcating it from its surroundings. Yet these spaces are negotiable, changeable, and the point of engaging in spiritual practice is not merely to feel secure in a sacred space but to grow increasingly aware of the mysterious and transcendent aspects of the sacred as well. Practice-oriented spirituality makes full use of the opportunities for exploration that are available in a complex market society, but it is also a way of imposing discipline on personal explorations. Above all, practice requires responsibility on the part of the individual practitioner rather than on the part of some community or the marketplace.

Practice-oriented spirituality can best be nurtured by practice-oriented religious organizations—that is, by churches, synagogues, mosques, temples, and other places of worship that define their primary mission as one of strengthening the spiritual discipline of their members. Such organizations will strive to give members both roots and wings—roots to ground them solidly in the traditions of their particular faith, wings to explore their own talents and the mysteries of the sacred.[18] In spiritual practice, religious institutions need to be conceived as facilitators, rather than as ends in themselves. Instead of drawing people in to do God's work in the organization itself, they need to send people out to do God's work in the world. In this view, clergy must serve as models of spirituality, rather than as guardians or shopkeepers.

An emphasis on spiritual practice is also a way of retrieving balance in the contemporary debate over the future of American democracy. For some, the solution to contemporary social ills is to chastise U.S. culture for its individualism, calling for a return to an idealized community that encourages loyalty, self-sacrifice, and civic responsibility. For others, the solution has been to assert the priority of fairness, rights, social justice, and strong institutions capable of protecting individual freedom as well as minimizing the human costs inherent in any complex system of economic exchange. The one solution errs in demeaning the individual and in valorizing largely unworkable notions of community; the other overemphasizes rationality and social programs. Spiritual practice invokes the tradition of hard work, individual initiative, and responsible civic participation that has served the United States in the past and that is still widely shared at present. In emphasizing the need to reflect and to deliberate on the ultimate sources of one's moral commitments, this tradition denies that either communities or legal systems have all the answers and insists that effort must be devoted to questions of value if one is to live more than a mediocre existence. The facile shopping for quick-fix solutions to spiritual problems has not served the United States well nor has the hope that people could simply settle into a spiritual community that would solve their problems. An important part of what must be done, therefore, is to recover an understanding of both the value and the urgency of spiritual practice.

In the final analysis, any challenge is best faced by first taking careful stock of where we are. My aim in writing this book is to help us understand how our spirituality—individually and collectively—has been reshaped by the social forces to which we have been subject in the twentieth century, not only so that our appreciation of the century past may be enriched but also so that our ability to meet the challenges of the century ahead may be enhanced.

CHAPTER *Two*

In the House of the Lord

ℛichard Foster's popular 1992 book on prayer opens with a passionate statement about Americans' insatiable longing for home. "For too long," Foster writes, "we have been in a far country: a country of noise and hurry and crowds, a country of climb and push and shove, a country of frustration and fear and intimidation." God "welcomes us home," Foster asserts, "home to serenity and peace and joy, home to friendship and fellowship and openness, home to intimacy and acceptance and affirmation."[1]

Foster's claim that spiritual happiness can be found by conceiving of God as an intimate friend may be debated, but the sacred home to which he appeals is recognizably a prominent idea in U.S. culture. Indeed, one way Americans have commonly understood their personal spirituality is as creating a sacred home in which to dwell. Foster's imagery of an intimate, happy, loving home conjures up traditional themes that remain appealing even at the end of the twentieth century.[2] But these themes have also been changing. Conceptions of spirituality rooted in familial, household, and other spatial imageries are grounded in social experience; thus, they have been altered by changes in the U.S. family in particular and in the social landscape generally. An example will set the stage for considering how these conceptions have changed.

AND I SHALL DWELL

Ned Stewart, a middle-class man in his late fifties who wears thick glasses and a blue cardigan sweater, has an understanding of spirituality that was shaped by growing up in the 1940s and 1950s. He was raised in a working-class neighborhood on the outskirts of Atlanta. Ned's parents sent him to Sunday school at the Baptist church they attended regularly. He recalls vividly one Sunday when he was seven years old. "The teacher was reading the Twenty-third Psalm. She read, 'Surely goodness and mercy shall follow me all the days of my life and I shall dwell in the house of the Lord forever.' I said to myself, 'I want that. That describes the kind of life I want to have.'"[3] It was a pivotal moment. At the end of the worship service that morning, Ned walked down the aisle and shook the preacher's hand. He didn't understand what he was doing, but he knew it had to do with joining the church and becoming part of "God's kingdom."

The desire to dwell in God's house continued to make sense to Ned as he grew older. Indeed, the Twenty-third Psalm still provides a narrative around which his orientation toward spirituality is constructed. Ned is a man who takes spirituality seriously. But he repeatedly returns to metaphors of home, place, security, and dwelling to describe its place in his life. After talking for several hours about his life, he says his faith can probably be summed up in one sentence: "Surely goodness and mercy shall follow me all the days of my life and I shall dwell in the house of the Lord forever."

Ned emphasizes metaphors of dwelling because he grew up in a community where family, church, and neighborhood were closely integrated: they provided a sheltered haven in which to dwell. His father was a lawyer who held an appointed office in the county, was active in local politics, taught Sunday school, and served on the deacon board at church—a public figure whose roles connected the family with the church and the wider community. His mother taught school before marrying but quit to raise Ned and his brother and sister. Other than going to church, she spent most of her time at home. Both parents were deeply devoted to their children and to the community. Ned's father had lived in near poverty during the Depression and he wanted to provide a good living for his children. But he was also committed to helping the needy, often by providing free legal advice. Ned's mother, worried by a younger brother who had become an alcoholic, focused on the moral training of her children but also helped start a rehabilitation center.

Church and family were virtually indistinguishable as houses of God. Every meal began with the family saying grace. At night Ned always said the following prayer with his mother: "Gentle Jesus, meek and mild, look upon this little child. Keep me safe until the morn." Looking back on his childhood, Ned believes his parents worked as hard as they did in order to keep the place in which they lived free from evil. There were often reminders (wayward relatives, public catastrophes) that it was not possible to keep the world safe, and this realization brought both parents closer to God. But they also succeeded fairly well at sanctifying their daily lives. It was hard to disconnect spirituality from the spatial metaphors of home and family.

AN EPIC QUEST

To understand what spirituality means to a man like Ned Stewart it is necessary to consider the extent to which U.S. culture associates spirituality with the idea of inhabiting a space that has been sacralized. Americans have never been animists, who believe that certain places literally embody the divine. Indeed, their formal theology distinguishes sharply between creator and creation. But Americans do believe that the sacred is more readily available in some contexts than in others: Christ's body and blood in the Eucharist, divine truth in sacred texts, vivid imagery of heaven as a literal place, cemeteries and shrines designated as hallowed ground, and special buildings consecrated as places of worship.[4]

Americans' attachment to sacred places is easy to miss because we have always been a transient people—"almost nomadic," the historian James Bryce wrote in 1888—a people whose credo is "here today, gone tomorrow."[5] Yet we take our homes, communities, and nation so seriously that we often invest these places with sacred meaning. Indeed, the sense of place that pervaded Americans' sense of spirituality in the years after World War II was in many ways not so different from understandings of spirituality that had been present throughout American history.

The first European settlers came to the New World because it offered a place in which to worship. They established colonies as holy places bound covenantally between people and God. Their daily lives were filled with manifestations of the supernatural—including superstitions about graveyards, illnesses, crops and animals, the moon, stars, the seasons, and holidays.[6] Much of the imagery that emerged during the founding of the republic pictured America as a promised land, a new Israel, a celestial city—all images of sacred space. The laws that were to play such an important role in protecting individual rights were built on arguments that European settlers were more civilized than North America's indigenous peoples, and these laws thus privileged another way of sacralizing space: homesteading took precedence over hunting and gathering.[7] To be civilized and to be chosen of God came early to legitimate Europeans' struggles to occupy the land. Waves of new immigrants during the nineteenth century extended this imagery, as they came to the United States in search of a new home and a better life.[8]

The Puritan legacy was an especially strong source of connections between spirituality and sacred space. Through their ideas about being a chosen people, their congregations, and their distinctive dress, the Puritans drew a close relationship between God and the places in which they lived. As the historian Daniel Boorstin explained in 1958, "The Puritan beacon for misguided mankind was to be neither a book nor a theory. It was to be the community itself."[9] Conversion, baptism, and communion functioned as rites of communal initiation, and periodic witch trials helped to define community boundaries.[10] Puritan clergy seemed intent on erecting high walls around consecrated space.[11]

The immigrant experience added a new conception of sacred space. Historians Oscar and Mary Handlin recognized that this experience was centrally about leaving home, seeking a place, and retrieving the lost home. "Always the migrants left because they had to," they wrote. "Yet in moving away, they wished to retain, preserve and strengthen the values of home. . . . Wherever [they] arrived, the need to re-create the place home had been became an overwhelming concern."[12] Native American writer Louise Erdrich characterizes European expansion into the New World in similar terms, calling it an "epic quest" to "find home," including "a grounded spirituality."[13]

It is not surprising that European Americans' spirituality came to have a strong connection with territoriality. Many of the immigrants had been reared in "territorial" congregations. They came from Scandinavian countries where Lutheranism was understood to be a territorial religion, from Catholic countries that divided their populations into local parishes, and from Jewish settlements that were geographically focused. In their new communities, the legal demarcations that governed conceptions of space—townships and counties—were often arbitrarily defined by land surveys; thus, religious communities were the more meaningful ways of defining social space.[14] "The church building itself," one historian has written, "became both the rallying point for the community and the main physical manifestation of new fellow-feeling."[15]

In an influential 1954 essay, historian Sidney Mead declared that "space came to take precedence over time in the formation of [Americans'] most cherished ideals." His argument, reminiscent of Frederick Jackson Turner's famous thesis about the role of the frontier in shaping American character, was that space itself had always been a decisive factor in how Americans understood their spirituality. From earliest times, European settlers became a new people because they were residents of a new land. They built settlements and described themselves as settlers—later as homesteaders. They inscribed religious practices within the boundaries of their settlements and lived peaceably with practitioners of different beliefs as long as all kept within their own spaces.[16]

Judging from their letters, immigrants often held a plain, uncomplicated image of God that was not connected to formal doctrine or for that matter to Jesus, Mary, sin, salvation, or religious rituals, but they stressed that God was close, always present, watching over the people and protecting them: their God was one with whom they could dwell.[17] Once they resettled, many immigrants lived in ethnic neighborhoods with the church or synagogue physically in the space they inhabited. Interviews with immigrants are replete with memories of going on Sundays from church to the park or to shops, with stories about walking to church or synagogue, with accounts of ethnic festivals being held at their place of worship, and with statements about being "home people" who seldom strayed far from their neighborhoods.[18]

The early decades of the twentieth century were deeply influenced by the immigrant experience; large numbers of people were themselves recent immigrants or were the children of immigrants. For many, spirituality was practiced within ethnic enclaves that gave it a distinct geographic identity. A man who still attends the same Hungarian Reformed church in which he was baptized in 1924 recalls that the church was always his second home. The first act of the previous generation when they came to the United States, he explains, was to build a church that doubled as a kind of social center for the community. For him, spirituality will always be associated with that special place.

A Jewish man who was born shortly after his parents' arrival in the United States in 1915 recalls vividly the link between faith and space that resulted in frequent turf wars between Jews and Catholics during his childhood. "We traveled in gangs for our own protection," he explains. "If you crossed anybody else's turf, you'd better be careful that you did it in company with somebody else, or at least have a group that was physically able to defend each other." Although he is still interested in spirituality, he misses the sense of being located in a sacred space like the one he knew as a child.

"Back home," wrote Will Herberg in 1955 (referring to Europe), "the church (or synagogue) had been, for most of [the immigrants], the meaningful center of life, the repository of the sacred symbols of community existence." Whether this was true is debatable, but Herberg was right in asserting, "As soon as they touched land in the New World, they set themselves to re-establishing [this center]."[19] Indeed, the church was probably more closely connected with home and community in the United States than it was in many parts of Europe. As an older man—who remembers growing up in the 1930s in a Methodist community where both his parents had been raised and where his father had started a blacksmith shop in the 1920s—observes, "Everyone went to church every Sunday and said a prayer at every meal. It was all just a part of our life. We didn't think it was unusual. It was just a normal thing to do."[20] His spirituality was normal because it was so deeply rooted in the place where he lived.

Another older man, a retired carpenter named Lee Ackerman, provides a graphic sense of how closely intertwined spirituality and consecrated space could be. As he reflects on what it has meant to be a person of faith, he is drawn to one of his earliest memories. He is walking home from church on a sunny Sunday afternoon in the fall, stopping at his grandfather's house and being given a brittle piece of black YNS licorice. As he reflects on this scene, he is able to articulate other features of it that linger in his memory. The road down which he has been walking is called Ackerman Road because it was the site of his grandfather's farm. The church from which he has come is a small, wooden structure, nearly square, with white stucco exterior walls, and on the inside are four rows of wooden pews facing a pulpit about ten feet long, in front of which is a wooden desk that holds papers used by the Sunday school superintendent. Lee remarks, although it was not part of his earliest memory, that the people who built the church early in this century paid $700 for the materials—and wondered how they could raise such a huge sum of money. He knows, too, from having walked the road so many times that the distance from the church, past his grandfather's farm, to his own house is exactly half a mile. Just beyond is where the Hollises lived, and over yonder, on the other side of the church, is where the Midlers lived with their five children, one of whom later married the

Hollis boy, with whom he often sat on those long Sunday mornings on the hard wooden pew.

Lee Ackerman dates his personal encounter with spirituality a few years after this. As was its custom, the church invited an itinerant evangelist each year to hold a series of revival meetings, and when Lee was nine, the evangelist was the Reverend I.N.H. Beame, who came and preached for two weeks, during which he stayed in the Ackerman's spare bedroom because they lived so close to the church. Toward the end of this fortnight, Lee decided to "accept Christ" and was baptized in the stream that ran down behind the church and through the back of his grandfather's farm. He says, "That's the thing that sticks out in my mind as the most vividly real."

It is unclear from his comment whether accepting Christ or being baptized in the stream was "most vividly real." In fact, the two are intertwined, just as his sense of spirituality is almost imperceptibly interwoven with his rootedness in this place. The stream in which he was baptized has been in the family for three generations and is now owned by one of his cousins. The people who attended the church lived nearby, forming a community of friends and relatives. The pastor, Benjamin Hottle, was a layman, or "free minister," as the people called him, who gave sermons and presided over meetings but earned his living as a farmer. Sometimes he took turns with Lee's grandfather, who was also a free minister. The Midlers were all related to Benjamin Hottle. So were the three Funk girls, who taught Lee's Sunday school class. There were also two large families of Kramers in the church.

As he talks about his spirituality, Lee uses the words *Christ* and *church* almost interchangeably, and he places both in a spatial context. "Christ was supposed to be the center of our lives," he asserts. When asked to explain, he says, "The church was the center of our lives. Our life revolved around the church. Going to church was the most important thing for us to do." Noting that there were no Little League teams in those days and that the church discouraged going to movies and dances, he says his family's "social life" focused mainly on the church. The annual church picnic, he recalls, was "the highlight of the year."

For many Americans of this generation, spirituality was concentrated more in churches and synagogues than it was practiced at home. Yet a study of autobiographies written during the first half of the twentieth century found extensive remarks about the devotional rituals of families as well: before the advent of radio parents read to children from such works as *Pilgrim's Progress* and John Foxe's *Book of Martyrs,* morning or evening prayers were often said aloud, and table grace was a common feature of family meals.[21] Ray Stannard Baker's memory of his father praying is typical: "I can see the little boy who was myself kneeling there on the carpet with his nose buried in the queer musty-smelling upholstery of the living-room chair, listening intently to what Father said to God."[22] For him, God and home were forever intertwined.

Lee Ackerman's home was also a place in which a spirituality of dwelling was reinforced. As an extension of the church, it was part of the sacred space in which Lee came to understand spirituality. Besides the Reverend Beame, most of the other evangelists and traveling ministers stayed there: George Landis, A. C. Bauer, Joe Whittaker. Lee remembers them well. Whittaker was the one who ate with his plate precariously close to the edge of the table. Bauer went out in the mornings and chopped wood for exercise. Landis played the saxophone. They'd sit around after supper and tell stories until bedtime.

The home was a sacred space for Lee in other ways too. Every morning before he left for school, his parents called him and his three siblings to the dining room for Bible reading and prayer. Usually, the children would take turns reading. At every meal, his father said a prayer, and in the evening Lee said a prayer before going to bed. Lee learned early that God was always watching him, so it didn't make sense to misbehave and try to hide it. He says that disobeying his parents and disobeying God were "one and the same thing." He also memorized verses, proudly displaying a plaque on his bedroom wall that he received for memorizing a certain number of them. He was especially fond of the picture on the dining room wall showing Jesus talking to the children.

Experiences such as these were reinforced by an ideal of domestic tranquility that arose with the middle class in the nineteenth century and dominated thinking about the home during the first half of the twentieth century. Associated with the development of commerce, industry, and the middle class, this ideal emphasized marital stability, the rearing of children, economic autonomy, and devotion to moral standards of personal discipline.[23] As homes became more comfortable, they took on greater symbolic significance (as havens, castles, and habitats). Keeping them well furnished and spotless took more of the family income and became more closely identified with the roles to which middle-class women were to aspire (often with prompting from the clergy). As Lee Ackerman's experience suggests, homes also became sacralized through the purchase of family Bibles, by being adorned with religious pictures, and through the practice of daily devotionals.[24]

Writing in 1939 about his upbringing in Wilmington, Delaware, *Saturday Review* editor Henry Seidel Canby captured an important part of the domestic ideal. "Home was the most impressive experience in life. Our most sensitive and our most relaxed hours were spent in it. Time moved more slowly there, as it always does when there is a familiar routine with a deep background of memory. . . . The ideal was . . . a house where the family wished to live even when they disliked each other."[25] Such homes were fairly recent inventions, and they lived perhaps more in memory than in fact; nevertheless, it is clear that the home was not only a cherished place for many Americans but also where spirituality was primarily located.[26]

Indeed, as the middle class expanded, the family placed increasing emphasis on spirituality within the household, thus heightening the sense that sacredness and familial space went hand in hand. Parents were expected to nurture the spiritual development of their children and to set an example for them by praying and reading sacred texts in their presence. Devotionalism increasingly took on elements of the family itself. As religious historian Ann Taves observes in her study of nineteenth-century Catholic devotionalism, the spiritual world began to be conceived as a household in which "everyone takes on a familial role: God is the father; Mary, the mother; and Jesus, the elder brother to all angels, saints, and other Catholics, both living and dead."[27] The spiritual world thus became near, like one's own family, and its nearness allowed practitioners to ask for and receive special graces and favors, much as they might from a parent or sibling.[28]

SPIRITUAL DWELLING IN THE 1950S

By the 1950s, Americans were living in a new era, separated from their immigrant roots and from the nineteenth-century ideal of domestic tranquility by two world wars, a depression, and the invention of atomic weapons. But the very novelty of the era seems also to have been part of a renewed quest to create a sacred space in which to dwell. Writing from a British perspective, sociologist Os Guiness observes in his book *The American Hour* that "'the fifties for Americans is what 'the myth of the nineteenth century' was for an earlier generation of Europeans."[29] It was, Guiness argues, a decade characterized both by nostalgia and by a real emphasis on the values of an earlier era. Small-town life, congregations, and Americanism, Guiness says, were the "three pillars" of stability in the 1950s. Significantly, all three created sacralized space in which the burgeoning postwar population could live.[30]

Though separated by a generation or more from the old country, many Americans still lived in ethnic neighborhoods that linked a particular concept of God with family and place. For the two million Jews who immigrated to the United States between 1870 and the 1920s, benevolent societies (*landsmanshaftn*), along with synagogues and families, provided a significant "home away from home," and these organizations continued to do so after World War II. Indeed, at least half of these societies were organized around the particular towns and villages from which groups of immigrants had come, while the remainder linked immigrants with extended kin, fellow believers, and members who shared the same occupations. The *landsmanshaftn* reproduced the ethnic and religious customs of the immigrants' places of origin, giving them a place to meet and kindred spirits to meet with, as well as fulfilling such important functions as burying the dead, arranging weddings, helping families bring other members to the United States, and eventually assisting survivors of the pogroms and the Holocaust.[31]

Besides the immigrants millions of Americans whose ancestors had arrived during the nineteenth century now populated the small towns and villages of the heartland. Of them, journalist David Halberstam has written, "They lived in God's country, a land far from oceans and far from foreigners, and they were all-powerful in their own small towns."[32] About the only people who did not have strong spatial attachments, Halberstam observes, were vagrants, Hollywood sex sirens, intellectuals, spies, and communists—all of whom were spiritually suspect.[33]

In many ways, therefore, the emphasis on sacred space that characterized American culture at mid-century marked continuity with the past, and yet the fifties was also an aberrant decade, differing from the past in ways that reinforced Americans' tendency to associate spirituality with home, congregation, and family. The baby boom was the first in history to be accompanied by vaccines and antibiotics capable of greatly reducing the risk of childhood illness and death; thus, parents could invest their children with the implicit expectation that immortality would be theirs on earth through the longevity of their children and grandchildren. The immigrant experience was also changing in ways that made Americans more settled in the Promised Land. First-generation immigrants had sought a new home, but remained permanently as transitional figures in a strange land. They wrote letters home to their relatives that mentioned heaven as another shore on which families apart could one day be reunited. Successive generations lost contact with relatives abroad; theirs was more fully the Promised Land in the United States itself.[34]

Correlatively, images of the afterlife began to shift in all branches of popular religion. Polls showed that most Americans believed unquestioningly in the existence of an afterlife. But getting there was now easier, for heaven was readily available to all who tried hard, either by living good lives or by saying a simple prayer that expressed their trust in God, and it was temporally more distant, complementing a full life on earth rather than threatening to cut it short. Indeed, popular depictions of heaven increasingly used worldly images to show what it was like, by implication arguing that heaven was not such a bad place because it was at least as good as the here and now.

None of these changes left Americans any less sure of their beliefs about God; it simply became more possible to believe that God was an immanent being whose presence shined on all respectable Americans in their everyday lives. Among Christians, theology increasingly reflected the popular mood by focusing on the incarnation of Jesus, rather than the mysterious or distant character of God, and by making the Savior a friend who could be trusted for help, rather than a judge interested in counseling people about their sins. Those who thought about it said it was a shame that such a good man had been crucified; in the United States, he would have been treated better.

Popular theology also shifted subtly in the way it described the kingdom of God. Two world wars, the Holocaust, existential philosophy, and new interest in so-called premillennial theology among evangelical Christians made it increasingly difficult for clergy to argue that the kingdom of God was literally coming into being in North America through science, technology, and enlightened democracy.[35] But if a spirituality of dwelling was diminishing in this sense, it was nevertheless increasing through a new tendency to associate the kingdom of God specifically with the local congregation and with the good works of its members. In contrast with the former view, the new one gave Americans a specific place in which they could go and be in the kingdom of God.

MONOPOLIZING SPIRITUALITY

Having focused so much of their attention during the 1940s on war, it is not surprising that many religious leaders in the 1950s resorted to military analogies when they talked about spirituality. But it is striking that much more attention was devoted to images of *territory*. Just as a physical body was a space that might be invaded by an army of germs and therefore needed to be protected by a sterile field, so the soul was deemed to reside in a sacred space that required geographic fortification. Moral decay came from going into the wrong parts of town, from associating with the wrong people, and from frequenting dance halls, bars, or drive-in movie theaters. Colleges and universities still adhered to rules designed to prevent "undesirable" groups from attending, and *in locus parentis* was accomplished through close supervision of resident students. Some states and many municipalities restricted the sale of alcoholic beverages within their borders. The new "activity church" or "program church" encouraged people to spend more time on sanctified turf by sponsoring socials and potluck dinners, young people's groups, Sunday school classes, men's prayer breakfasts, and ladies' aid societies.

Indeed, the place where Americans could know God best was the local congregation—their house of worship. By the 1950s, religious leaders had succeeded in rendering spirituality virtually equivalent to participating in a local congregation. Compared with the nineteenth century, when fewer than half the population claimed membership in a local congregation, now at least three-quarters of Americans belonged to a local house of worship.[36] One study, conducted in 1956, put the figure at 80 percent.[37] Religious leaders, sometimes amazed by their own success, pointed to the growing need for new congregations.[38]

Despite their alleged individualism, Americans were understandably concerned about whether they fit in with their neighbors, often aspiring to the life-styles they saw depicted on television, and keeping company with their families and friends.[39] These social emphases extended to their religious congregations. The God who seemed present yet invisible and inactive in the rest of life could be consciously invoked whenever enough people chose to do so. God was not simply present in their midst because of some omnipresent quality but because they invited Him to enter into their corporeal body.

With growing awareness of the human dimensions of symbolism and ritual, clergy also worked hard to create the right kind of ambiance in morning worship services, partly through the continuing power of the spoken word but also increasingly through the full liturgical experience, including the corporate offering of hymns, the mood set by the organ and by stained glass windows, and the accouterments of dress, carpeting, vaulted ceilings, welcoming foyers, and convenient parking. If Americans worried at some deep level about the atomization of their society, they could count on their congregations—to borrow a line from poet Denise Levertov—"to give to the Vast Loneliness a hearth, a locus."[40]

Several developments during the first half of the twentieth century helped to extend organized religion's monopoly over spiritual practice.[41] First, divisions between social class were muted, whereas elsewhere they left working-class families subject not only to the appeal of radical political movements but also to the attractions of noninstitutionalized spirituality. Indeed, in the United States, working-class spirituality was organized increasingly by new congregations that gradually brought popular expressions of piety under the control of the clergy. Second, a strong program of "homeland missions" helped to spread churches and church buildings throughout the nation. And, third, the strongest cultural definition of piety outside of organized religion became atheism or unbelief—that is, to not be churched was to be without piety at all rather than to subscribe to some alternative form of spirituality. Thus, it was often considered an act of extreme nonconformity for someone to remain unaffiliated.[42]

In the 1950s, each of these developments was accentuated. Economic growth forged a new cultural alliance between the working class and the middle class, causing many in the working class to imitate the middle class and to aspire to similar life-styles, including religious attendance. After a moratorium on religious construction during World War II, new churches and synagogues went up at a rapid pace. And the main definition of nonchurchedness now became not only atheism, but atheistic communism, which was too dangerous politically for anyone to subscribe to lightly. The established churches were thus engaged in a battle not so much against noninstitutionalized popular piety as against each other, against sects, and against atheists and communists.[43]

Yet, if the historical influences shaping U.S. religion are temporarily set aside, one might find it surprising that a religious tradition in which the universality of God's grace, as well as God's omnipresence and the capacity of all people to call on God and to know God, had been emphasized for centuries would have given rise to a situation in which God was in fact perceived to be more vividly present in certain buildings than in others. U.S. clergy wrote of the church as a universal and invisible entity, denying that there was anything holy about church buildings or particular congregations. Nevertheless the 1950s were the apex of a century and a half of church construction and membership drives, the result of which had been to triple the portion of the U.S. population who claimed membership in local congregations and thus to extend the dominance of organized religion over popular expressions of spirituality.[44]

In many communities the church was still the most imposing structure on the visual landscape. Across the Great Plains, church buildings
could often be seen from long distances, just as water towers and grain
elevators could. In the huge working-class districts of Chicago, Detroit,
and Philadelphia, treeless streets lined with row houses were marked as
neighborhoods only by the towering church buildings and parochial
schools that appeared at regular intervals. The modest, garageless Cape
Cod houses that made up Levittown were unimposing compared with
the occasional church or temple that went up on the edge of such communities.[45] In smaller towns, religion remained even more visibly a part
of public community space, as the authors of one study remarked:
"Church-going is of major importance . . . simply because it constitutes
so great a part of the publicly visible community activity. Church activities involve relatively large groups of people and occur in conspicuous
places at fixed times. A large part of the attention of the community is
captured by activities centered in the churches."[46]

Many of the customs reinforcing organized religious participation had
such long histories that Americans needed to pay little attention to them.
However, formal mechanisms helped to keep these customs intact.
Catholics were expected to attend Mass and to participate in confession
regularly. Simply residing within parish boundaries was not sufficient;
weddings, funerals, priestly visits to the sick, and the right to send children to parochial schools depended in most instances on being an active
member in good standing. Protestants varied in how strictly membership expectations were enforced, but mainline denominations tended to
restrict communion to members, counseled newlyweds to become members at the church of their choice, and often required attendance at membership classes as a condition for baptizing infants; smaller denominations often upheld these restrictions through creedal arguments, defenses
of particular church traditions, and informal practices of social inclu-
sion and exclusion. Jews followed customs similar to those of many
Christian organizations but also levied synagogue fees and encouraged
bar mitzvahs and memberships in burial societies and benevolent asso-
ciations as a way of reining in the loyalties of participants.

These customs brought strong social pressures to bear on spirituality. A woman born in 1926 of Irish immigrants remarked tellingly, "It
was very important to conform, to not bring disgrace on the family."
Conformity depended on the tight integration of church with family and
of both with the community. Catholic children worried about disgrac-
ing their parents because the neighbors would find out, because it would

make a difference to aunts and uncles and grandparents, and because their misbehavior at school would be reported by the nuns to their parents (or misbehavior at home, to the priest). Another Catholic woman provided a vivid example of how closely intertwined church and neighborhood remained. When asked where she grew up, she responded "Saint Rita's parish and then in Saint Thomas's parish"; she also identified her first neighborhood as a married woman by its parish name: Sacred Heart. Four decades later, she explained, "We just never wanted to leave the neighborhood. We had such wonderful friends. We were very close."

But if congregations became more important in the 1950s, it was partly because they could not be as easily taken for granted. Compared with the ethnoreligious neighborhoods that had been built up during the previous half century, more Americans now lived in suburbia, where life was more intentional and more diverse. The sociologist Herbert Gans captured an important dimension of its cultural impact in a 1957 study of Jewish life in a Chicago suburb. "In the city they had lived so much *with* Jews that there was little need to worry about living *as* Jews. But in Park Forest their neighbors were as likely as not to be Christian, and the latter's proximity made them conscious of the difference, all the more so as they felt that these neighbors saw and treated them *as* Jews."[47] The response to this imposition of one's religious identity was in many cases to create new places in which to affirm it. "The temple," wrote Irving Howe, "[was] modernized, bland, affluent, well staffed, sumptuously built; . . . it combined house of worship, community center, Sunday school, social hall, and hangout for the young."[48]

It was not enough for Americans simply to visit their houses of worship once or twice a week (although, in reality, that is what most Americans did). Clergy wanted their flocks to be at home with God when they came to their places of worship. Congregations became comfortable, familiar, domestic, offering an image of God that was basically congruent with the domestic tranquility of the ideal home. In popular imagery, the sacred, the practice of spirituality, and particular geographic places were closely connected, and these places—whether church buildings and temples or the houses in which people lived—were sacralized not simply as convenient places to meet or as mere houses, but as *homes,* with all the cultural significance that this word implied.[49]

For Americans of the 1950s, spirituality of dwelling was thus quite different from that of people who might have designated some distant spot, such as a hermitage in the desert or a quiet meadow by a bubbling stream, as a special place in which to access the sacred. Spiritual places were above all homes (habitats, dwellings), and homes were not only physical structures implying some stability but also places of fellowship.[50] To have a home thus meant living in social space, both within and among one's neighbors.[51]

A spirituality of home implied warmth and fellowship, indeed, unconditional acceptance, expressed in godly abundance by fellow inhabitants. Spiritual homes were the kind of places that loving mothers could best provide, and the role of maternal images in shaping local congregations should not be underestimated.[52] Despite the dominance of male clergy in most religious traditions, women outnumbered men at religious services by a substantial margin, did most of the teaching of children in Sunday schools, prayed more visibly and regularly at home, and took charge of their offspring's religious instruction. In one national study, 80 percent of persons born before 1940 remembered that they had been sent to Sunday school as children; 60 percent said religion was very important in their families while they were growing up; half said their parents read the Bible to them; and nearly a third said they had had family devotions.[53] Mothers were the dominant figures in all these experiences.

The connections among devotional practices, the home, and sacred objects are especially evident in people's memories of this period. Catholics who were raised during the 1950s generally describe their parents' daily religious life in terms of attending Mass, going to confession, saying novenas, and praying the rosary. A woman from a Presbyterian family remembers how her family had a little box on the dining room table filled with short prayers or "daily graces" that various members of the family read aloud at each meal. Another Protestant remembers drifting to sleep at night with stories from the Bible coursing through her mind. Her parents read a few verses to her before she went to bed and generally read some Scripture and said a prayer at meals. The Bible itself was tangible evidence that God was close, and the cardboard manger scene under the tree at Christmas and the Easter sunrise services at church made her feel especially close to God. A Jewish man recalls how his mother "used to light the candles on Friday night, which was a very traditional Jewish thing to do, the ushering in of the Sabbath. We used to have our Friday evening Sabbath meal, which always consisted of the same thing for twenty years." His experience corresponds well with the remark of another observer, who wrote that "the Jewish God is a Household God."[54]

As these examples suggest, Americans did not neglect the need to pray, to read sacred texts, and to meditate on God's leading in their lives during the week at home. Statistics collected during the 1950s confirm this impression. Nationally, a poll taken at the start of the decade showed that 42 percent of Americans prayed at least twice a day, while one at the end of the decade found that 69 percent said table grace aloud with their families every day.[55] People undoubtedly prayed in their own ways and for their own personal desires.

But most instruction on these matters also treated spirituality as an element of liturgy and thus as something over which religious organizations had control. Catholics and Jews understood the annual liturgical calendar not only as a guide to the celebration of holy days, the seasons, and the natural rhythms of the planet but also to the cycle of prayer and worship that was to accompany each day. Prior to the Second Vatican Council, devotional practices among Catholics blurred the line between spirituality practiced at home or in private and spirituality practiced at church and during worship services. Devotional guides provided prayers in English that could be said silently while the Mass was being performed in Latin (some were in fact called "paraliturgical").[56]

Among Protestants, private devotional practices were also linked with official places of worship. Episcopalians were provided with morning and evening prayers in the official prayer book of their denomination. Presbyterians found instructions in the constitution of their church (which many studied as part of membership classes) for extending their congregational participation into the crevices of their daily lives. That one should not be divorced from the other was inescapable in the language itself: "Besides the public worship in congregations, it is the indispensable duty of each person, alone, in secret, and of every family, by itself, in private, to pray to and worship God."[57] Symbolically, one participated in these devotional activities not as a lone seeker in search of God but as a church member whose behavior was inscribed inside the liturgical cosmos of a religious tradition. As one woman observes in explaining her mother's devotional behavior, "She was raised in the faith, made all her sacraments, and was married in the church. I don't think she ever needed to ask why."[58]

THE INFLUENCE OF SOCIAL CONDITIONS

The particular way in which Americans expressed their desire to dwell with God was reinforced by their day-to-day experiences in their homes and communities. What demographer Paul Glick called "the familistic period" was in full swing.[59] After declines prompted by the Depression and World War II, marriages and births dramatically increased. By 1957,

the average age at first marriage was twenty, and the fertility rate was
3.8 children per woman. This increase had an enormous impact on family life-styles. By 1955, 65 percent of all new houses were being constructed with family rooms. By the end of the decade, fully a third of all
households included children under the age of six, and more than half
included children under age eighteen.[60]

Americans' spirituality of dwelling was reinforced by the family-centeredness of the 1950s. Homes and congregations acquired special
spiritual significance because they were the places where children were
being raised. An older woman who immigrated from Greece in 1939 remembered how much her life in the 1940s and 1950s centered around
the church as a result of its role in rearing children. "A lot of mothers,
they got children, they multiply. Lots of youngsters. Our little church
needed to be bigger. They don't have cars. Didn't go to the outskirts. So
we built it bigger right here. With our nickels and dimes, we built this
beautiful church." It still makes her angry that people started moving
away in the 1960s. The close connection between families and congregations was also evident in a 1953 survey conducted nationally among
Episcopalians. The study showed that even unmarried and divorced people were flocking to the churches, apparently attracted by its familistic
emphasis. The authors of a later study based on the data argued that
congregations functioned as "surrogate families."[61]

Another factor that probably reinforced Americans' sense of spiritual
dwelling was their attachment to their extended families. A study just
after this period found that city people reported, on average, twenty-seven relatives with whom they were personally acquainted and who in
most cases lived close enough to visit at least once in a while. The extent
of these connections is indicated by comparisons in a follow-up study
some fifteen years later showing that the total number of kin acquaintances had dropped by about a third, and, perhaps more significantly,
they lived farther away; phone calls permitted people to keep in touch
with parents and children, but siblings and cousins ceased to be as important, and less tangible types of sharing and support were exchanged
among kin members. For the earlier period, then, family served as a kind
of community that actually had a geographic center and that provided,
among other things, a place in which religious practices could be observed.[62] Grandparents also played a particularly important role in connecting local space and spirituality. Prior to the advent of nursing homes,
retirement villages, and extended-care facilities in the late 1960s, most
older people (85 percent) lived close to at least one of their grown chil-

dren, and more than a third shared living quarters with adult children.[63] "Grandma lived above us on the second floor," a Jewish man recalls, "and her sister was on the third floor. We used to share everything.
At night I would say the She'ma Yisrael with her. 'Hear O Israel, the
Lord our God, the Lord is One.' On Sundays we would drive to another
town to visit my other grandmother." A Hispanic woman also has a lingering sense that spirituality is connected with a place because her grandmother lived with her family. Sometimes she can still feel her grandmother—dead now for many years—sitting on the bed beside her while
she is praying.

After World War II another significant development that probably influenced conceptions of the sacred was what might be called the do-
mestication of the male breadwinner. Despite the long-term emphasis on
domestic household duties that had arisen in the nineteenth century,
these had been performed largely by women. After World War II, a growing number of men worked at desk jobs or in occupations that required
only the standard forty-hour workweek. New emphasis was placed on
leisure activities, such as gardening, remodeling projects around the
house, and spending time with children.[64] Popular television programs,
such as *Make Room for Daddy, Father Knows Best,* and *Ozzie and Har-
riet,* depicted fathers who worked but who seldom spent time at their
jobs and who were devoted companions of their wives and children. Fathers did not necessarily shoulder many household duties, but they were
more available to fill out the symbolic roles of the spiritual household.
"Dads were . . . steady and steadfast," Halberstam has written. "They
symbolized a secure world."[65] God the father could thus be more easily
imagined as part of a spirituality of dwelling. Indeed, interviews reveal
that fathers were a tangible manifestation of spirituality for many people in this era. For example, Ned Stewart talks fondly of seeing his father preparing his Sunday school lesson each week at the dining-room
table and recalls understanding God's love better because of seeing his
father helping sick neighbors.

The 1950s were also characterized by scholarly treatises emphasizing
the need for Americans to feel "located," to have "roots," and to know
their "place." "Being religious," Herberg wrote, "is, under contemporary American conditions, a fundamental way of 'adjusting' and 'belonging.'"[66] Curiously, looking back on this period with more recent
terms in mind, such as *self-esteem* and *self-fulfillment,* one cannot help
noticing the frequency with which another word is used: *self-location.*
When the question "Who am I?" arose, as it did increasingly in these

years, advice columnists attempted to respond by suggesting that people
were troubled by spatial dislocation and that they needed to find a space
in which they could belong in order to know who they really were.

The dominant fact of social life was that growing numbers of people
were no longer linked to an identifiable space. As often as not they
were recent immigrants who still felt uprooted, the children of immigrants who were ambivalent about their ethnic traditions, veterans who
had been geographically and psychologically displaced during World
War II, and itinerant nuclear families trying to make a new start for
themselves in the burgeoning suburbs. Growth in cities, the spread of
newspaper and radio communications, and the emergence of television
signaled the dangerous possibility of everyone's becoming an isolated
individualist with no distinctive place to provide a strong sense of personal identity.

Still, the preferred way to cope with these dislocations was to search
all the harder for homes that would be as nurturing to the soul as they
were comforting to the body. In the 1950s Americans became known as
a nation of joiners. If lifelong ties that spanned generations no longer existed, people would nevertheless create new domestic bonds for themselves. They joined civic groups, clubs, and religious organizations in
droves, and they made sure their children did the same. The suburbs that
housed so many new families, such as the Levittowns of Long Island and
Pennsylvania, were places to live, places to plant trees and to fill up at-
tics; they were homes.[67]

The anthropologist Mary Douglas has observed that "home starts by
bringing some space under control." It need not be a single or unmov-
able space, but there must be some regularity about it: in the appearance
and reappearance of its furnishings, its inhabitants, and the moods associated with it.[68] Similarly, a spiritual home was one in which the hearth
had been prepared, where religious duties had been performed, and
where contributions had been made; and heaven was a place where one's
treasure had been stored. To inhabit a spiritual home included making
a pact with God about one's children, promising to bring them up properly in return for providential protection. A congregation was a spiritual
home if it reinforced this pact and if it solidified parents' control over
the space in which they lived.

As homes, these spiritual sanctuaries were thus fortresses whose walls
needed to be protected from exterior threats so that life inside could be
kept under control. The denominational and interconfessional conflicts

of the 1950s can be understood in this light. Were spirituality an amor-phous, eclectic, or purely personal quest, it might have developed in ways that rapidly blurred the boundaries between the various traditions. But spirituality was a location in which one's selfhood was defined. To be a member of one denomination meant keeping a certain distance from those of another tradition. The occasional sparks that flew when chil-dren ventured into the wrong neighborhood or the squabbling that clergy carried on with their counterparts from other faiths helped to keep the fortress walls intact.[69]

And if the local enclaves in which people worshiped were sacred fortresses, the nation in which they lived was even more in need of be-ing inviolable. It, too, was sacred space, a place in which spirituality and identity were forged together. Being a good American was a way of ex-hibiting faith, and both depended on keeping intruders out. Commu-nism, of course, was the most feared intruder of all, for it championed a different style of government as well as a different vision of humanity, and it was known to be intent on corrupting the United States by send-ing in subversives to eat away at its core. Indeed, when a poll was con-ducted in 1954 to find out why Americans thought there was a religious revival, the most commonly given answers focused on uncertain and troubled times, fear of the future, fears of war with the Communists, the atom bomb, and memories of World War II.[70]

Having played such an important role in World War II, Americans in the fifties also saw their country fulfilling a divine mission in the post-war world. The nation itself was a sacred space, a launching pad from which democratic and what were increasingly referred to as "Judeo-Christian" values could be spread abroad. By the end of the decade, it was literally a launching pad, demonstrating its scientific prowess by sending rockets into outer space. Meanwhile, it fought Communism in Korea and faced down the Russians in Eastern Europe. These feats, how-ever, were not without cost. Americans feared that their fortress could be invaded at any time. They spent increasing amounts on national de-fense, built bomb shelters, and searched for subversives in their midst. "Our own nation . . . is less potent to do what it wants in the hour of its greatest strength than it was in the days of its infancy," complained Rein-hold Niebuhr in 1952.[71] To buttress their strength, Americans repeat-edly declared their trust in God: in 1954, the phrase "one nation under God" was added to the pledge of allegiance, and "in God we trust" was printed on the currency.[72]

AT HOME WITH GOD

Despite the surge in popular piety, observers frequently cautioned that spirituality in the 1950s was superficial. It was a kind of formulaic religiosity, a faith in faith itself, a simple affirmation in the existence of God, a belief that all would be well if one worked hard. Critics noted that people went to religious services but did little during the week to express their faith at work or to carry principles of justice and charity from the pews to the poor in their communities. Herberg wrote that Americans displayed "a religiousness with almost any kind of content or none, a way of sociability or 'belonging' rather than a way of reorienting life to God."[73]

In retrospect, this apparent shallowness can be understood in terms of the closeness with which spirituality and place were associated. Being at home means having the answers before one has questions. Once one moves in, a home is mainly a place to take for granted. Religion functioned this way. It offered people salvation or identity or a sense that what they were doing was right simply by virtue of belonging to a particular faith and of participating on a fairly regular basis. Ninety percent of what it took was, as the saying goes, simply showing up.

To say that faith was shallow also implies a lack of introspection, at least of the kind that mystics had traditionally practiced or even of the kind that was to become more popular during the 1960s and 1970s. Although psychoanalysis was beginning to attract some interest among religious leaders, most people in the 1950s were not deeply introspective about their faith or about their inner selves; they did not feel they had spaces within themselves that needed to be explored. When Americans argued for "deeds, not creeds," they were not simply reflecting a pragmatic spirit; rather, they were oriented toward action because their selfhood was defined more by roles and by the exterior location of the individual and less by an inward structure to which creeds might be attached.

Another reason why self-reflection was not more often a part of spirituality is that such reflection requires a conceptual division between the inner world and the outer world. But true homes are places where no acute division exists between the private, inner self and the self that acts and is on display to others. Their very lack of introspection was thus indicative of how effective Americans had been in creating a spiritual home for themselves. "When the divinity that rules the world and distributes the unknown and unjust gifts of destiny is ... familiar and close . . . as a father is to his small child," philosopher Georg Lukacs had written, "then every action is only a well-fitting garment for the world."[74] For middle America, the habitual spirituality of churches and temples was, indeed, a well-fitting garment.

There was no contradiction, then, between the lack of depth that characterized spirituality in the 1950s and the regularity with which Americans participated in religious activities. One followed naturally from the other. Although homes are private places, daily life within them is intensely open to the scrutiny of fellow occupants, meaning especially that members are supposed to be available at specified times for collective activities. Their presence is required; they are not supposed to be gone all the time or to disappear at the wrong times. This intermittent mingling is a demonstration of loyalty, a signal that one can be trusted, that one's intentions are good, that one is faithful. In spirituality, if one is faithful in showing up for prayers or singing the right hymns or attending services, then one is part of the community that God blesses.

In retrospect, it is difficult to argue that the 1950s was a high-water mark in personal spirituality, except for the fact that attendance at religious services consumed the energies of more Americans in those years than it has in subsequent decades, and that there was a kind of habitual affinity between the sacred and the places in which people lived and worshiped.[75] Indeed, the relative ease with which spirituality was associated with attendance at religious services and the concern that many observers expressed about its shallowness suggests that spirituality may have become livelier and more vital for many people in subsequent years when it was also more diverse and problematic.

THE LIMITATIONS OF SPIRITUAL HOMES

A place that lacks depth, that does not encourage self-reflection, and that requires conforming to social expectations can of course be a stifling place in which to live, rather than simply a comfortable dwelling.[76] Indeed, all homes carry a price, and the price Americans paid in the 1950s for their spiritual homes was often one of denial. Some denied that millions of Jews had died only a few years previously in the Nazi Holocaust. Many denied that millions of African Americans did not enjoy the basic freedoms on which the ability to gain an education, earn a living, and maintain a decent home depended. Although the threat of nuclear annihilation was increasingly a reality, many Americans denied that it was a threat worth taking seriously. They also denied much of their own

past—for example, by depicting themselves simply as the latest in a long
series of generations who had built homes and led orderly lives, ignor-
ing the disruption that had accompanied a century of immigration and
more than a century of war, let alone the violence that had been done to
indigenous peoples and the physical environment.

The imagery of spiritual homes as safe, secure dwellings is often an
idealized picture. The reality of home is much different. The nest gets
fouled, pipes burst, the roof leaks, illness strikes, and people die. In contrast to the surrealistic world of advertising and television, homes are
places of sadness as well as joy. And this fact tempered the spirituality of
the 1950s. People knew that the power of positive thinking would not
save them ultimately. The spiritual ground in which they located themselves included the hospitals in which they would die and the cemeteries
in which they would be buried. As time progressed, it also became
harder—especially for young people—to maintain the sanctity of the
spaces in which they lived, for changing social realities and new realiza-
tions raised fundamental doubts about the plausibility of spiritual homes.

The difficulty of maintaining a spirituality of dwelling is evident in
the life of Ned Stewart. During the past two decades, he and his wife
have tried hard to give their son the same kind of sheltered spiritual world
in which Ned was raised. But the difficulties they have faced are indicative of how hard it is for many Americans to maintain a spirituality of
dwelling in unsettled times. Ned himself offers a graphic image. When
he went away to college in the late fifties, he arrived at a huge building
dedicated to the pursuit of knowledge. Its vaulted ceilings towered over
him. Having always thought of religion as the center of his universe, he
looked for the campus chapel. It was a tiny structure, minuscule in comparison, set off near the edge of the grounds. He says, "I realized I was
a minority in the seriousness with which I took my faith." The social milieu is also dramatically different than it was when Ned was a boy. He
grew up in a state—like the United States as a whole—that had about
fifty people per square mile; he now lives in a county with approximately
thirteen hundred people per square mile. Of these, nearly 40 percent have
moved within the past five years; scarcely anyone lives within walking
distance of work; more than half are in marriages that will end in divorce; and the crime rate has been steadily rising.[77]

Another important change is Ned's realization that even the secure
space in which he lived as a child was not as pure as he once thought. Ned
took it for granted that the black maid was not allowed to mingle with
white people. A decade later, he was active in the civil rights movement.

He recognizes that both his parents were deeply prejudiced and knows he has not escaped being influenced by their thinking. He admits, "They believed that black people were ordained to be a race of servants—'hewers of wood and drawers of water,' as the Bible says—and these servants should be treated fairly but not accepted socially as equals." As he grows older, he becomes increasingly concerned about the "moral deterioration" of the United States, but he also recognizes that the "golden age" of his childhood is not one to which he would want to return. "The views I grew up with are not the right ones either, particularly the blatant racism."

Ned has tried to follow his father's footsteps in religion. He teaches Sunday school, serves on committees at church, and helps with Boy Scouts. He feels his work as a chemistry teacher is a way to serve God, and he devotes long hours to his teaching. But his life is scattered in a way his father's was not. He attends church in one community, teaches in another, and helps with Boy Scouts in a third. The spheres of his life do not overlap, except in his own schedule, and thus he has to figure out who he is and where he feels most at home. There is no "community" in which to be known the way his father was. Even his church life has been negotiated rather than habitual as his parents' was. His wife grew up in a different denomination than he did; Ned participated in several different denominations while he was in college and, when he returned to the Baptist church found it unfamiliar. The family now attends a Presbyterian church, but Ned fears he may be "just a Baptist in Presbyterian clothing." Intuitively, he also senses that the world cannot be sanctified the way his father felt it could. He and his wife sometimes attend a small support group, but they seldom see the people in it from one week to the next. His students have so many different problems that Ned feels all he can do sometimes is just to pray.

Without a sacred place in which to dwell, Ned also finds that his relationship with God is more ephemeral. "I sort of run into God periodically," he says. "Usually when I'm least expecting it." Ned still says his prayers every day; most days he even reads the Bible at home. But God is less a part of this everyday world than of the spaces outside it. For instance, God sometimes speaks to Ned when he is on a camping trip with Scouts; at other times, when he is driving from place to place; and, on other occasions, Ned feels God calling him to some other place entirely. "I'll just get a strong feeling that I should go someplace. I don't understand it. But when I get there I feel there must be a reason."

As this example suggests, changes in established religion are part of the reason why a spirituality of dwelling is harder to maintain than it was a few decades ago. In the 1950s, the average Protestant church consisted of about a hundred confirmed members, virtually the same size of churches a half century earlier, and these members tended to live in the same community; over the next twenty-five years, this figure would double and the number of "megachurches," numbering members in excess of a thousand, would increase significantly.[78] Besides overall growth, the character of congregations would shift dramatically as well; whereas three-quarters of all Protestant churches were still in small towns and rural areas on the eve of World War II, they would relocate predominantly to suburban areas over the next two decades.[79] When congregations are large and impersonal, and when congregants are geographically scattered, it is hard for members to feel that the congregation is truly where they can dwell with God.[80]

Yet it is important to recognize that images of a safe, secure spiritual dwelling have continued to inspire nostalgia and to be regarded as a normative standard in many quarters. If the 1950s was a decade in which adults emphasized home, it has become a time that children from that period look back on with nostalgia. Family researchers note the frequency with which people now in their forties and fifties lament the breakdown of the family, worrying that life has become too complicated and expressing a desire to "go back home again." For these people, the 1950s was indeed a time in which home and family prevailed. Their world was sheltered. Most of their mothers stayed home to care for them; most of them watched idealized versions of home on television; and the vast majority participated in congregations and Sunday school programs that emphasized belonging.[81] Nostalgia for this period means that spirituality is often defined even more sharply in conversation with an idealized image of a spiritual home than was true of the 1950s itself. There is still the longing for home, to which Foster and others appeal, but an even deeper sense that home has been lost.

Much of the change that has contributed to this sense of spiritual loss is rooted in shifting patterns of family and community behavior. The changes Ned Stewart illustrates are not atypical. In 1950, half of the American population still lived on farms or in towns of fewer than ten thousand people. By 1970, that proportion had dropped to 36 percent. Many of the other changes that took place during the 1960s and 1970s can also be observed in national statistics. Between 1960 and 1979, the proportion of white families who lived together as married units declined from 76 percent to 64 percent. The changes among African American families were even more pronounced, with married families declining from 60 percent to 43 percent of the total. In addition, the number of divorced people who did not remarry edged up from 1.9 percent of all households in 1950 to 2.3 percent in 1960 and then rose to 5.8 percent by 1979. And after the 1950s, birthrates declined steadily, from 118 per thousand women in 1960, to 88 in 1970, and then to 66 in 1976. This meant, of course, that fewer families were centered around child rearing.[82]

A spirituality of dwelling was particularly vulnerable to these kinds of change, for its conception of a sacred order depended on the capacity of families, local communities, and congregations to provide tangible symbols of divine presence and to organize religious behavior, both public and private, around the familiar habits of ordinary life.[83] Assuming that spirituality could be taken for granted, moreover, made it easy for people to miss the fact that it would erode when the social conditions on which it was based were no longer present. Gradually, this kind of spirituality seemed to make less sense because both the habits and the habitations that had sustained it were changing. Increasingly, spirituality would have to be practiced more actively and consciously, rather than being an automatic cultural response to the world.

Many people of course continued to center their spirituality in religious congregations long after the 1950s. Indeed, many Americans speak of their congregations as communities, families, or homes, and their commitment to these congregations reinforces their conviction that God supplies them with a sacred place in which to dwell. Yet the fragility of these convictions is often evident as well.

Kim Lacy illustrates how spirituality and the quest for a home came together—in her case under a gothic spire—and then left her with a gnawing desire for something else when the resulting dwelling could no longer be taken for granted. She attended a Methodist church as a child, and much of her life was centered around the activities of the church. In college, she switched to an Episcopal church. It was less familiar, but she was attracted by the Anglican liturgy. She attended college close to her home and remained in close contact with her parents and siblings.

Her sense of being uprooted did not come until she moved more than a thousand miles away to attend graduate school, and even then she was able to create a safe place in which to practice her faith. Almost immediately, she settled into an Episcopal church in her new community, and it became her new home. She joined the choir, found new friends, and soon met the man who was to become her husband. "It didn't take long at all," she explains, "because I got connected with a small community.

It was a community that was meeting to do vigil Eucharist on Saturday nights. It was led by a priest who had a great interest in liturgy, which was exactly what I was interested in. And we had a group of twenty to thirty people who got together every Saturday at 5:30 to have dinner, sometimes to do educational stuff, and just to hang out and talk. These were the golden days of my association with institutionalized religion because it was *heaven*. I would look forward to it; I would plan for it. I did music for it. I would spend time in the library finding, you know, a fifteenth-century hymn for that Sunday and get together a bunch of friends, and we would do it at the service. I mean, it was *heaven*; it was just incredible. It was just what I thought church ought to be."

As Kim talks about her experience, it sounds too good to be true. And it was. At least her sense of being in heaven didn't last. Three years after she arrived, Kim went abroad for a year, and when she returned found that she had outgrown the group. The leadership had changed and her interests had changed. Still, in a sense, the wider parish provided her with a surrogate family. She was married in the church a couple of years later. Her husband was an active member, and she served on a number of parish committees. During this time, nothing caused her to question her faith or her involvement in the church. Indeed, she says she had a very simple faith and wondered why others didn't believe the same way; it was a comfortable spirituality that could be practiced habitually in a sacred space.

But in her thirties the cumulative impact of the changes she had experienced began to seep into her consciousness, and when her own life course shifted dramatically Kim found that even the wider parish was no longer able to provide her with a satisfactory sense of family. With a husband and child, she needed it less in one way, but in other ways she needed it more. She was beginning to think more deeply about her faith, about who she was, and about the relationship between her own spirituality and conditions in the outside world. From reading about feminist spirituality, she became increasingly troubled by the extent to which the church was "male-dominated" and realized that society is in a "dreadful state" because of all the violence, conflict, and inhumanity. She says she became "very uncomfortable at church, very uncomfortable." She attributes this feeling less to her concerns about social issues than to what was happening in her own life: her mother's death and her daughter's birth. Both drove home her sense of vulnerability. It was painful to watch her mother die, and it was shocking to realize how totally responsible she was for her daughter's well-being. Now, she is no longer able to concentrate on the liturgy. It has ceased to be enough, and in questioning it, she has also been forced to think hard about her faith, her role in the church, and the central role that the church has played in her marriage. She worries especially about finding some place to worship where she again feels totally comfortable so that her daughter does not pick up her negative views. Sometimes she goes to another church, a smaller one, where there is a greater sense of the feminine nature of God, and she sits there and cries because it feels so good. Yet there are times when she feels the service there is "nutty as a fruitcake."

She summarizes, "My spirituality is in shreds, essentially. It's in shreds because, basically, my spirituality has always been centered on church services, you know, on liturgy. And when that relationship goes awry, I feel as if things are in very bad shape right now." Her voice cracks. "The whole thing means a tremendous amount to me." Then she adds, "Maybe if I could find the support I need, the right kind of encouragement—but right now I just feel like I'm in disarray and disappointment. Not a good place at all."

Part of what people experience when the church is no longer a "good place" is that they are again without a home and so they talk about needing support. But the breakdown of institutional support also means that spirituality at the personal level becomes precarious. Once carried by the rituals, activities, and conversations that were part of the institution, it now has to be carried alone. Kim puts it this way: "My personal faith journey has always been pretty passive in the sense that it has been fed by the institution. And now that I no longer have the institution feeding it, it's kind of splat on the ground, sitting there without any help." She says she is finding it much more difficult to "construct something for myself now in the absence of being able to get it passively by going somewhere on Sunday and receiving it." Having become less habitual, her spirituality now has to be negotiated.

And when one's home is lost, the validity of one's routine spiritual practices is likely to fall into question as well. Some people, of course, cling all the more tenaciously to their practices, using them to provide the security of a lost home. But the practices themselves may lose their meaningfulness, and people then are no longer as sure of the specific creeds they have said or the specific rituals they have performed. Their beliefs become, as Kim says, "darkened and cobwebby." All that may be left are generic ideas that still seem to make sense as a result of personal experience even if these ideas cannot be framed in creedal language. For instance, Kim says that she believes only in God as goodness—"the goodness one can find in an act, in another person, as the good instincts that people have as opposed to the destructive instincts that people have." Jesus, salvation, and religion also have a more generic meaning. "I think that historical religion was probably some sort of attempt to civilize ourselves—or to make sense of destruction; I mean to make sense of what it means to be mortal, to die, and how to deal with that." She says this all sounds pretty "feeble" but admits that she has little connection to creeds at the moment.

The way her spirituality has shifted as a result of her loss of community is also evident in her current inability to pray and in her disinterest in seeking answers in books or through other devotional guides. She wishes she could do these things, and expects that she will be able to in the future; but without a strong sense of what she believes, these activities are difficult to pursue. Yet she experiences her present searching, painful as it is, as an opportunity for growth. Believing that faith is essentially siding with good instead of evil, she looks for a spark of goodness in every person she encounters in her work and tries to affirm that goodness. It sounds corny to her to say that she is looking for Jesus in them, but she says this is still the basic idea.

DISTANT LANDS

In the late 1960s, Bob Dylan's popular song "No Direction Home" asked listeners how it felt to be on their own, without direction home. Sociologist Robert Bellah answered a few years later, "To most of us in America today it doesn't feel very good."[84] Previous generations of pilgrims and sojourners, Bellah observed, at least knew where home was, even if they had become lost. In contrast, he wrote, "We don't even know where home is; for us there is literally no direction home. There is an immense nostalgia and longing for home, for being at home, but our reality is an acute, radical homelessness."

For most people, home is a point of orientation, a familiar place that provides their bearings. In his study of flood victims, for example, sociologist Kai Erikson found that people who had lost their homes were literally disoriented.[85] They no longer knew who they were or were as capable of telling time, remembering common dates and names, or finding their way. As sacred space, a spiritual home offers a center, a focal point, a place to stay or a place to return to. But home has increasingly become a point of departure rather than a place to live, a staging area to be occupied temporarily, because circumstances prevent people from tarrying too long. Rather than devoting a great deal of effort to building a spiritual home, many people engage in fleeting activities that put them in a safe place for a few moments. Feeling the compulsion to move on, they visit briefly at national shrines and in ornate houses of worship.

Home becomes metaphoric, as literary scholar William Paulson writes, "The fireside is the . . . site not so much of traditional family or community life but of urban loners, dandys, and intellectuals in their moments of melancholy."[86] Or as Kathleen Norris observes in her book on spiritual geography, people attempt to rediscover their identity by making pilgrimages, visiting the villages of their ancestors.[87] Yet these pilgrims often find that they are not fully comfortable in such places because they—the pilgrims and the places—have changed. And thus they may realize there is no place where they can make their spiritual home.

Still, a spirituality of dwelling lingers, despite the difficulties people experience in sustaining it. To live without a sense of sacred space is to fear that the world has succumbed to monolithic secularity. Reliance on technology, business, and government policy to solve prevalent social problems is symptomatic of the extent to which the landscape has indeed become secular. Yet the quest for sacred space continues, often with a kind of frenetic zeal. U.S. fundamentalism can be understood as a prominent example of the continuing attraction of a spirituality of dwelling. Fundamentalist churches create high walls between themselves and the secular culture. Larger ones hope to provide total communities in which to live—places to read, to watch videos, and to play sports, as well as to worship. Fundamentalists' efforts to bring prayer and Bible reading back into the public schools can also be understood as a quest for sacred space. Were it simply a matter of having the time to pray, most Americans—including schoolchildren—could easily fit the three or four minutes they pray into the quiet time in their beds before they go to sleep or after they wake up in the mornings. What concerns fundamentalists is not the lack of time to pray, but the fact that schoolrooms are a physical place in which God appears to be excluded. Having the right to pray there, even if that right is never exercised, means that this space can be part of a sanctified world.

The continuing desire for a place—a spiritual home—is also evident in the current interest in communal values, retreat houses, sweat lodges, and Native American religions. Those who have somehow made a portion of the earth their home are the envy of those who have been less fortunate. Nature itself provides an image of sacred space. Spiritual practitioners drawing on Eastern traditions sometimes light candles at the four corners of a small space in their homes to sanctify this space. Growing numbers of Americans spend weekends at retreat centers that give them a holy place in which to focus on spirituality. For example, on the island of Iona (off the coast of Scotland), people seeking physical or emotional healing come regularly from the United States and elsewhere to the transept of an ancient Celtic church, place their hands on one another's shoulders, and quietly pray. Candles glowing in the darkness, chanting, and the church's thirteen hundred year history help to charge the space with sacred power. People who have practiced a la carte spirituality attest, in one man's words, that the experience is like a "homecoming."[88]

The quest for a spiritual home is sometimes expressed artistically as well. One of the women interviewed works as an artist. She has been creating sculptures by gluing pieces of wood to a large panel of plywood and then covering the pieces with brightly colored acrylics. She prefers to get wood from houses that are being torn down—"wood that has been loved and caressed as part of a home." She says the spatial arrangement of the pieces is intended to convey the idea of a journey. But the spaces in between are "little nesting areas." She explains, "My work talks of shelter, refuge, home. It speaks of that sacred space that we each have within us—where we can go to at any time, gather our energies, and then be in the world again."

For this artist, sacred space is close at hand. Uncomfortable with the thought that there is anything sacred about their own homes however, many Americans appear to search for spirituality in distant lands. Watching the late Joseph Campbell on public television, they become intrigued with the idea that the sacred is located in Palenque, Delphi, or the Lascaux Cave.[89] Most viewers of course have never been to these places; few may have any idea where these places are. Mass communication brings foreign places into people's homes but leaves them feeling like tourists rather than like people who truly dwell in sacred space.

Architect Thomas Bender writes, "What is significant about sacred places turns out *not* to be the places themselves." The power of sacred places, he argues, is their capacity to marshal an individual's inner resources and to strengthen that person's convictions.[90] It is thus unnecessary to travel to a shrine in Tibet in order to find a sacred place. Like home, a sacred place is where the heart is—not where the heart yearns to be but where people are willing to invest the time and energy required to construct a home and to live there. At its best, making a home is a practice, an act of love. "The extra touch put into a door by its builder, the love with which a new marriage bed is built, the window added to see a favorite tree outside," says Bender, "all echo that love."[91]

The wisdom of the old adage that "it takes a lot of living to make a house a home" is that homes are not found, but fashioned; not bought, but built; and not easily established or replaced. Writer Wendell Berry says that homes are created by building—layer on layer—an accumulation of stories and lore and songs. And there must be, he observes, a "centripetal force, holding local soil and local memory in place."[92] Building a spiritual home also involves defining a center of one's life and erecting boundaries around the perimeter of one's life. "If there are no centers and boundaries," writes Richard Feather Anderson, "it is difficult to know who you are and where you are."[93] But contemporary life is fluid, an ooze that seeps out in all directions. It is hard to know where the center of a suburb is, hard to feel centrally connected to an employer who is seldom seen, and hard to sink roots for a family whose members come and go according to their own schedules.

Thus, for some, spirituality becomes a search for novel ways to retrieve a sense of sacred space. One woman says that sacred space is a hospice she has created as a place to do the difficult work of dying. For another, sacred space is the mystical sense of energy he creates as he rides his bicycle. Another joins with friends to form a group called Sacred Space, in which feminist concerns can be shared. Still another creates sacred space on canvas by depicting bodies and pastoral scenes. Some resanctify their living spaces by rediscovering the rituals of lighting candles, by setting up altars in the corner of their bedrooms, and by kissing the mezuzah as they go in and out of their doors. In all these instances, the act of creating space signifies intentionality in a way that living within a taken-for-granted dwelling does not. Space has remained essential to the spiritual quest; yet its meaning has been transformed, and for many, spirituality has come to be practiced in ways that do not emphasize space at all.

CHAPTER *Three*

The New Spiritual Freedom

*S*hirley Knight turned twelve in 1960. Her parents had divorced when she was seven. When she was little, they took her to church every Sunday, but it was usually a different church each Sunday. They thought it was important for her "to explore what was out there." In fourth grade, she attended a Catholic boarding school, and in fifth grade, a private school run by Quakers. In sixth grade, she went through confirmation class at an Episcopal church and in seventh and eighth grade attended Sunday school at the Methodist church. During high school, she attended a Christian Science church.

Shirley's spiritual odyssey continued when she went to college at a large state university. Some students from a fundamentalist Protestant group befriended her, but Shirley soon felt uncomfortable with them. By the end of her freshman year, she was attending services at the Catholic Student Union, attracted by the beauty of its rituals. During her sophomore year she studied in Italy, where she learned more about Catholicism. A course in Buddhism the following year broadened her horizons, and she was soon reading books about other world religions. After graduation she moved in with her boyfriend, who was "into yoga and very spiritual." Within a year she had broken up with him. She had also worked at seven different jobs.

One day Shirley was sitting at work feeling sorry for herself, thinking, as she recalls, that "nothing is working for me," when a new customer walked in and struck up a conversation. Shirley married him two weeks later. He was involved in Alcoholics Anonymous and interested in Sufism. They spent their honeymoon visiting spiritual retreat centers in Europe. Coming home disappointed, they settled in Virginia and became active in Alcoholics Anonymous. Shirley recalls that she loved the group because the people in it were "so spiritual."

After a decade in Virginia, Shirley, her husband, and two children moved to the Southwest, where they joined an Adult Children of Alcoholics group, and Shirley started taking classes from a Jungian therapist. Through the Waldorf school that her children attended, she became interested in the teachings of Rudolf Steiner, called anthroposophy, and soon began driving to a retreat center on weekends to learn more about it. At the moment, she summarizes her religious beliefs by asserting that they focus on "spiritual freedom and moral imagination."

For people like Shirley Knight, the 1960s and 1970s provided new opportunities to expand their spiritual horizons. The 1960s began with Christian theologians declaring that God was dead; it ended with millions of Americans finding that God could be approached and made relevant to their lives in more ways than they had ever imagined. Campus ministries forged new brands of politicized spirituality. Evangelical churches and conservative denominations grew quietly in the suburbs. After the Second Vatican Council, Catholics began hearing mass in English and participated more actively than before in Sunday services.[1] New religious movements of Asian origin, such as Zen and Hare Krishna, spread in metropolitan areas, as did the humanistic spirituality of such groups as Esalen, EST, and Scientology.[2] So-called underground churches and Jesus freak organizations emerged, and monasteries and religious communes began to attract new followings. For many people, it was difficult to know which spiritual path to follow.

In retrospect, the 1960s had a dramatic impact on American spirituality. Research indicates that many people were influenced by the turmoil of these years to adopt a freewheeling and eclectic style of spirituality.[3] In addition to baby boomers like Shirley Knight who matured during the 1960s, many older Americans participated in the religious changes of this period, and many younger Americans have been influenced by it indirectly, thus giving the period much wider significance than can be understood by considering generations or cohorts alone.[4] What has not been adequately considered is how activists in the 1960s and their subsequent critics reshaped Americans' understanding of freedom itself, and how this new understanding contributed to the decline of a spirituality of dwelling and to the rise of a spirituality of seeking.

NEW HORIZONS

Adam Westfield is especially articulate about how the 1960s shaped his views of spirituality. Born in 1942, he grew up in New England, attended a private secondary school, graduated from an elite university, and then embarked on a career in business. Looking back on his childhood, he says his parents taught him the importance of family, trying hard, and being good, but left him to discover spiritual values on his own. He senses a strong shift in the attention given to religion in his family history. "I think my parents' generation had a much more intensive sort of religious pre-history [than I did]," he explains. "My father had been brought up in Massachusetts and had gone to church two or three times a day. My mother's family had all been preachers in the Unitarian church. I think by the time I came along they were both a little weary. They certainly didn't evangelize their children."

Being conditioned to seek spirituality on his own, he was eager to break out of the subculture in which he was raised. For a long time, however, "I was not aware that there were any other cultures at all," he says. His first awareness came when his parents took him on a trip that included driving through a large city. His father had a small statue of a black Buddha in a cabinet at home, so when the boy spotted a black person for the first time on the trip, he shouted, "Look, Dad, it's the Buddha!" In retrospect, he says, "It's amazing. I lived in a time capsule, sort of Lake Wobegon, a place that time forgot. Everybody was white, and there were forty families that just sort of lived together [in my town] from 1942 to 1960. It's amazing."

As a child, Adam associated religion with a kind of stodgy, tight-lipped, strictly disciplined New England asceticism. It was a spirituality of dwelling that blended imperceptibly into the fabric of the town. Only after college did he start to reflect on the meaning of his own spirituality. He attributes his new interest in spirituality to the more open setting in which he was working. Many of the people were black. One of his closest friends was Jewish. Adam started to realize that whatever spiritual path he took, he would have to come to terms with the racial and religious prejudices in his background.

During the 1960s his spirituality was deeply influenced by the civil rights movement. Adam appreciated the freedom to explore new ways of expressing his spirituality. During the Vietnam war he had to confront impulses toward violence for which his middle-class upbringing had not prepared him. Turmoil in his marriage was also to affect his spirituality. He remains involved in a church, but his spirituality is quite different from that of his parents.

Other people describe different avenues to experiencing new spiritual freedoms. Nancy Nystrom, like many teenagers during the 1960s, experienced the turmoil of the decade as conflict within her own life. Her parents were devout Catholics. During the 1950s they raised her in a secure home embellished with the trappings of organized religion. Her first memories are of Catholic statues "all over the house," of saying the rosary and the Lord's Prayer with her mother, and of conversations about God, sin, and divine punishment. She remembers being terrified of God. "I had a naturally curious mind," she says, "but I was afraid to move, afraid to explore. I felt doomed, helpless, powerless." For her, a spirituality of dwelling felt constraining.

When she was in seventh grade, Nancy quit attending the Baptist church her parents now attended despite their objections. "I hated the church, the minister, and God," she recalls. But in eleventh grade her parents sent her to a Catholic high school, and Nancy started thinking again about God. The principal told her it was more important to be spiritual in her daily life than to attend mass and confession. Everyone was friendly to her, and for two years she found a temporary home that made her feel secure: "I just wanted to *belong*." Still, thoughts about God reminded her of her childhood fears, so she postponed any serious investigation of spirituality until she was in college.

"During the hippie era, I began on my own to read a little about Eastern religions," she recalls. "I doubted Christianity, and I still felt very estranged from God, but I believed in reincarnation. My brother was reading a lot about the occult, and that got me interested in numerology and Tarot. I read the Seth books by Jane Roberts. Seth was allegedly a spirit guide. I never just embraced these ideas automatically. I had a lot of questions, but I believed some of the things, like the idea that each person has a spirit guide who is available if you want them. I also started going to a spiritualist. And I thought a lot about the Ten Commandments. I wasn't sure they were from God, but I did feel they were a kind of code imprinted on me and that they were a good way to live."

The main result of these explorations was an enhanced sense of freedom. Nancy recalls, "I somehow felt *freer*. I felt as if I had more control over my own life. I felt released from the shackles. I still couldn't quite get a grasp on my life, but I was free of the angry God and hypocritical church experiences of my childhood." She still feels this way. She no longer seeks counsel from spiritualists. She knows herself better than she did before and finds it easier to make up her own mind. "There's just something inside my soul that says God is good." She says organized religion did not help her discover that; she needed to find it on her own. To be in charge this way is liberating. Images of freedom come easily to her. Sometimes she imagines herself floating like a balloon. When she prays, she imagines herself freeing her thoughts to rise like little balloons toward God.

Nancy's journey began in reaction to a family and church environment that she found patriarchal and constraining. But she was also a product of her times. Indeed, her parents paved the way. Like a growing number of people in the 1950s, her parents switched denominations—from Catholic to Baptist—in hopes of finding a spiritual home more to their liking. Nancy was put off by both denominations' claims to having absolute truth. She decided that if it were possible to switch, it was possible to do without organized religion entirely. She was also raised to believe that things could be improved if people thought for themselves rather than clinging to the past. Her parents favored the civil rights movement and voted for John F. Kennedy. Nancy says the social reforms of the 1960s "turned up a little flame" inside her that said she should be "part of making things right." The Vietnam war made her angry because she did not think it was making things right. Eastern religions and the hippie culture were a breath of fresh air. She admits she was naive, but she found them liberating because they appealed to the best in human nature.

UNDERSTANDING THE NEW FREEDOMS

A decade earlier, few observers of American religion had foreseen the kinds of spiritual exploration in which Shirley Knight, Adam Westfield, and Nancy Nystrom engaged during the 1960s. Schooled to think that spirituality depended on the tight-knit bonds of ethnic and religious attachments, they saw only the likelihood of spirituality diminishing as these attachments weakened. Indeed, the 1950s' revival in established religion was regarded as a temporary phenomenon because of the social forces working against it.[5] Intense, introspective spiritual searching was the last thing anyone expected; as Abraham Heschel lamented, speaking of Christians and Jews alike, "The self is silent; words are dead, and prayer is a forgotten language."[6]

The upsurge of interest in spirituality in the late 1960s is all the more impressive when viewed against these predictions of declining interest in spirituality. The new quest for the sacred blossomed despite the breakdown of social arrangements that had given religion its communal base. The fact that it could blossom this way attests to the fact that spirituality was indeed shifting from an attachment to place and becoming increasingly eclectic.

Although the 1960s was an unusual decade, filled with radical ideas and shocking behavior, it corrected some of the aberrations that the previous decade had brought to spirituality. The clinging to safe, respectable houses of worship in which a domesticated God could be counted on to provide reassurance was being challenged by religious movements that reasserted some of the mystery that had always been part of conceptions of the sacred. Americans in the fifties chose largely to remain where they were, opting for security rather than risking their faith in a genuine search for spiritual depth; however, in the 1960s many Americans, having learned that they could move around, think through their options, and select a faith that truly captured what they believed to be the truth, took the choice seriously, bargaining with their souls, seeking new spiritual guides, and rediscovering that God dwells not only in homes but also in the byways trod by pilgrims and sojourners.

The sixties questioned middle-class, white-bread definitions of who God was and of where God could be found, making it more uncertain how to be in touch with the sacred. In this process, more Americans drew inspiration from the struggles of the poor, from the rich spiritual traditions of African Americans, from other world religions, from rock music and contemporary art, and from changing understandings of gender and sexuality. If the result was more complex, it was at least more true to the broad variety of human experience.

The mood of the sixties was also indebted to nearly a century of U.S. and European commentary on the growing anonymity of modern life, ranging from Karl Marx and Ferdinand Toennies to Sinclair Lewis's *Babbitt* to William Whyte's *Organization Man* and David Riesman's *Lonely Crowd*. In these depictions, the spiritual homes—Marx's "heart of a heartless world"—that had provided warmth, succor, and identity in the past were becoming increasingly sparse as a result of large-scale industry, the assembly line, the bureaucratic workplace, the city, and finally the suburb. Whereas it had once been possible to have a distinct, nuanced, public sense of who one was as a result of living in a particular neighborhood or attending a certain parish, now, according to these interpretations, one had only a numbing feeling of anonymity. In the suburb of the 1960s, just as in the factory of the 1890s, each person was an interchangeable part, all fundamentally the same in outward appearances. Whatever distinctive characteristics of spirit set the individual apart from others were largely invisible to those same others. The growing desire to escape was thus less of an inclination to leave home for the sheer sake of gaining one's independence than of wanting to flee the stale sameness of modernity that was threatening to engulf one's very soul.

The religious efflorescence of the 1960s was also rooted in long-standing traditions of freedom in American religion. These traditions not only emphasized the right of individuals to choose their own faith but also provided a set of arguments about the basis of this right. For instance, Thomas Jefferson had offered two grounds for the free exercise of religion that remained part of thinking in the United States two centuries later (despite some changes in understandings of basic terms). One was that the human spirit was naturally inclined to think freely, to be curious, to examine alternatives, and to be influenced by arguments and opinions. The other was that any conviction arrived at short of such free exploration was somehow less than genuine. It was, in Jefferson's view, similar to being coerced, and thus tending "only to beget habits of hypocrisy and meanness."[7] Although these arguments focused mostly on preventing the state from interfering with religious expression, they were also associated in Jefferson's mind with the need for people to be free of religious influences that might encourage them to pay homage to one church or pastor rather than seeking another more in keeping with their deepest moral convictions.

Throughout the 1960s, interpreters of the religious scene supplied connections between what was happening among U.S. youth and larger, historical frameworks. Rather than viewing the new experimentation as a complete break with the past, these interpreters saw continuity with important features of Western religion.[8] These interpretations nevertheless presumed that people were still searching for spiritual homes, albeit different ones from those of their congregations or families.

Indeed, much of what attracted public attention were experiments, such as communes, underground churches, and student groups, that fit this conception of the pressing need for new spiritual homes.[9] Freedom was understood as a desire not so much to discard all forms of religious organization as to move from organized religion to new religious communities. Freedom would thus at least be constrained by such leavening influences as the need to get along with each other and to get things done. Religious tradition could embrace some of these alternatives.

It was less clear whether religious leaders could embrace a new mentality that placed less emphasis on community of any kind. People who were searching on their own were assumed to be potential members either of alternative communities or of established religious organizations. The possibility that they might remain permanently on the road was less desirable, particularly because the source of their seeking was taken to be alienation from institutions they did not like. Nobody quite understood that they were also being pulled by a freedom they did like, nor that this freedom was quite compatible with the increasingly fluid environment in the United States.

It is possible with hindsight to see not only that freedom was at the heart of the spiritual quest of many Americans during the 1960s but also that the meaning of freedom was changing. Western religious thought has generally held that individuals choose among various courses of action and therefore must have freedom to exercise this choice. Because individuals are likely to choose evil, however, some means of guiding their choices must also be present. Conscience is an inner voice guiding individual choice. It restrains individual choice by reminding people of their social responsibilities or by reflecting time-worn social norms. The key to understanding how the 1960s reshaped ideas of spiritual freedom lies in the difference between freedom of conscience and freedom of choice.

Conscience speaks authoritatively about right and wrong. It does not connote shades of gray as much as it does obedience or disobedience to clear standards. It is thus, as the sociologist Emile Durkheim emphasized in his classic treatise on religion, a feature of community.[10] Individuals who live in homogeneous communities with authoritative standards of right and wrong can be mentored by an internalized voice. This voice is binding, meaning that freedom lies in the right to voluntarily obey or disobey rather than having to conform to some arbitrarily imposed or coercive standard. Freedom of conscience implies an absence of external intrusion into such communities. The sacred space is morally inviolable, and yet it provides freedom within its boundaries for individual talents and convictions to be expressed as long as primary loyalty to the community is maintained.[11]

In contrast, freedom of choice becomes important when individuals must make their way among multiple communities. Decisions are required about entry and exit into particular communities and about whether to participate in any community. Under such conditions, the internal voice decides less between right and wrong and more between better and worse. Freedom to choose implies having available an array of options. The ability to make good choices depends on exercising the right to weigh these various options.

Norman Mailer's essay on the "hipster," which in many ways presaged the mood of the 1960s, illustrates the emerging emphasis on freedom of choice. A person of character, Mailer wrote, is not so much one who can distinguish between good and bad as one who can realize possibilities in the face of growing uncertainty. To make choices is the hallmark of freedom because every situation poses "a new alternative, a new question" and because emphasis is placed "on complexity rather than simplicity." True freedom comes from liberating oneself from the repressive "superego" of the community and from developing one's own moral imagination through a process of experimentation.[12]

THE RIGHTS REVOLUTION

For many people, these new ways of thinking about spiritual freedom can be traced to the civil rights movement. Government was the agent most capable of intruding on taken-for-granted freedoms of conscience. In the 1960s, government was perceived as a threat by many who thought it was interfering in their local communities, but it also offered new freedoms to those who felt unable to express themselves adequately. The civil rights movement, calling on government to protect freedom of conscience and being resisted for the same reasons, became one of the prominent places in which freedom was redefined—and in ways that would influence not only civic discourse but also understandings of spirituality.

In 1958, Martin Luther King Jr.'s book *Stride toward Freedom* appeared, quickly selling more than sixty thousand copies and receiving favorable publicity in nearly all religious and secular periodicals. King argued that principles of freedom found in Christianity and in the U.S. democratic tradition needed to be rediscovered and extended so that all Americans could enjoy the fruits of liberty. His argument reflected a progressive view of history in which the forces opposing freedom would eventually succumb to those favoring it but not without the active efforts of interested parties. Indeed, King saw a special role for African Americans to fulfill in bringing the claims of freedom to the forefront of public attention.[13]

Although King resorted sparingly to the idea of conscience, he did call on all Americans to heed the "national conscience" in working together for racial justice. Freedom was thus associated explicitly in his treatise with freedom from oppression, with the attainment of individual and collective dignity, with civic responsibility, and with the spiritual health of the nation. The quest for freedom was a way of ridding the United States of evil and of elevating its status as a "colony of heaven" in which all people were "one in Christ."

King's understanding of freedom emphasized the internalized voice of right and wrong that was common to a spirituality of dwelling with God. It was rooted in communal traditions within Christianity and in understandings of U.S. democracy to a greater extent than in the restless desire to experience alternative life-styles as a way of discovering new concepts of morality. In a broad sense, freedom was vitally important to the civil rights movement, as activists participated in freedom marches and fashioned themselves as freedom fighters. Yet its meanings were deliberately framed to give it continuity with U.S. political and religious ideals. Politically, it was a feature of democracy, an inalienable right to live without restrictions arbitrarily imposed because of race, color, or creed. Spiritually, it was rooted in a conception of brotherhood that implied a responsibility to treat others with equal respect and to respect the common values on which that brotherhood was established.

King's idea of freedom was thus constrained by a commitment to equal rights, justice, and love of the common good. It was also the type of freedom best understood within a communal or corporate context such as that in which a spirituality of dwelling was found. In his "I Have a Dream" speech King in fact repeatedly invoked metaphors of dwelling. He spoke often of African Americans living as exiles in their own land, shunted onto an island of poverty in a sea of prosperity. Freedom meant full participation in a place where human rights were inalienable and happiness could be pursued; it meant that all of God's children could sit down at the table together, join hands, and sing together of their beloved land.[14]

Freedom especially meant the opportunity, as theologian Joseph Washington Jr. added, "to enjoy the fruits and shoulder the responsibilities of the American society."[15] It was often described as the same kind of assimilation that European Americans had experienced—not a loss of ethnic identity, but the chance to build homes and communities and to pursue personal ideals without restrictions imposed by other groups. In the view of most religious leaders, true freedom was enhanced by being part of a religious community that respected the dignity of all persons.

The essential mark of spiritual freedom was thus the right not to pick and choose but to be included in "the household of faith."[16]

But the questions that some civil rights activists were raising about "the establishment" gradually became occasions for thinking about deeper meanings of liberation. As the 1960s unfolded, spiritual liberation came increasingly to mean a quest that deliberately took one outside social institutions. Cynicism resulted in questions being raised about the common values in which freedom of conscience was grounded. Other writers encouraged young people to "go into the wilderness" to confront themselves and to spend time meditating about the mysteries of life. They should be, Jack Kerouac had written, "mad to live, mad to talk, mad to be saved, desirous of everything at the same time."[17]

For many of the people we talked to, the civil rights movement was indeed their point of departure, teaching them that diversity is good and that personal exploration is desirable. A woman who still attends church but who expresses her spirituality through a wider variety of social service activities attributes the decisive shift in her orientation to a summer camp she attended in 1961, when she was a junior in high school. The camp, sponsored by several of the churches in her area, was an attempt to bring the civil rights movement to the local level by putting teenagers from predominately white neighborhoods into mixed racial settings for the first time. She says the interaction began to "open" her consciousness. A few years later she participated in a summer work program sponsored by the American Friends Service Committee. She learned a lot, not only from the inner-city residents she was helping but also from fellow volunteers. "They were quite liberal in social philosophy," she remembers. She began to realize how important it is "to understand where different people are coming from," and she was inspired by the people she met who were disadvantaged.

Gradually this woman came to believe that there are good people wherever you go. She began to think that denominational differences and doctrines were less important than serving others. She was especially influenced by the Friends' teaching that, as she puts it, "God can speak through anyone; there's not just somebody appointed by God to carry out his will, but God works through everyone." Over the years, she has followed these inclinations, switching from church to church, sometimes remaining uninvolved, expressing detachment from theological arguments, and feeling that she is seeking God in her own way.

Jim Sampson provides the clearest example of how the civil rights movement started to reshape people's ideas about the meaning of freedom itself. Jim is a retail clothing salesman in his late fifties. When he was a teenager, King preached at the African American church Jim attended with his family in Philadelphia. The sermon had a deep impact on Jim because he had been raised to take what people of faith said with utmost seriousness. The spirituality Jim was raised with is best characterized as a spirituality of dwelling. He says his earliest memory having to do with religion is simply that "religion was everywhere." It was on the lips of his grandmother, with whom he spent a great deal of time. "She would stand with her hands folded behind her, look up, pace up and down the hallway, and talk to the Lord," Jim remembers. He recalls in detail the Baptist church he went to several times a week as a child: the foyer, the double doors leading into the sanctuary, the arrangement of the pews, the pulpit, and the cross behind it. All his friends went to the church.

What Jim remembers most about King's sermon was its emphasis on God's love for all people. He says it pricked his conscience. A few weeks later, Jim's conscience was pricked again, this time by his own pastor's preaching. "I really came in touch with my spirituality—with my purpose here on earth," he recalls. The Christian message of love and redemption became his own. "Part of my core values," he says.[18] At this point in his life, Jim understood spiritual freedom largely as the freedom that comes to a person whose conscience is guided by deep immersion within a Christian community. Describing this understanding as "freedom in Christ," he explains that he felt clearer about what was right and what was wrong. King became a tangible symbol of what was right, an "icon," somebody who Jim wanted to follow. But several years would pass before the opportunity came.

When Jim graduated from high school, he had no money to attend college, so he took a job working for a carpenter. Within months he was drafted. After two years in Vietnam, he returned to find his neighborhood engulfed by the civil rights movement. Jim still believed in "God and country," as he puts it, but he immediately joined one of the civil rights demonstrations. Protesting for the freedom of his people seemed like the right thing to do.

Jim says the civil rights movement affected his spirituality mainly by fueling his anger. During one of the protest marches, police turned off the street lights, causing the marchers to panic, and then beat many of the marchers with clubs. Jim's uncle, one of the deacons at his church, was in the hospital for days. After this episode, Jim sided increasingly with the militant wing of the movement being led by Bobby Seale,

H. Rapp Brown, and Malcolm X. He started questioning whether the core values he had learned in church were right.

After King was assassinated, Jim's anger turned to cynicism. Then his cynicism deepened when the only job he could find—as part of a new affirmative-action program sponsored by the city—was washing trucks. Having been unable to achieve freedom in one way, he increasingly turned to seeking it in another. For the next several years he tried to enjoy life as much as possible, even though it was often difficult. On two occasions he and his girlfriend sought an abortion. Eventually they married and had a son, but his wife left him a few years later.

Jim recalls this period as being so traumatic that he was unable to face most of the people he knew. He interacted less with his family, found new friends, and quit going to church. He says his core values did not change. But he did come to think of spirituality in a new way. Rather than associating it with his place in the church, he thinks of it in connection with the wider array of choices he has made. "I'm just as comfortable with Muslims or Catholics as I am with Baptists," he observes. "I feel that God is in all of us. I'm open to more ideas." The greatest change, he says, was that he found trying to be obedient to God oppressive. It became necessary for him to "push out the boundaries."

Apart from the civil rights movement, the 1960s promoted a mood of openness that encouraged people to respect diversity and thus to move freely among different life-styles and world-views. Many of the people we talked to took pride in having triumphed over their parents' religious, ethnic, and racial prejudices. Having gotten to know people of other backgrounds, having lived through or learned about the civil rights movement, and in many cases having married someone from a different faith were decisive experiences. They felt that life was better as a result.

Adam Westfield is one example. Even though he came from a long line of educated and professional people, he believes there was much prejudice to be overcome. "My father was definitely bigoted," he admits, "and my mother would never say things particularly, but I do remember her saying, 'It would probably be better if you didn't marry a Catholic or a Negro.' What's interesting about that comment is that Jews weren't even on the chart. I ended up marrying a Catholic, and I felt pretty good about it." Moving toward a more tolerant outlook on life was especially meaningful for him.

Another way in which people started to open out was by experiencing and reflecting on the struggle for equality between women and men, a movement that had grown independently of the struggle for civil rights but that often drew on the same sources for inspiration. The spiritual implications of this struggle were often profound because people came to believe that the teachings of their own religious traditions were fundamentally biased against women. People who came to this conviction were thus compelled to reject some of their religious assumptions and to think how to find inspiration in new interpretations or in other traditions.[19]

Adam Westfield is again an example. Asked how the feminist movement had influenced him, he remarks, "The religious texts—I don't think it's just the Torah and I don't think it's just the Bible—have really done women an incredible disservice. And that's such an understatement. In my heart I know that women are my equal in the same way that I know and feel that a black person is my equal, or that a Jew is my equal, or whatever. I feel it. I feel it really passionately and deeply. So I'm very sympathetic with any feminist activity. I would call myself a feminist to the extent that a man can."

A woman in her late forties—a life-long member of a Lutheran church—also remembered the vivid impact feminist thinking played in her spiritual development. "Talking once with our minister we got onto the topic of how God may view women. The discussion turned to the fact that it was women who first discovered that Christ had risen from the tomb. That led to the fact that it was Mary, again a woman, who first knew of the coming of the Christ child. But even more interesting was the story of the shepherds. He indicated that in those days the shepherds were also young women!" As a result, she feels more like she has a part in God's scheme.

As the sixties progressed, millions of Americans came to be influenced by changing understandings of gender and by a new interest in feminist views of spirituality. In one important respect, feminist spirituality reinforced the more familiar emphasis on freedom of conscience, especially by focusing greater attention on the internal voices of which conscience was composed and often by insisting that these voices be informed by egalitarian and cooperative social relationships.[20] Yet, in another sense, they also contributed to the growing emphasis on freedom of choice. Choice of life-styles and careers, as well as the right to participate equally in religious services and institutions, played a role in reshaping understandings of freedom. More important, religious symbols themselves became fungible, severed from automatic connections with their meanings because their patriarchal imagery was being questioned.[21] Increasingly, it proved possible—even necessary—to be intentional about the ways one chose to embrace the sacred.[22]

THE FLUIDITY OF LIFE

Whether they applauded or lamented the changes taking place, social observers in the 1960s and early 1970s uniformly emphasized the fact that life was becoming complex in ways that challenged the viability of established institutions. Theologian Michael Novak (prior to becoming a "neoconservative") wrote that communication technology was destroying the ability to live within stable geographic places. Instead, "the camera zooms in, pulls back, superimposes, cuts away suddenly, races, slows, flashes back, flicks ahead, juxtaposes, repeats, spins." Our very sense of reality, he argued, becomes more fluid.[23]

Social theorists who in the 1950s had written of the need to construct strong institutions in order to keep the terror of chaos at bay were now reinterpreted.[24] If institutions were truly human constructions, then they needed to be questioned, debunked, and perhaps replaced. Facing up to the terror would liberate us. We might be able to withstand more chaos than we had imagined. Institutions, above all, existed not so much to get the work done as to perpetuate a myth that work was being done. Social life was largely a fiction of smoke and mirrors. Once people realized that, they could create their own realities.

But the emphasis that many Americans placed on questioning established social conditions was itself rooted in social conditions. Freedom of choice was the rallying cry of consumers even more than it was of civil rights activists and hippies. Indeed, it is interesting to recall the enormous expansion in consumerism that took place during the 1960s; it has been overshadowed by the political unrest of the period but may have had consequences that were equally profound. At the end of World War II, consumer products were invariably scarce, and the corner grocery or local hardware store remained at the core of retailing. By 1960, retailing had already expanded enormously, including the invention of large chains, such as Korvette's, which took in more than $150 million in that year. In 1954, a Chicago businessman, Ray Kroc, had witnessed a new idea on a trip to California that would revolutionize the way Americans ate, and by 1960 more than two hundred McDonald's restaurants had spread across the country and were rapidly being joined by other fast-food chains. Over the next three decades, more than eight thousand McDonald's would be added. Americans learned two important lessons from these developments: one, that you could shop around for some of the essential services that had always been provided at home, and, two, that not only was it valuable to obtain services at a good price but convenience—especially in the amount of time it took—was a valuable commodity itself. Above all, Americans were deliberately being taught to shop as never before. The generation who came of age during the 1960s was the first cohort of young people to have been reared in a fully commercialized consumer society and to have been exposed to television advertising since birth. Between 1950 and 1960 national expenditures on advertising had doubled, and between 1960 and 1970 they doubled again.[25]

Religious entrepreneurs started to imitate the strategies of advertisers and retailers. Drive-in churches and drive-through confessionals made headlines as innovative, if bizarre, adaptations of business ideas to the religious world. Less visibly, clergy shortened sermons to accommodate the time demands of their parishioners, religious bookstores began to appear, the bookstore chains that developed in shopping malls started to carry Bibles and inspirational books, and college campuses started to provide tracts and sign-up sheets for religious organizations as a cafeteria-style approach to promoting religious interests along with other student activities.[26] Spirituality, like hamburgers, was increasingly something one could get quickly and in a variety of places.

If the consumer revolution encouraged Americans to choose, so did new ideas about the family. In May 1960, the Food and Drug Administration approved Enovid as an oral contraceptive. By the end of 1961 more than four hundred thousand women were taking the Pill. This figure rose to 1.2 million a year later and reached 2.3 million by the end of 1963.[27] Journalists heralded the development as a new era of freedom for women. Religious leaders recognized its moral implications but could scarcely have predicted its wider social impact. During the 1950s, the average time between confirmation class and birth of first child for U.S. young people had been only seven years; by the end of the 1960s, in large measure because of the new contraceptive technologies, this period had more than doubled to fifteen years. Since the time between confirmation and parenthood has always been one in which young people could drop out of established religion and turn their attention to other things, the doubling of this period was of enormous religious significance.

In a study of Presbyterians, the effects of these social developments were much in evidence: young adults who became religiously uninvolved were significantly more likely than those who stayed "churched" to remain single or to divorce, to have no children, to move more often, and to live farther away from their extended families.[28] More broadly, there appears to be a relationship between the loss of family or community ties and a propensity toward eclecticism in one's attitudes and activities. For instance, research on musical consumption and artistic taste shows that eclecticism in these areas has increased steadily, that it reaches higher levels among single or divorced people than among married people (taking account of age differences), and that it is reinforced by geographic mobility.[29]

Thus, if the 1950s had sanctified the nursery and the family room, the 1960s encouraged those who had been reared in these places to explore the wider world. Whereas the fertility rate had been 3.8 children per woman in 1957, by 1973 it was only 1.9, the lowest it had been in U.S. history. During the same period, the number of young women who remained unmarried increased by a third, and the divorce rate soared. Other trends also signaled a more "liberated" orientation toward family: the proportion of first births occurring outside of marriage rose from 5 percent in the late 1950s to 11 percent in 1971; a spectacular eightfold increase occurred during the 1960s in the number of household heads who were reported as living apart from relatives while sharing their living quarters with an unrelated adult "partner" of the opposite sex; and the number of persons reporting in surveys that they had engaged in premarital sexual relations increased, as did homosexual activity.[30]

Accompanying these changes in life-style was an enormous rise in exposure to new ideas and information. College training was perhaps the major source of such exposure. Between 1960 and 1970, college enrollments jumped from 3.6 million to 8.6 million students.[31] Another way of gauging the impact of this expansion is through the declining numbers of Americans who had not graduated from high school: in 1950, fully two-thirds (66 percent) fell into this category; by 1970, fewer than half (48 percent) did; and by 1990, the proportion was less than a quarter (22 percent).[32] Young women, whose numbers on campuses tripled during the 1960s, were particularly influenced by these changes. In contrast to their mothers, whose twenties were spent mostly at home raising small children, young women in the sixties and seventies were much more likely to be living in dormitories or apartments and studying literature and the social sciences or preparing for careers in the professions.[33]

Opening out was being promoted actively by government and business as well. A "mobile, fluid labor force" was championed by employers who wanted workers willing to move as new jobs and markets demanded. Realizing from the war effort that goods and services needed to be brought together in more complex ways than ever before, policymakers approved a new forty-one thousand mile interstate highway system in 1956, and oversaw its construction during the next decade and a half. As teamsters and vacationers scrambled to benefit from these new resources, it should not have been surprising that new rumblings of the spirit would be expressed in books such as Jack Kerouac's *On the Road* or in the music of the Rolling Stones.

The emphasis on choice and exploration would have made little difference, however, had it not been for another important factor. Prosperity made it possible for growing numbers of Americans to take advantage of the new opportunities available to them. The relative prosperity of the 1960s is evident in the fact that per capita income grew by more than 3 percent each year between 1960 and 1975 (adjusted for inflation), compared with growth of less than 2 percent annually during the following fifteen years. Another indicator of how this growth affected people is that families living below the poverty line fell from 22 percent of the population in 1960 to only 12 percent in 1975; in comparison, most of the growth in the subsequent period benefited the rich.[34]

Rising prosperity meant that people like Shirley Knight, Adam Westfield, and Nancy Nystrom had opportunities to explore new spiritual horizons that their parents and grandparents did not have. Young people who matured during the 1960s were able to take classes in college that exposed them to other religious traditions. Many of them traveled, sometimes to places that sparked their religious imaginations. Many were able to major in the humanities or social sciences, rather than specializing in subjects that may not have exposed them to new ideas about religion.

THE CONFRONTATION WITH EVIL

Although it is generally pictured as a time of hedonism and self-exploration, the 1960s was even more a decade in which Americans who had tried to build a safe world in the 1950s came to terms with the continuing reality of evil. They did so not in a profoundly theological way but through public events and personal traumas that could scarcely be ignored.[35] If meaninglessness and boredom were (as commentators argued) the wellsprings of youthful unrest, concern about suffering primed the pump. Indeed, new interest in freedom was inspired as much by a desire to understand and alleviate suffering as it was by sheer self-indulgence.

Adam Westfield remembers how the death of President Kennedy affected him. When Kennedy was elected, Adam recalls, "he was all tan and he looked amazing. He was one of us who had gone out and done it, and was leading the Free World, and we could too. I am different in my ambitions and my view of the world because of him." Kennedy's death was a serious psychological blow. "When he died, we were all numb. It was a huge event." But Adam also says "it seemed random." Thus, the deaths of King and Bobby Kennedy had a more radical effect on his thinking.

Most of the people we interviewed who remembered the deaths of the Kennedys and of King spoke of the shock to their values. In an instant, the familiar world was shattered, and the fantasy world of better tomorrows came to an end; in its place was the frightening reality of a world capable of generating evil. A woman who turned fourteen the day Kennedy was killed puts it well: "I was brokenhearted when he died. How could the world kill this man who was supposed to bring so much good to the world? I really believed that he was going to bring good. It was horrible. Everything went crazy."

Almost three decades later, Nancy Nystrom breaks down and cries as she describes how she felt when she heard that King had been shot. Such emotion can be understood only in relation to the spiritual meaning with which the civil rights movement was charged. Nancy was typical of many younger people who believed that God's work must somehow be done through social reforms because it was not being accomplished by the churches. Working hard on behalf of human betterment became a kind of religion for her. When these efforts met with violent resistance, the basis for that religion had to be rethought. "I wondered," she recalls, "what is prevalent? Good or evil?"

Military service during the war in Vietnam was another way in which young people came to a growing recognition of evil. Adam Westfield had always been taught to defend his country. When he was drafted in 1968, he came to realize that there was evil within himself. He explains, "I don't think there's any sensitive and caring human being who goes into basic training and doesn't get changed dramatically. What the Army does is it makes you anonymous. It shaves off all your hair, it keeps you from sleeping, so it really turns you into a nonperson, which is really alarming. One person had told me before I went in, 'They'll break you.' And they do. That's what military discipline does. I also discovered two things. It's fun to march. You walk along and it's fun. It feels good: click, click, click. It's this deep human thing, for boys anyway, fun to march.

The other thing is they give you this really light little thing made out of aluminum or something, with a handle on it, and you carry it around like a little briefcase, and it can fire four hundred bullets a minute. You push the trigger and you hit the target a hundred yards away or two hundred yards away. That was great; I loved it. It struck me that men like to kill, that it's fun. That's a scary thought that doesn't leave you—that I have that in me."

Discovering evil—in the society or in yourself—may not lead to a new interest in spirituality. But, for many of the people we interviewed, this discovery started them on a journey that led away from the simple religious truths they had learned as children or, in other cases, the simple secular pleasures they had taken for granted as children. For Adam Westfield, this was the start of his quest to learn how to be tolerant, how to wage peace, and how to encourage what he calls "moral civic action." In her book, *Dakota*, Kathleen Norris draws an even stronger connection between the confrontation with evil and the possibilities for liberation. "For one who has chosen the desert and truly embraced the forsaken ground," she writes, "it is not despair or fear or limitation that dictates how one lives. One finds instead an openness and hope that verges on the wild."[36]

The person we interviewed who best illustrates the wild hope that Norris describes is Diane Mason. A woman in her forties who runs a mental-health clinic, Diane was deeply influenced by the evil she witnessed in the 1960s and early 1970s. She was sixteen when her brother came home from Vietnam. He was drinking and using drugs, trying hard to forget the killing. Shortly after he was arrested for disturbing the peace, the church where her parents taught Sunday school asked them not to come back.

Diane says she didn't lose her faith in God, but she did lose confidence in the church. From that point on, she decided to live by her own rules. She experimented with drugs until she graduated from high school. In college, she majored in drama because it was an outlet for her desire to be creative. Before she graduated, her restlessness took her in a rusty Volkswagen bus to the Florida Keys, where she lived for a year. During the year she decided she wanted to have a baby. She met a man, got pregnant, and eventually came home to live with her parents. Diane was exercising her freedom to explore spirituality as well. She took courses in world religions in college, read books about Tibetan Buddhism, and learned to meditate. She dabbled with the psychic teachings of Edgar Cayce, talked with friends about Native American spirituality, and read the Bible. Whenever people asked her her religious preference, she said, "Christian and Buddhist—and Jewish and everything else."

But a spirituality that emphasized freedom to choose anything did not end simply in dabbling or self-indulgence. Through these years, Diane was haunted by her brother's mental anguish. As he went from hospital to hospital, she became increasingly interested in learning what she could do to help. At first she volunteered at a crisis-intervention center. She took courses in psychology and toyed with the idea of becoming a social worker. For a brief time she held an office job at a clinic. Eventually she worked her way up to her present position. Most of her work now involves networking—she solicits donations to keep the clinic afloat, brings health professionals together, and provides services for people like her brother.

The lesson that Diane gained from trying to make choices about her spirituality—and about her life—was that the most important aspect of spirituality is doing. She isn't sure what to believe. Nor is she sure that what one believes matters. Her spirituality frees her to do good. "I just believe that we are what we do," she asserts. "I live my spirituality. It's in everything I do. The reason I exist in this reality is to make it better." The connection between this view of spirituality and the pain she witnesses in people like her brother is that helping to alleviate this pain energizes her. "I've watched how their faith has helped them survive," she says. "It gets them through the night. I see miracles. I see people come alive." She summarizes, "I mostly see God through the work of other people. And my work is acknowledging the God in others." In many ways Diane Mason's spiritual journey has been characterized by choices she made mainly to find out where they would lead. She has exercised a great deal of freedom in making these choices. Yet her view of God became so inclusive that she was led to see God even in the people she was trying to help. She hopes that her work is helping to liberate them. She knows it is helping to liberate her.

SPIRITUALITY TAKES WING

The most significant impact of the 1960s for many people's understandings of spirituality was a growing awareness that spirituality and organized religion are different and, indeed, might run in opposite directions. Although many Americans continued to participate in churches and synagogues, younger people increasingly pursued spirituality in other venues, and even the religiously involved found inspiration from a wider variety of sources. Underlying these changes was the shift in fundamental understandings of freedom that I described earlier.

Whereas freedom of conscience had once emphasized an absence of intrusions into one's place of worship, freedom of choice now gave the spiritual quest increased importance and encouraged seekers to make up their own minds in matters of the heart. The poet Maya Angelou, experiencing a spiritual awakening during the 1960s, wrote lyrically of the exhilaration associated with this new sense of freedom: "I am a big bird winging over high mountains, down into serene valleys. I am ripples of waves on silver seas. I'm a spring leaf trembling in anticipation."[37]

Academicians were among the first to challenge the monopoly of established religion and to suggest why the faithful might want to look elsewhere. The groundwork for these attacks had been laid a generation earlier by theologians wrestling with the need to modernize in order to accommodate changing social realities. Dietrich Bonhoeffer had written of a "religionless Christianity," which would be free of the political entanglements that characterized the European churches for so many centuries.[38] Harvey Cox, living in Berlin just prior to writing *The Secular City,* read Bonhoeffer's works and was deeply influenced by them. Cox argued that "dereligioning" was a good thing because it freed people from oppressive moralities and made them think hard about their own spirituality.

Others took up similar themes. In a lecture given at Harvard Divinity School, Robert Bellah asserted that "the biblical tradition provides insufficient resources to meet the desperate problems that beset us." Rather than clinging obstinately to this tradition, he suggested, Americans needed to understand the wisdom of Native Americans, the experience of nothingness expressed in Zen Buddhism, the prophetic elements in African and African American cultures, and the encounters with Mother Earth in primitive and shamanistic religions.[39] Combining Christian and Marxist imagery, philosopher Norman Brown encouraged Americans to "leave the place where we belong. The Proletariate has no fatherland, and the son of man no place to lay his head. Be at home nowhere."[40]

Critics within organized religion were not attempting to debunk Christianity or Judaism but to show that a spirituality of dwelling was too narrow. Indeed, many argued that religion had become sacrilegious, worshiping customs and organizations rather than the Creator. Their imagery was of a spiritual home, but one too neat to be lived in. They wrote of chains and confinement, intolerance, nationalism, closed systems, authoritarianism, and heavy-handedness. To live within a sacred habitat was to be tribalistic and thus to dwell among people of limited imagination. It was reminiscent of Nazism and similar to communism. Its familism was too secure, bestowing "on all its members an unquestioned place and a secure identity," answering questions before they were raised.[41] Whatever the new era was hailing, it would be open to all manifestations of truth. It would be tolerant, respecting the insights of all peoples and faiths; it would give people room to doubt, to express their views, and to explore new horizons.[42]

Clergy, too, were becoming increasingly worried that congregations were not doing enough to attack the status quo. In a cross-denominational survey of clergy in California conducted in 1968, more than half (52 percent) agreed that "Protestant churches have become too aligned with the status quo in the United States to become major agents of social reform." Nearly this many (43 percent) agreed that "as long as the churches persist in regarding the parish or the local congregation as their normative structure, they will not confront life at its most significant point."[43] Hoping that parishioners would remain loyal to the faith even if they were disillusioned with their churches, these clergy often played a hand in the changes that were taking place. Nancy Nystrom, we saw, was influenced by the priest at her high school who counseled students to love their neighbors instead of dutifully attending mass. Another Catholic woman who had dropped out of the church found support from a priest at a marriage-encounter weekend who told her, "Many of theology's greatest ideas have come from people who were not part of the church."

Many of the people we talked to had thus come to find special meaning in the contrast between spirituality and religion. For them, spirituality was a broader term that signaled the value of drawing insights from many sources, whereas religion was simply the particular institutional manifestation of different traditions. Adam Westfield explains the distinction in these terms: "if one could ever be so smart as to understand Moses and Buddha and Lao Tsu and the Bantu elders from many centuries ago, I think you could come very close to a common human spirituality and the fundamental goodness of man." Religion, to him, means something like denominationalism, whereas spirituality is more the core of different religions. Spirituality, he says, "is closer to nature and closer to oneness with the planet."

Such broadening has been evident in other studies as well. One study tracked down a large number of adults who had participated in confirmation classes at churches in the 1960s. It found that after two decades fewer than a third remained in their denomination, while nearly half (48 percent) had become "unchurched." Of the unchurched, a relatively small portion (8 percent) claimed to be entirely without religious interests. Most still entertained some religious views, participated occasionally in organized religion, but largely pursued spirituality in their own ways. Indeed, they legitimated their spiritual eclecticism by identifying themselves as religious liberals and by espousing universalistic views of salvation and individualistic orientations toward theological authority. Nine out of ten thought it possible to be a good Christian or Jew without attending religious services; eight out of ten thought individuals should arrive at their own beliefs independent of any religious organizations; and seven out of ten thought all religions are equally good ways of finding ultimate truth.[44]

Other evidence points to the wide variety of ways spirituality was being pursued.[45] According to a 1977 Gallup Poll, 4 percent of the population said they currently practiced Transcendental Meditation, 3 percent practiced yoga, 2 percent said they were involved in mysticism, and 1 percent claimed membership in an Eastern religion. Among people under age thirty and among college graduates, these figures were approximately twice as high as in the population as a whole.[46] In addition to Eastern religions, many Christian groups provided alternative styles of worship that would alter how people perceived their relationship to congregations. One woman who was in college at the time remembers joining a group called the Church of the Open Doors. She reports, "We went to people's houses and met there rather than at church itself. We were trying to get closer to what Jesus's teachings really were as opposed to all of the trappings of organized church. And we had many interesting discussions. One that stood out in my mind was how much you would help someone you didn't know, someone you saw with car trouble or something, whether you would chance being taken advantage of yourself to stop and help the person and what was the right thing to do."[47]

The impact of some of these changes was clearly evident in 1978, when a national study of religious participation was conducted. Of the people in that study who had been born between 1944 and 1960, nearly half were single or divorced, a majority had lived in their present community fewer than five years, more than two-thirds had changed residences in the past five years, two-thirds had stopped participating in religious organizations for a period of at least two years, and only 13 percent currently attended a church or synagogue weekly. The fact that only one in eight was an active church-goer was especially striking, given the fact that 66 percent had attended regularly as children. Dissatisfaction with established religion was evident in attitudes as well as in behavior: three quarters agreed that "most churches and synagogues today have lost the real spiritual part of religion," and a majority felt that "most churches and synagogues today are too concerned with organizational, as opposed to theological or spiritual issues."[48]

The study also revealed a little suspected fact about the religious defection that was taking place among young people: in addition to the liberalizing influences of the classroom and the counterculture, defection was most likely among young people who were being severely affected by the dislocations of social change: semiskilled workers, sales and service workers, divorced persons, African American men, people who had moved more often, and those earning lower incomes.[49] The longer-term significance of these developments was also suggested in the study. Of those in the 1944–1960 birth cohort who had children, only half were exposing their children to formal religious training of any kind, compared with 86 percent who themselves had received religious training as children. Significant exposure was even lower: only 34 percent were sending their children to Sunday school classes, whereas 63 percent had themselves attended such classes.

Wilma Nichols illustrates how easy it had become by the mid-1970s to pursue spirituality outside an established congregation. She was in her late thirties, recently divorced, and raising two children on her salary as an office manager when we interviewed her. She had grown up in a devout Catholic family, gone to college, married a Protestant, and become dissatisfied with the church after the priest advised his flock one Sunday morning that they should quit reading newspapers and watching television in order to avoid temptation. Otherwise, she had not been influenced by the civil rights movement, the campus protests, or any of the turmoil of the 1960s. Indeed, she says she hardly thought about life at all during those years. When her husband fell in love with one of her friends, she decided it was time to start thinking.

"God figured it was time to get my attention!" she explains. At first, she sought help from a therapist who counseled her to get even by having an affair of her own. That advice rekindled Wilma's childhood thoughts about what was right and wrong, including the spiritual basis for such thoughts. Soon after rejecting the therapist's advice, she had to make a thirteen-hour drive for a business trip, and a friend loaned her a set of tapes to keep her company. They were by a businessman who combined Christian themes with motivational appeals. During the trip, she stayed with a family that participated sporadically in the activities of several different churches. That experience broadened her thinking about how one can benefit from churches without having them become stifling. Soon after, she picked up a book on self-love by a prominent television preacher. Finding it more helpful than attending church, she started reading similar books. "There was a lot of Christian ethic in them that was not expressed in religious terms," she recalls.

Wilma Nichols eventually became involved in a local Lutheran church, partly because she wanted her children to experience church. But her individual quest for spirituality left her convinced that no church could fully satisfy her. Participating in a Bible study group and serving on the church council soon bored her. "It showed me the negative aspects of organized religion," she says. Periodically she takes long walks in the woods because this is where she feels especially close to God. She likes the Lutheran emphasis on "faith alone." Reading about Martin Luther, she has been drawn especially to his dictum "Believe boldly; sin boldly." She has a new therapist with whom she enjoys talking about spirituality. "We both know a lot of people in the religious community," she says, "but it's not easy in that environment to talk about spirituality." Indeed, her journey is especially telling because it shows the wide variety of sources on which people can draw for spiritual inspiration.

Although, as we have seen, some clergy themselves encouraged spiritual seekers to find the sacred outside organized religion, a more typical response was to reassert the more traditional dwelling-oriented understanding of spirituality. As if to define themselves clearly, many churches responded to the changes of the 1960s and 1970s by reaffirming their identity as spiritual homes and by encouraging members to return home from their wanderings. For instance, a woman who attends a mainline Protestant church "most Sundays" explains that she goes primarily because it provides a refuge from the rest of her life. She can sit there alone with her thoughts, focus on who she is, perhaps forgive herself for some mistake she has made, and have her values reinforced by being around other good people. Her reason for continuing to attend one church is that it has become familiar to her. Particular teachings are not important, even the pastor doesn't matter; she just knows her way around.

The more important consequence of these changes, however, was in private conceptions of spirituality. For people who have been opening out, it is often difficult to draw a clear distinction between those activities that have sacred or spiritual significance and those that do not. Asked whether he meditates, for example, Adam Westfield says he jogs five miles every morning and comes up with some "pretty interesting thoughts," but he is not sure whether it is "just the endorphins" or something else. Similarly, when asked whether he listens to religious music, he responds, "Is Mozart religious? I've got this sonata that's unbelievable. I play it every morning, and I don't get tired of it. It must be religious. I don't know."

Ultimately the freedom that triumphed in the 1960s was freedom to feel one's own feelings and to experience one's own sensibilities. How one might deliberately go about seeking a relationship with the sacred also underwent serious rethinking. Americans still believed that deliberate effort was valuable. But prayer and Bible reading rooted in habit were no longer as highly valued. Devotional routines that reinforced unthinking loyalty to family and church diminished in importance compared with those that encouraged people to think for themselves. New translations and paraphrases of the Bible proliferated, attracting readers who wanted to think about cant phrases in new ways. Many people saw value in learning about other world religions as ways of sharpening insights about their own. Devotional practice took on added meaning for those who sought to include breathing techniques, exercise, chanting, or emotional work, all in an effort to make spirituality a "whole person" activity.

But devotional practice in another sense was devalued. People were told they needed to escape the security of their religious enclaves and to participate fully in the world. Like Jim Sampson and Diane Mason, they learned that the sacred could also be found in secular society. In work or at play, it was possible to experience moments of transcendence without knowing any special creeds or performing any religious rituals. Thus, one could read Cox's *Secular City*, for example, and find no mention of prayer, meditation, family devotions, or Bible reading. Ordinary work and play were sufficiently sacred to remind the enlightened of God's kingdom. Similarly, ethicist Gibson Winter's *Being Free* encouraged Americans to be critical of technology on religious grounds, but it was enough to form a critical attitude rather than having to adopt an alternative lifestyle or to engage in devotional practices.[50] Faced with the realities of secular society, critics as different as Charles Reich and Theodore Roszak argued that consciousness should (and probably would) be transformed, but doing anything special to communicate with the sacred received little attention.[51]

In the most widely read treatises, therefore, subjectivity was elevated as a central concern, opening the way for increased attention to the interior life (see Chapter 6). But intentional action toward social or personal transformation was often implicitly devalued. Writers pondered feelings of alienation and meaninglessness and counseled readers that life could be better if they only released their inner thoughts from bondage. And, in this respect, the new arguments were not so different from the advice of positive thinkers and thought-reform specialists of the past. Americans did not have to sacrifice comfortable life-styles as long as they paid attention to how they felt about their lives. The specific spiritual disciplines found in Transcendental Meditation, Zen Buddhism, kundalini yoga, and various "human potential" groups attracted widespread attention but were generally marginalized in popular interpretations as esoteric practices. They were depicted as magical cures that would soon disappoint their devotees or as the teachings of gurus whose dress and language set them apart from mainstream culture. Devotional practice could thus be experimented with as part of a counterculture but just as easily abandoned once the counterculture was no longer in vogue.

Nancy Nystrom illustrates these understandings. She feels her spirituality is stronger than her parents' because she has had to struggle harder with hers. Over the years, she has gotten over most of her previous hatred of the church. She imagines she might even start attending church again in the future; it would feel good, she thinks, to worship with other people. In the meantime, she thinks a lot about God and about spirituality. Various activities prompt her to do so: listening to classical music, conversations with a friend. But she does not actively do anything to cultivate her sense of spirituality. Other than her "thought balloons," she does not pray. Her view of freedom is heavily imbued with the value of being in control, so prayer seems to her like asking God to serve as a crutch. Meditation is more interesting but not something she practices regularly. She explains that God is always present, so it makes sense just to meditate "when the spirit moves me." Sometimes she talks to God in the bathtub, and sometimes she prays just as a way of doing something nice for someone else. The way spirituality influences her daily life is thus to quiet her thoughts. She feels less impatient when things go wrong and more capable of making them go right.

THE LIMITS OF FREEDOM

By the end of the 1970s, many of the new religions that had been formed during the preceding decade were being described as "cults." The mass suicide that took place in Guyana in November 1978 among the followers of religious leader Jim Jones fueled the tendency to view religious experiments as bizarre, antisocial movements led by misguided, charismatic figures. In this interpretation, people forsook the faith of their parents, escaped the uncertainties of their own lives, and allowed themselves to be brainwashed by authoritarian cult leaders. The result was submersion in a totalitarian community that resembled a theocratic family, only with higher walls against the outside world.

There were plenty of examples, especially from former cult members and from so-called deprogrammers, to support this interpretation. More common, however, was a form of religious experimentation that involved short-term exposure to a variety of leaders, ideas, and spiritual disciplines. Typical accounts of spiritual journeys took the form: "I tried everything from A to Z," perhaps followed by a list starting with aikido and ending with Zen. But much of the impetus to experiment was short-lived; experimentation staggered to a halt once the Vietnam war ended and the economic downturn accompanying the oil embargo of 1973 forced young Americans to become serious about finding jobs and paying their bills. Yet the idea that spirituality needed to be pursued on one's own and perhaps even in tension with social institutions did not die easily. A decade later most Americans still thought it was important to arrive at their religious values on their own and to be skeptical of accepting the words of religious authorities.

The lingering question from the standpoint of organized religion, of course, is why the churches and synagogues did not oppose—or oppose more vehemently—a cultural development that was to contribute so greatly to the weakening of religion's traditional monopoly over spirituality. The answer can be found only partly in liberal tendencies in mainline theology or in inadequate organizational responses to demographic shifts. Moderate mainline denominations, Catholics, Jews, and evangelical Protestants also participated in the redefinition of spirituality that took place in the 1960s. The reason for this participation was organized religion's own desire to promote intense spiritual conviction in the face of a rising tide of secularism, scientific agnosticism, and implicit indifference bred from taking spirituality for granted as part of one's lineage and community. In order to mobilize increased commitment, religious leaders opted for two seemingly innocent proposals: that the faithful could gain knowledge only by being exposed to a variety of arguments and counterarguments, and that faith was ultimately a matter of inner conviction more than of rational or scientific persuasion.

As they endorsed the ancient teaching that "the truth shall make you free," religious leaders took an important step toward accommodating the growing cultural diversity of the period. No longer able to prevent parishioners from learning about spirituality in ways other than those prescribed by established religious bodies, the leaders of these organizations chose, in effect, to argue that their own traditions did not stand in the way of freedom but offered true freedom. Americans who heard this message often took it quite literally, acting as if the truth on which freedom depended was less important than the exercise of freedom itself. In the future, organized religion would thus be able to compete with other media that also offered spiritual freedom, but its leaders would have to work harder to say what freedom entailed, and they would find themselves engaged in a broader arena of competition from which there was no return.

Individuals who left their spiritual homes also found it difficult to return to them or to find alternatives. Some of the people we interviewed were trying to make the world their home, thus maximizing their freedom to pick and choose. When the whole universe is perceived as God's home, there is enormous freedom to roam; but no particular place can ultimately be more sacred than any other. For example, Wilma Nichols believes God loves everybody. "Would he reject anyone from his house?" she asks. "God has a limitless capacity for forgiveness, so I doubt it." Looking back on her Catholic upbringing, she says it was a necessary first step, like learning the multiplication tables. There was security and order, "but I had to reject it as a young adult." Searching for spirituality on her own was a taxing experience, so she is glad to have found friends who share her journey. Nevertheless, she still imagines herself living in a huge house that she continues to explore. "I have an abiding feeling that new doors are still waiting to be opened." She adds, "There are lessons in spirituality to be learned outside those avenues that advertise themselves as spiritual places."

Other people had returned to a sacred space more narrowly defined where they could feel safe and secure. To an outsider, they sometimes appear to have rejected the pronounced freedom offered by the 1960s, but it is clear that even their search for a spiritual home was influenced by the idea of choice. One man illustrates these influences with particular clarity. Todd Brentwood was attending a Catholic high school in the late 1960s. He recalls that these were "turbulent times" in the church as well as in the society. The result was a "big change" in the school that led him to become "more liberal" and "antiestablishment" in his thinking. Although he had been active in the church since infancy, he now found himself confused. "I couldn't really tell what the church's teachings were." When he went away to college, he found himself without spiritual support. "There was no rail that I could hang onto for spiritual guidance. Everything had to come from me." His response was to embrace a *carpe diem* view of life. "Everything was transitory. Get it while you can. Gather ye rosebuds while ye may, for tomorrow ye may die." He played college basketball, studied, worked at UPS, and enjoyed life.

By the late 1970s, Todd was at a turning point. Deciding that the purpose of life is to achieve happiness for oneself, he had become part of the Me Generation. He became a coach because basketball made him happy. At the high school where he worked, he taught his students to question authority and to dream their own dreams. But he was lonely. His marriage had ended in divorce. His *carpe diem* attitude made it hard to pursue—or to take pleasure in—long-term projects because acquiring the skills for these projects was contrary to keeping his options open from day to day. He also began to realize that he desperately missed his mother, who had died when he was thirteen. He wanted a home, spiritually as well as socially.

Like a growing number of Americans, Todd sought a spiritual home in an evangelical church. It offered fellowship (his new girlfriend attended there) and a compelling message about Jesus as the answer to life's questions. But Todd's new commitment was not a repudiation of his freedom. Indeed, his choice illustrates that conservative Christians were also influenced by the liberating themes of the time. Although he became a "born-again" Christian, Todd did so on his own terms. He says he retained his critical, questioning attitude toward what he heard at the church but was able to participate because the service gave him "a good feeling inside." As he read the Bible and developed a stronger belief in Jesus, he was propelled mainly by the "inner happiness" that resulted. This happiness allowed him to ease up on himself a bit. He decided that "Christian morals"—broadly defined—provided a good basis for life and that he should "find the path the Lord wants you to take." This attitude gave him a new sense of freedom. Unlike church-goers who he says are "just programmed," he feels he has a "more open approach to things." His favorite book is Stephen Covey's *Seven Habits of Highly Successful People*. He likes it because it emphasizes "your inner self" and gives him confidence that the right decisions in life are consistent with the "moral fiber" that runs through the Christian approach to life.

For people like Todd Brentwood, evangelical Christianity is a new home that offers security in a world gone wild. But it is a commitment that rests lightly on their shoulders. The moral certainty it provides is almost self-legitimating: when Todd makes decisions he now does so with the feeling that he's probably doing God's will. And going to church is a way to feel good and to make friends rather than a deep, enduring commitment to truth. Just being there gives him "peace of mind" and makes him "lighthearted." Todd says his spiritual journey "has mostly to do with individuals," even though he admits the church had an "indirect" effect. He says Christianity isn't a religion; it is just a way of life based on love. In his daily life, it helps him to relax and be himself.

If my argument is correct, then, the 1960s did not simply introduce new religions that encouraged Americans to be more eclectic in their spirituality; rather, during the 1960s the nature of freedom itself was contested and redefined. The freedom that living in a secure community of like-minded individuals offered was gradually replaced by a freedom to exercise choice in a marketplace of ideas and life-styles. Freedom of choice was attractive to those who in fact were confronted with an immense array of alternatives. Yet most people recognized that some choices are less healthy than others and that exercising choice for its own sake is not always the most desirable alternative. As a way of reining in freedom of choice, a new emphasis was also placed on the dangers of external constraints, such as those imposed explicitly by government or implicitly by technology. In the process, freedom came to be more subjective. In spirituality, freedom of conscience thus came to mean paying attention to the inner voices of feelings, and freedom of choice meant exposing oneself to alternative experiences that would help develop these voices.

The concept of freedom that emerged during the 1960s proved to be unstable because it did not sufficiently take into account the social forces shaping it. It made freedom largely into a matter of life-style, subjective opinion, and choice. The grand narrative of religious and philosophical tradition was replaced by personalized narratives of exploration and expression. As critics have observed, it was not clear how a society could be ordered in these terms. People needed reasons to limit their choices other than the sheer fact that they were exhausted or broke.

Freedom of choice was also unworkable in the terms that visionaries of the 1960s had themselves articulated it. People could not be motivated simply by a historical narrative that envisioned ever greater freedom and sophistication. Coming to terms with the evil embedded in U.S. society required more than a critique of the 1950s; it required a realistic appraisal of what life could be engineered to be. It was not possible to have biblical faith without religion, nor was it likely that people would continue to speak of God if they had no reason to speak to God. They would have to work harder to incorporate insights from African Americans and feminists instead of simply talking about them. The need was not for a different metaphysical canopy that valued freedom less. It was to discover through practical living how to maintain spiritual freedom without losing the essence of spirituality itself.

Were it only that the 1960s encouraged Americans to value their religious freedom or to leave the homes of their upbringing in search of more fulfilling spiritual mansions—were this all that took place—the 1960s would be of only passing interest. Instead, the 1960s brought together a quest for spiritual freedom with rapidly changing social conditions—a quest that had a wide variety of unanticipated results. Rather than either becoming more secular or starting new religious organizations, Americans after the 1960s had to think hard about what it meant to be spiritual. Their freedoms and their circumstances combined in ways that encouraged them to experiment, and these experiments opened up new possibilities that were more puzzling than they had imagined.

CHAPTER Four

Desire for Discipline

*I*n popular memory, the late 1970s and 1980s stand in sharp contrast to the 1960s and early 1970s. Whereas the earlier period championed freedom, the later one reasserted moral strictness. Spiritual diversity blossomed in the 1960s; fundamentalism flourished in the 1980s. Champions of religious conservatism argued that they were waging a war to correct the excesses of the 1960s. Yet the truth of the matter is that there was a great deal of continuity between the two periods.

Although the efforts to promote spiritual discipline during the 1980s were generally well-intentioned, and despite the fact that they reintroduced older concerns about personal morality into public debates, they failed ultimately to reshape the individual behavior of most Americans. The reasons for this failure are twofold: the social setting in which most Americans conducted their lives was quite different from the settings in which traditional understandings of spiritual and moral discipline had prevailed; and the proponents of spiritual discipline emphasized it in ways that reduced it largely to a therapeutic device having little impact on actual behavior. In a word, culture watered down the new preachments about moral and spiritual discipline to the point that these arguments could easily be reconciled with the way most middle-class Americans were already behaving, and thus discipline came to be a symbolic way of expressing concern about the wrongdoing of others more than a means of recapturing some lost sense of certainty about the sacred itself.

The struggle for spiritual discipline that gained prominence in the 1980s—and that continues—is thus of interest because it demonstrates how powerful the shift from a spirituality of dwelling to one of seeking has been. Were Americans' conception of the sacred still rooted in tight-knit communities and congregations, it might be possible to impose strict ideas of discipline on their quest for spirituality. But spirituality that results from a process of negotiation is harder to control. Such spirituality can provide personal guidance; it can create order in daily life; it can even be governed by well-specified rules. Yet it remains a feature of life in a complex world that requires individual choice and that elevates feelings as a major criterion on which choice is based. To understand these connections, we must pay attention to the specific meanings that spiritual discipline came to have in the 1980s and beyond.

THE SOFT LOGIC OF TECHNIQUE

Ken Maynard was in his early twenties when he "became a Christian" while watching a Billy Graham revival on television. The year was 1978. Having dropped out of high school to join the Navy, he was now finding it difficult to get a job. His parents had not taken him to church when he was a child. But, as he began attending an Assemblies of God church, he found the guidance he needed to put together a stable life. He quit visiting taverns and eventually landed a steady job driving a forklift tractor at a warehouse.

Amanda Schmidt was raised in an evangelical church. Her parents were deeply religious people who read the Bible and prayed with their children every day. When she was thirteen, Amanda accepted Christ as her personal savior. Now in her twenties, she teaches elementary school and is attending graduate school part-time to earn her master's degree. It will be from a Bible college, just as her undergraduate degree was. She attends an independent Bible church that is more conservative than the one in which she was raised. What she appreciates most about it is its "dedication to the truth in Scripture."

When asked what he considers the most serious problem in the United States today, Ken Maynard responds immediately: "the lack of self-control." He elaborates, "Everyone's out of control. There's no right or wrong. There's no standards, no absolutes. I think that's the basis right there. That there's no absolutes. You need absolutes. I mean, children need absolutes or they'll run out in the street, or they'll plunge through a window or who knows. Put their hand in the lion's cage. There has to be absolutes. Without them pandemonium sets in. It is setting in, yeah. That is it for me as far as I'm concerned. There are no absolutes, and we must have them."

Amanda Schmidt says almost the same thing. She believes the most serious social problem is "that we are raising children to believe that there are no absolutes." The reason this worries her, she explains, is that "it leaves you empty." In recent years, she thinks Americans have become "absolutely free to choose whatever [they] want to." And when this happens, "you can live however you want to." In contrast, she believes "that there is a God and there are absolutes." If she did not have these absolutes, she fears, "I would have nothing to hold onto; my life would be empty; I would just be floundering around."

The reason Ken and Amanda are interested in absolutes is not because they want a coherent set of arguments with which to answer philosophical questions. Like many other Americans, they are looking for practical rules that will guide them in their daily lives. They pray for God's guidance when they are faced with difficult situations, and they read devotional books that tell them how to live a Christian life. Although they have affiliated with conservative Protestant churches, their quest for moral and spiritual discipline is part of a long tradition in U.S. culture.

Discipline has been emphasized not only by those favoring a rigorous approach to spirituality but also by teachers, parents, and community leaders who regard it as a means for attaining worldly success. To be disciplined is to be steadfast in the pursuit of one's goals, avoiding diversions and harnessing one's energies, the way an ascetic Puritan or a rugged, self-sufficient pioneer might live. Discipline is thus the mark of a responsible, hardworking citizen who can be trusted to plan for the future and to look out for his or her own interests. In religion, spiritual discipline has carried similar connotations. A disciplined believer is a disciple who follows the teachings of the Lord, paying close attention to obedience as a mark of good behavior and realizing that a good life in this world, if not also in the world to come, is best attained by living according to a strict set of moral standards.

In the 1950s, social critics were already worrying that Americans were becoming undisciplined. Riesman's *Lonely Crowd* decried the decline of inner-directed personalities who had known what they wanted and devoted themselves wholeheartedly to pursuing it. C. Wright Mills's popular books *Power Elite* and *White Collar* were, among other things, diatribes against the erosion of the Calvinist ethic and the emergence of a comfortable middle-class life-style that was seemingly without purpose.

Mills, like the generation of literary figures that had preceded him, could admire the working class more than the emerging professional and managerial elite because of the simple, disciplined pursuit of basic values the working class symbolized.[1] By the end of the decade, religious leaders were also expressing concern that Americans were being pampered too much by their churches. Discipline was needed, they argued, in order to rebuild decaying slums or, in the suburbs, to build character in children.

In retrospect, one of the ways religious leaders might have tried to bolster the moral and spiritual discipline of middle-class Americans would have been to cultivate what Teresa of Avila had called the interior castle: focusing attention on the complexities of the self, emotions, thoughts, and desires; encouraging people to pray and to meditate; and developing character through self-knowledge. Despite the interest in spiritual discipline that had developed in some alternative religious movements during the 1960s, most Americans were ill-equipped to understand or appreciate what it might mean to explore the interior castle. Intense introspection of this kind remained generally less popular among religious leaders than the more active style of congregational involvement that had been championed during the 1950s.

The common way of strengthening individual believers was through techniques of personal discipline that could be used by busy people in the midst of ordinary life. By the mid 1970s, these techniques came from such different sources as psychotherapists, conservative religious moralists, self-help groups, and various champions of economic self-interest, all of which performed a similar function in personal life. They offered clear-cut methods, often formulated in simple "how-to" language, that individuals could follow to improve themselves.

Such techniques of personal management were not unknown in U.S. culture. Children had been reared according to "Dr. Spock" or other popular psychological manuals that instructed parents, step by step. Parents were taught to follow advice books about keeping family budgets or remodeling their houses or preserving their marriages. Dale Carnegie courses offered simple formulas for winning friends and influencing people. Increasingly, such techniques were also applied to the life of the soul. Religious books and magazines in the 1950s and 1960s were filled with practical advice on how to cultivate good devotional habits: recipes for praying in the morning, ten easy steps for teaching children how to do the same, checklists for reading the Bible, and (increasingly) flow charts showing how to make decisions about difficult moral and ethical issues.

Technique of this kind overlooked the need to probe deeply into the inner life, as psychologist Rollo May had observed in the 1950s. Believing that people suffered from a "vacuum" of orienting symbols and values, May argued that the contemporary tendency was to rely on tools. "It is not surprising," he wrote, "that a plethora of books on . . . *techniques* and *methods* comes out at just the time when people have difficulty experiencing the power of their own emotions and passions."[2] He added that subjectivity is lost when people focus externally on tools, rather than internally on their own being, and that tools can alienate people from themselves because the self comes to be viewed as an object that can be manipulated, processed, and programmed.

Americans in the late 1970s and 1980s were thus predisposed to favor a kind of spiritual discipline that consisted of applying techniques to various aspects of personal life in the hopes of improving themselves. "How-to" books continued to dominate the publishing industry, with best-selling nonfiction titles generally focusing on issues of money (including personal finances, taxes, and consumer advice) and sex (such as erotica, romance, relationships, and bodies, including diets). The same logic was evident in discussions of spiritual discipline.

Ken Maynard makes regular pilgrimages to a Christian bookstore near his home. His tastes are eclectic; he reads books written by religious figures in the past and ones that help him to understand the Bible. But the ones he enjoys most are study guides that give him techniques for improving his spiritual life. He says they keep him on an even keel. Amanda Schmidt belongs to a fellowship group for single women. The group uses devotional books that show how to apply difficult verses from the Bible to daily life. Amanda also reads on her own. Her favorites are what she calls "Christian living" books. Some of them take characters from the Bible and show how people nowadays can follow their example. Amanda says they clarify the principles by which she tries to live.

Neither Ken nor Amanda believe that their relationship with God can be reduced to a few simple formulas or techniques. Both emphasize God's grace and the support they receive from other Christians. But they are especially attracted to guidebooks and to formulaic prayers as a way to bring discipline to their lives. As they do for other people, such techniques impose a relatively soft form of discipline that permits practitioners to realize results without having to pay too high a price. As sociologist Jacques Ellul observed in his widely read book *The Technological Society,* this emphasis on technique may also be a way of quieting anxieties aroused by living in an increasingly insecure world and by being plagued with metaphysical doubt.[3]

Indeed, many of the people we interviewed who were old enough to have experienced them said the freedoms of the 1960s were an unsettling if not a frightening experience. For them, the quest for discipline became a way to flee the insecure world of the 1960s and achieve a moderate style of living. Whether because of the explicit quest for religious freedom or simply the uncertainty that came from changes in communities and families, the new freedoms produced enough discomfort to prompt a desire for "normalcy."[4]

THE CALL FOR DISCIPLINE

During the 1970s, personal discipline did come to be emphasized—in a wide variety of ways—as a key to curbing the excesses of the 1960s and to restoring toughness to American character. In religious circles, one of the most influential of these efforts was James Dobson's *Dare to Discipline,* which was published in 1971 in response to the liberalism of the 1960s and which sold over two million copies during the next two decades. Dobson encouraged parents to spank children when they were disrespectful, to provide strict moral guidelines, and in other ways to abandon the indulgent philosophies of child rearing that, in his view, had resulted in the excesses of the previous decade. One of the men we talked to who was raising teenage sons in the late 1970s said he and his wife used *Dare to Discipline* almost like a Bible. He thought it was especially important for children to know who was in charge. Otherwise, they would rebel and become "pretty messed up" because "there were so many confusing things in the world." The value of a book like Dobson's, he explained, is that it provides "spiritual discernment."[5]

The desire for moral and spiritual discipline also became evident among parents who forsook the public school system in order to educate their children themselves. One of their strongest complaints was that the schools had become morally and scholastically lax. Another was that God had been excluded from the classroom. As one man observed, "When I was growing up, we took turns reading a chapter from the Bible in school every morning. It's no wonder there are so many problems now." People like him thought it important for parents to take responsibility to keep the culture of chaos at bay by charting a strict course for their children. As another of the men we interviewed explained, "We're resolved about how we want to raise our children. What's more important than that? We're not going to go to all the trouble and expense of having children and then turn them over to someone else to raise!" For him and for many other parents, this conviction meant that mothers should not take on full-time work outside the home; it also meant setting a clear moral and spiritual example for one's children.

In public life, new concerns for moral and spiritual commitment were also being voiced: in efforts to combat sexual permissiveness, in the "war" on drugs, in policies oriented toward forcing welfare recipients to take increased responsibility for their own lives, in the beginnings of a movement by conservative Christians to put strict moral standards back on the national agenda, and in discussions of the need for spiritual discipline itself.[6] Looking back on the period, commentator William Bennett described it as a time of recovering from the "spiritual torpor" that had reached a high point in 1968. The 1980s, he said, was a decade in which Americans became aware of the "nightmarish world" that would come about unless they started searching for spiritual discipline.[7]

Less visible to the mass media, new interest in spiritual discipline was also being generated in religious circles by the church growth movement. While liberal denominations experienced decline, conservative churches appeared to be growing. Thus, the logical conclusion was that stiff doctrinal and moral demands needed to be made on parishioners in order to make churches grow.[8] Conservative evangelical Protestantism did become one of the primary vehicles for emphasizing moral and spiritual discipline. Television preachers, such as Jerry Falwell and Pat Robertson, also called for a return to strict standards of moral and spiritual discipline.[9] Religious leaders in mainstream Protestant and Catholic circles increasingly emphasized spiritual discipline as well. If freedom had been attractive a decade earlier, its appeal was now diminishing as leaders saw the consequences. Many worried that drugs and sex went along with a lack of spiritual discipline. Others worried that spiritual freedom was merely an expression of the consumerism that characterized the wider society. Thus, religiously grounded discipline needed to be emphasized as a way of helping people resist the pressures of the marketplace.

To a considerable extent, the concern about discipline also reflected a sense in the public at large that private life was becoming increasingly difficult. For many, moral standards were not as clear as they once were. Family schedules were more complicated. Two-career couples and single parents found it difficult to raise children. One study found that 90 percent of Americans agreed that "the job of parent is more difficult today than it used to be." Nearly the same number (89 percent) agreed that "parents today often feel uncertain about what is the right thing to do in raising their children." By a margin of 55 percent to 8 percent, respondents also thought the moral or religious training of children was worse than it had been ten years earlier.[10]

Nowhere was the call for moral and spiritual discipline more evident than in the rhetoric and symbolism of the Reagan White House. Toughness, faith in God, and a return to simple and straightforward moral principles were prominent themes.[11] Calls for personal discipline extended beyond antigovernment sentiments and free market economics to focus attention on the underlying spiritual and moral order on which Americans' lives depended.

Although it was tenuously linked to ideas about spiritual discipline, uncertainty in the economy also disposed some people to think seriously about the need for discipline. The 1980s were characterized by economic setbacks that caused many Americans to wonder whether they could realize their material ambitions. Business failures, which had remained constant during the 1970s, doubled between 1980 and 1982 and then rose another 50 percent by 1986; in contrast, new business incorporations stagnated during the 1980s after having doubled in the 1970s.[12] The shift in economic circumstances was also evident in the fact that household savings, which had risen during most of the period since World War II (adjusting for inflation), reached a high in 1982 and then fell to about half this level by 1987.[13] In real terms, median family incomes fell by about 6 percent in the decade after 1973, compared with a rise of nearly 50 percent in the previous decade and a half. To compound these difficulties, taxes took more than a fifth of family income in the late 1970s, compared with only about an eighth in the early 1960s.[14] Some people found the idea of spiritual discipline attractive as a way of pursuing economic success; others, as comfort in the face of economic failure.[15]

The call for spiritual discipline also came to be associated increasingly with the idea of sexual restraint. The generation that came of age in the 1960s found that sexuality was an exciting topic, both in its own right and as a way in which transcendence could be experienced. By the end of the 1980s, especially with the spread of AIDS, sex had become less a symbol of life than of death. To restrain oneself was thus to minimize sexual activity, to be abstinent if unmarried and to be faithful in marriage. By extension, it also meant being against homosexuality, pornography, and, insofar as it was symptomatic of a promiscuous attitude toward sexuality, abortion on demand. Maintaining strict control of sexual functioning was deemed desirable not simply as a matter of health but as evidence of conformity to a divinely ordered morality.

More broadly, moral and spiritual discipline was promoted in the name of social order itself, almost as if clear rules for individual behavior could substitute for the sacred dwellings in which Americans were presumed to have lived in the past. The call for discipline was framed in individualistic terms rather than in the communal stories of those who emphasized home. Discipline became a way of providing order, not by subjecting people to the authority of a place but by temporally arranging and legitimating their activities. "Be careful little hands what you do, for the Father up above is looking down in love," the children's chorus says. Discipline connotes an act of will, a conscious decision, creating not only an imaginary home but a model for living by providing clear guidelines to follow and by instructing practitioners that the abundant life is best achieved through self-restraint rather than through self-expression.

But it is important to look closely at the kinds of moral and spiritual discipline that became popular during the 1980s. As Americans tried to re-create orderly lives for themselves, they did so by accepting many of the new social realities to which they had grown accustomed. Freedom of choice was not so much curbed as criticized. Discipline was taken out of the communal contexts in which it had been understood by a previous generation and, despite new calls for community, was left largely to the discretion of individuals. In short, discipline came quickly to reflect the life-styles that matched Americans' personal interests and thus had both ambiguous and unanticipated consequences.

DISCIPLINE AS DETACHMENT

Etymologically, discipline refers to practice or exercise, an activity of the disciple, in contrast to doctrine or theory, which is the domain of the doctor or teacher. Discipline is thus embedded in asymmetric relationships, connoting respect for authority, obedience to hierarchy, a willingness to sacrifice personal freedom in order to acquire skills beneficial to some larger cause—ideas that run inherently into conflict with Americans' emphasis on self-interest and personal gratification. Yet discipline can also be justified on utilitarian grounds as a means for achieving individual ambitions. This emphasis on the practical aspect of everyday life was a vital ingredient of the arguments about moral discipline that came into prominence in the 1980s. It also meant that theoretical understandings of discipline would be compromised by the demands of ordinary experience.

The new meaning that discipline acquired in the 1980s is well evidenced in the life of Jenny Chambers. Having graduated from college in 1974, just in time to experience the severe setbacks in the American economy during the next decade and a half, she provides an example of how uncertainties in the wider society influenced individual Americans. Unsure of what major to pursue in college, she concentrated in both psychology and economics, worked at a summer camp to gain experience, and dropped out for a while between her junior and senior year in order to think about what she wanted to do. After graduation, she lived with her boyfriend for a year and a half, then married him, and about a year later had her first baby. Over the next decade she had three more children, worked for at least ten different companies, and lived in four different houses. She also helped her husband build up a business with fifty employees, watched helplessly as the business fell apart, declared personal bankruptcy, supported her husband through several career changes, and helped him start another business. Her life has been more chaotic than she ever imagined it could be.

Jenny was reared in an affluent, mainline Protestant home by parents who valued education, independence, and thinking for oneself, and who thus encouraged her to explore the full variety of options open to her but who also emphasized strict moral discipline. For them, discipline meant living an orderly life in the family, at work, and at church. Jenny's father learned discipline in the Navy during the Korean War and by working for his father. He remembers being sent out in a driving rainstorm to make door-to-door calls for his father's brokerage firm. Jenny's mother was also a stern disciplinarian; for example, Jenny remembers being roundly scolded one time by her mother for borrowing a few dollars from a friend. Jenny was too young to have experienced the full force of the counterculture in the 1960s, but she admits that the sixties loosened things up to the point that her living with her boyfriend before marriage was not considered scandalous.

When Jenny and her husband started having financial (and marital) troubles, she joined a conservative evangelical church. It was more rigorous in its teachings than the mainline church her parents attended, and it appealed to her as a way of finding stability in her chaotic life. Jenny says she found biblical answers, fellowship, and guidelines for living a spiritual life from day to day. A women's discipleship group became important to her, and she started trying to be disciplined in her devotional practices, reading her Bible and praying every day, as well as attending church. By all indications, she was heeding the call for discipline that was gaining popularity in evangelical circles and in the wider society during the 1980s. But what she learned was a new kind of discipline that reflected the uncertain times in which she lived.

For Jenny's parents, leading a disciplined life meant conforming behaviorally to expectations that were taken for granted within the family, community, and church; for Jenny, discipline mainly means detachment. Both views of discipline elevate the idea of submission—which has been an integral feature of religious and secular teaching alike—but do so in quite different ways. When George Washington remarked that "discipline is the soul of an army" or when early church writers spoke of "discipline in Christ," they had in mind the necessity of submitting to a program of instruction, as carried out by the military, the church, or some other institution, in order to become properly skilled as a functioning member of that institution. Submission of this kind required a profound modification of one's personal behavior, either through explicit conformity to certain rules, as in Jenny's father's naval experience, or through implicit conformity, as in following the norms of upper-middle-class respectability that governed the way Jenny's parents behaved at home and in public. Household discipline of this kind creates an orderly environment in which to live.

In contrast, the discipline of detachment implies a focus on attitudes, rather than on behavior; instead of bringing one's behavior under control, one learns not to care about control and to be content with circumstances as they are. Jenny says she has been learning to "give up" what she had been trying to control and to be more flexible. For instance, a devotional book she has been reading advises her to have a "freer attitude" toward life, which she says helps when her husband asks her to make some business calls for him. In short, becoming disciplined means learning to roll with the punches—a good thing to do when life is as filled with chaos as hers.

The contrast between these two understandings of discipline is as evident in the meaning of devotional activities as it is for other aspects of life. In the historic view, submission to church discipline included performing prescribed devotional duties, such as the daily office of personal prayer. Jenny's parents pray silently together each night before they go to bed. They do not expect to receive special messages from God during these moments when they are praying, and they do not regard prayer (or going to church) as a way of disciplining themselves spiritually; these activities are simply an established part of their routine. In contrast, the newer view of spiritual discipline focuses on its emotional effects. Jenny tries to pray for about ten minutes every day; this is a special time when she consciously detaches herself emotionally from whatever has been worrying her. She feels that God is able to "reward" her during these times because she has "opened her mind" to God.

By redefining discipline to mean little more than emotional detachment, religious leaders could reconnect their followers with an aspect of historic teachings but in a way that required few changes in how they lived and that, in fact, corresponded well with the cultural influences of the period. Whereas submission to institutional authority depended on respect for that authority, detachment could be defended chiefly as a means of leading a happier life. The one could be monitored publicly; the other—as an attitude—was entirely private. The older view was better adapted to circumstances that could indeed be controlled; the newer view, to unsettled times that were largely beyond control. Nor did the newer view constitute giving up much of the personal freedom that had become popular during the preceding decade. Instead, detachment was defined as a means of securing true freedom. As one of the more popular books on spiritual discipline explained. "Discipline has its corresponding freedom. . . . We are released to drop the matter, to forget it. Frankly, most things in life are not nearly so important as we think they are."[16]

DISCIPLINE AS A CHEERY ATTITUDE

A different understanding of discipline that also grew in popularity during the 1980s was the idea that people of faith should try hard to cultivate a happy, positive, cheery outlook on life. Although there were historic precedents for this interpretation, it came to be such a prominent aspect of evangelicalism that many religious leaders themselves commented on it, and it came increasingly to substitute for other meanings of discipline rather than simply being regarded as a by-product of faithful living. Like detachment, this view also emphasized feelings more than behavior, and both views implicitly took for granted that individuals could do relatively little objectively to control or change the circumstances in which they lived. Whereas detachment implies a kind of resignation or indifference, however, discipline as a cheery attitude suggests assertively taking charge of one's emotions, cleansing oneself of negative thoughts, looking on the bright side, and if necessary drawing on divine strength to do so.

Suellen Park, a Korean American who immigrated to the United States in the early 1970s, when she was in her early twenties, provides an interesting example of this orientation. She is a hardworking person who embodies many of the traditional meanings of discipline, and yet her understanding of spiritual discipline has been deeply influenced by the cultural forces she has been exposed to in the United States. Whereas Jenny's evangelicalism shows the marks of her journey through the 1960s, Suellen's stems from making the difficult adjustment to a new culture and, in the process, learning a thoroughly U.S. form of religious practice. She and her husband run a grocery store in a largely black section of a medium-sized city on the East Coast. "All the time I work, from morning to night," she says, "like a bore!" (Although she sometimes speaks in broken English, her words express vividly her understanding of spirituality and her reasons for engaging in spiritual activities.)

Suellen typically begins her day by driving her teenage son and daughter to school. It is a Catholic school that Suellen and her husband selected because it offers a more rigorous academic program than the local public high school (their daughter, a senior, has been admitted to an Ivy League college). Each morning they leave the house at seven o'clock, and Suellen uses the time to talk with her children about the day's activities, whether they have done their homework, and whatever problems she needs to discuss. When she returns home, she walks around the block a couple of times for exercise, also using the time to pray. "When I walk, I start to pray with the Lord's Prayer and the Apostle's Creed," she explains, "and then I start to pray over everything. When I come back, I'm ready for the day."

Generally, Suellen spends the rest of the morning cleaning, doing laundry, and cooking. She says her husband insists on having fresh Korean food, and her children refuse to eat anything but U.S. food, so she often spends two or three hours preparing meals for the day. At noon, she rests for a while, bathes and dresses to go out, spends a few moments in prayer, and leaves for work. Each day she works from one o'clock until ten o'clock. "When I work, I have a lot of things to do," she says, "lots and lots of paperwork, and I have two women in the office all the time because I have many employees."

Suellen did not have to come to the United States to learn the kind of personal discipline that keeps her going from early morning to late at night. Her father was a harsh taskmaster whose Confucian philosophy encouraged him to work hard, follow a strict code of moral discipline, and teach his children to do the same. "He made the list of things we children should do," Suellen recalls. "'Don't lie, don't steal and be respective to the parents, good rules. He put it on the wall. Every morning he made me memorize it. We were not allowed to do anything bad. He was very, very strict on that. We weren't allowed to play the card. He says, 'That playing card is simple pleasure, but it leads to the wrong way, so you're not allowed to play the card.' We weren't allowed to sing the popular songs either." From early childhood, then, Suellen learned to study hard in school and to do household chores, and when she was old enough, her father sent her away to college and encouraged her to emigrate to the United States. In many ways, Suellen epitomizes the kind of discipline that Falwell, Bennett, and others were advocating during the 1980s. Yet, as she talks about spirituality, it is evident that discipline means something different in this context than it does in the other parts of her life.

She feels especially grateful for the two women who help with the office work because both are interested in spirituality and Suellen enjoys talking with them about their thoughts and experiences. "Actually my faith grew because of them," she says. "When I look at them, they're different people, and I didn't know why they're different. They're strong, they're very nice, they're very clean inside, spirit is always bright. They don't complain, and they're so nice to other people. They always smile. I wasn't like that for a long time. I was crumbled and ugly. Inside is always boiling. I said, 'What's the difference between them and I?' because I am older than them and I have more experience in life, but I have lived so ugly a way. I said, 'What's wrong? What's wrong with me?' And then I start to learn from them. I watched them, and I realized they are leading a different kind of life. I found that they pray. They taught me how to pray. And when I ask, they give me an answer, they point it out in the Bible. It's not a direct answer. They tell me to look at it and think about it. And I asked them, 'Were you like this all your life?' and they say 'no.' And they're telling me a lot about how their baggage caused them to be that way, and yet now they're different."

These women, both Caucasians and both members of evangelical churches, have taught Suellen that leading a disciplined spiritual life means cultivating a cheery attitude. She says, "There *is* something that cleans me inside and makes my spirit clean and bright." This realization came to her about three years ago at a time when she felt desperate about the direction of her life. One day as she was crying and feeling sorry for herself it dawned on her that God wanted her to be happy. "Somehow I had some kind of an inspiration. After that day, everything looked different. My head was a lot clearer, just like I have a deep sleep and then got rewarded. It's more than that. I can't describe it exactly. But I realized that there is some kind of power that makes people clean, nice." Some people would call what Suellen experienced a "conversion" or being "in touch with the Holy Spirit." Certainly it was a sacred moment that opened her eyes to new possibilities, but it did not last. "After that I was going down again, up again, down again, up again, that kind of a life I went through. And every time I went down, I said, 'Something is wrong with me again. What is it?'"

This was when Suellen began to pray as she walked around the block each morning. "I started to pray and pray and pray and pray," she remembers. "Next day I up again. I was up and down, up and down. I found out in order to stay up what I should do. I talked to the people [at work], and they were really wonderful to me. They always help me out. They never criticize me because of my weakness, my bad feelings, my bad thoughts. They always help me out. And then I realized in order to keep up, I have to pray." Suellen describes some of the things she prays about. "Whenever I feel uncomfortable with someone," she explains, "I pray that morning, 'Lord, I am uncomfortable with this person, but I have to work with her today, so Lord, help me.' Every time I fear something, I start to ask for help from the Lord. That became my habit, right? And then I rely on him and then I start to be submissive to him, and I start to say, 'Oh Lord, take care of me."

She thinks her prayers put her in the right frame of mind so that she can be friendlier and more understanding with her customers. Part of the difference is that she feels better about herself. So she can smile and focus on their needs. She says God helps her to do this. She tries to go beyond her business dealings to give people encouragement and comfort. "Our store is in center of the black area," she says. "What I learned about black people [is that] the bottom of their heart is really good. They're not any different as people at all. Actually they are more concerned because they experienced all sorts of hardships, and they have more love." Believing that all people have this core of goodness within them, Suellen tries to say things that encourage this goodness to blossom. She tells about one woman who looks ugly sometimes because she is angry or worried, but the woman brightens up when Suellen treats her with respect. There is also a teenager who comes in every day. Suellen talks to him about his friends, about gangs, and about drugs. She says, "Jimmy, you're a very courageous person. You're such a smart person. Don't waste your life on anything but goodness."

Of course it is good for business to treat customers with kindness and respect; Suellen might try to do this even if she were not interested in spirituality. But, as she says, her spirituality protects her against the extremes of her up and down moods. As she talks about her customers, sometimes she seems proud, even sanctimonious. Yet she also admits her weaknesses. She tells people openly that she has trouble remembering names and numbers. She also says it makes her angry when people are snobbish, especially if they look down on her just because she is Korean. She loses her temper sometimes and yells at people, "Get out of my store. I don't need you. You have a dirty attitude!" Her spirituality doesn't make her perfect. "I shouldn't be doing that," she says, "but I do because my heart just can't stand it." But her spirituality does help her calm down again. "The important thing isn't status or money," she says. "They are just people that God is taking care of. They're in whatever situation, but they're basically just human. They're the same in the eyes of God."

Suellen's life, like Jenny Chambers's, has been difficult; both have had to struggle economically, even though both have been fairly successful. It might be argued that a disciplined spiritual life helped them achieve material success. Yet neither woman sees it that way herself. Instead, becoming disciplined in faith has mainly meant praying and reading the Bible every day, and thus each woman controls her emotions in a way that helps her get along with her husband and with the people she meets. Spiritual discipline works for them, and yet it works more to adjust them emotionally to their situations than it does to encourage them to live any differently than they might otherwise live. Discipline is hardly life transforming, even though it does play a positive role. By helping keep their emotions in check, it allows them to be happy in spite of the difficult situations in which they find themselves. They are living examples of what one popular writer on spirituality had in mind when she wrote that Christian discipline should consist mainly of "[not letting] our emotions flip and flop all over the place [and not] pouting and stewing."[17] Discipline helps them adjust to the complexities of life and to smile as they do.

DISCIPLINE AS REASSURANCE

Having a positive attitude as a result of praying every day can be a way of getting what one wants out of life, as advocates of positive thinking have often asserted. A more instrumental use of spiritual discipline is evident in people who regard their spirituality primarily as a way of receiving divine guidance. The quest for guidance is part of Americans' emphasis on practicality—similar to the desire that home appliances, government leaders, and scientists act to benefit daily life. *Application* is a key concept; the purpose of discipline is to apply it to daily life in order to achieve a goal, whether that be winning a war, learning to play the piano, or making money. Historically, spiritual discipline has often been conceived in this way, requiring disciples to master a body of sacred knowledge, acquire skills in faithful living, and seek divine guidance through their study of the Bible or the teachings of clergy. But historic teachings have also warned against trying to make God into an instrument for the pursuit of personal goals.

During the 1980s, the call for discipline emphasized divine guidance, both as a set of moral principles that disciples should follow and as a reward for praying and participating in religious services. But the meaning of guidance shifted subtly away from behavioral norms and focused instead on reassurance. People talked about receiving divine guidance, but what they meant, when pressed to explain, was that they felt better about what they were already doing. To be spiritually disciplined thus did not require a significant alteration in behavior, only engaging in token religious activities that provided reassurance. In the extreme, guidance ceased to imply a rigorous effort to understand and live according to spiritual wisdom; it came to mean receiving friendly suggestions from a God who had become a good buddy and was trying to help people make the most of their daily lives.

Birch Simmons is one of the men we talked to for whom guidance seemed to be central to his spirituality. A retired business executive in his late sixties, he has attended church nearly every Sunday of his life. When he was a boy in rural Indiana, his mother made sure he went to Sunday school and church regularly. He attended a denominational college where chapel and Sunday services were required. In the Navy, he continued to attend church. And after his daughter was born, he went every Sunday because he wanted her to receive a strong religious upbringing. He says he has even attended on Sundays when he has been traveling, both domestically and abroad.

Divine guidance runs through all his comments about religion. Reflecting on his boyhood, for example, he says the most significant thing about church was that he found direction from the Sunday school teachers. This guidance was especially important to him because his father had died when he was a year old. He thinks the time he devoted to taking his daughter to church was well spent too. He emphasizes that when she got married a couple of years ago the preacher was right there to give her advice and to get her marriage off to a good start (she herself does not mention this as having been significant).

But when Birch is pressed to give examples of how spiritual guidance has influenced his life, he fumbles for words. Mentioning that he has had to make decisions that were "pretty darn tough" in his business and in dealing with some of his family members, he says he has prayed on some of these occasions for guidance. He did not expect to hear a voice from heaven telling him what to do; he feels that life is too complex and that humans are too much in control of their own destinies for that to happen. But he did not devote deliberate effort to reading what saints and sages have written on these matters either; nor did he try to master any devotional methods that might bring him closer to God. Usually he prayed a perfunctory prayer on his own; in one particularly difficult situation, he asked his pastor to come and pray with him. What resulted was reassurance. "I think I made the right decision," he says; "it was a good use of my faith." What he received was not so much guidance as reassurance.

Many of the people we talked to held views similar to Birch Simmons's. They prayed from time to time, read the Bible once in a while, and went to church regularly, thus leading what they regarded as a spiritually disciplined life, and they sought divine guidance through these activities. They were unable to say that they had done anything differently as a result of being spiritually disciplined, but by having brought God into the picture at least momentarily they felt better about themselves. Birch Simmons expresses a common view when he remarks that his favorite sermons have "just enough reference to the Bible to make them meaningful" but are not "overshadowed by [the Bible.]"

People like Birch come away feeling reassured not because they have found specific answers, for they deny that God communicates with people this way, but because they have participated in an activity in which other, seemingly devout Americans like themselves are also engaged. Their faith in people is sometimes reinforced more directly than their faith in God—a point that Birch Simmons concedes. Indeed, this was probably one reason why millions of Americans started attending Bible-study groups and home fellowships during the 1980s. As they negotiated their own understandings of faith, the opportunity to share stories with kindred spirits reassured them that they were on the right track.

Research on such groups shows that an interest in spiritual discipline was one of the more common reasons for participating, but this interest did not connote personal sacrifices as much as it meant gaining a sense that one was a good person.[18] These groups did not demand very much—other than a couple of hours a week—and they did not impose rigid rules of behavior on members; instead, they gave people an opportunity to grope with their decisions, to hear others groping, and to come away feeling better about themselves for having looked chaos in the face and said, "I can stand it."

Jenny Chambers's women's discipleship group is an example. She attends every week and credits the group with having deepened her spiritual life enormously. What she likes best is what she calls the group's "inductive approach." Rather than having a leader who teaches the right answers or an authoritative text or study guide, the group looks up verses from the Bible and each woman asks herself, "What does this mean and how can I apply it to my life?" The answers that emerge from the group are thus relevant to the group but also tailored to fit the individual experiences, backgrounds, and needs of each member. Each woman can leave the group with some gem that helps her confront her life during the coming week, and yet those gems may all be different; indeed, they may be replaced by other gems the following week.

DISCIPLINE AS FAITH IN GOODNESS

By far, the most common understanding of spiritual discipline that emerged in our interviews was the idea that good-hearted people can discover good ways of living if they simply put their minds to it. In this understanding, having spiritual discipline does not mean following a set of divinely ordained moral rules; it means having faith that there are right ways to live, period. Leading a disciplined life thus means having faith in the existence of goodness or at least in the possibility of its existence. Being disciplined, even in this way, does not come easily or automatically, but it consists mostly of prayer as a time for reflection, a moment to think about one's life and to affirm one's faith that it is possible to do good. Spiritual discipline, in this sense, does not require much in the way of biblical or theological or moral knowledge, for it turns on the conviction that good living is basically common sense.

Among public figures, this understanding of discipline was evident in Ronald Reagan, the person who probably defined the spirit of the 1980s more than any other. As an actor, movie star, Californian, and divorcee, Reagan was an unlikely candidate to symbolize the new spirit of discipline. Yet throughout his presidency he not only symbolized this spirit but also gave it a distinctive interpretation. Reagan was fond of quoting

Theodore Roosevelt and of using the presidency, as Roosevelt had, as a bully pulpit. Favorite themes included the need for Americans to experience a spiritual awakening, to work hard, and to recover the moral standards that had made the United States great. He spoke often of the struggle for freedom, the battle against oppression, the heroics of those who had sacrificed and experienced pain, the bravery of men and women who risked their lives to escape tyranny, and the need to be constant in fighting for the truth. Religious convictions were also a recurrent theme. Faith was his guide, the Lord was his strength, God expected people to persevere, one's beliefs should be like a bedrock, and one's efforts to follow God should be active, enduring, and without fear. In one speech, quoting Eric Liddell, the Scottish runner featured in the film *Chariots of Fire,* Reagan drew an explicit connection with the muscular Christianity of an earlier era. "Where does the power come from to see the race to its end?" he asked, and he answered, "From within."[19]

If Reagan's words connoted toughness and control, his message nevertheless was more in keeping with the 1980s than it was a return to the rugged strength of Theodore Roosevelt. Reagan championed moral standards but seldom talked specifically about the content of these standards. He assumed they were commonsensical, within reach of all good people rather than requiring knowledge or training. He did not call on the public to make genuine sacrifices but promised that peace and prosperity would result from rolling back government. His defenders believed that everyone could achieve a good life simply by working hard and looking out for themselves. His critics complained that he was shallow, a manipulator of words rather than someone who truly knew what personal discipline meant. He himself denied that the spiritual discipline he advocated was dour or reserved. To be morally strict, he believed, was the avenue to laughter, prosperity, and happy times. One of his most perceptive interpreters wrote, "To represent toughness it is best to operate in a symbolic universe protected from the real-world obstacles that might threaten that toughness or expose its punitive character. Symbolizing toughness and staying out of touch, far from being contradictory, are mutually reinforcing."[20]

Many of the people we talked to who emphasized their own interest in leading a morally and spiritually disciplined life exhibited a similar understanding of discipline. They were concerned about the moral laxity they perceived to be threatening the United States, but, in standing firm on their religious principles, they were mostly trying to abide by common sense, performing symbolic acts that convinced them they were disciplined, and trusting their instincts, all of which was possible because they believed steadfastly in a kind of universal goodness. One woman spoke for many when she explained that her parents had put too much emphasis on discipline; for her, it just meant avoiding things that get you in trouble, like buying too much on credit or eating too much chocolate. She said she generally knows what is right and wrong because of her faith; when she prays, it is usually just for patience.

This view of right and wrong is compatible with living in a sacred dwelling where the habits are so familiar, the routines so taken for granted, that moral behavior is indeed second nature. But most of the people we talked to realized at some level that they no longer lived in such a world. The situations they faced at work or in their families were different from the ones their parents had faced. They could no longer respond in familiar ways but needed to improvise, making up what they said as they went along. A high school teacher, for example, says he tries to demonstrate his faith to his students but does so moment by moment, often without any clear sense that what he says is helpful to them. His faith does not tell him what to say, but his daily prayers give him confidence that whatever he says is good. Thus, he believes it is possible to do good, but this belief is hedged with uncertainty.

A Jewish man in his fifties who says he tries hard to bring his understanding of spirituality to bear on his medical practice offers a similar observation. "Sometimes what is positive in one situation is negative in another situation. Sometimes if somebody's in a lot of pain, if I reach out and touch their hand or physically touch them somewhere, I can feel a relaxation. So you have to stand back and think, 'Is this what I need to do or is it not what I need to do?' I think every day [that] goes by, every year [that] goes by, every week, month, year, I get better at it. Experience is the best teacher for that kind of thing." In the meantime, his sense of being in touch with God reassures him that he is doing the best he can.

GETTING WHAT ONE WANTS

As these examples suggest, the desire for discipline that Americans came to emphasize during the 1980s was influenced by the spirit of the times. Over the centuries, spiritual discipline has been understood to have implications for how people lived in ordinary life. Devotional practice was meant to influence ordinary behavior by serving, in John Calvin's words, as "a tutelage for our weakness," thus providing regularity to one's activities and periodic moments in which to entreat God for strength and to examine oneself. It was also the occasion for deepening one's under-standing of the divine rules of conduct set forth in religious texts, and it was a means of drawing close to the power and protection of God.[21] Cer-tainly for Saint Benedict it meant leading a rigorous life devoted to deep-ening one's relationship with God. The part that has been retained is less concerned with the awesome power of God and more interested in sat-isfying our need to feel good about ourselves. One young man was es-pecially candid when he remarked, "I'm a little bit afraid of getting too much into the discipline part!"

The reason too much discipline is frightening is that life in the United States is so complex that people generally do better by keeping their op-tions open. Prayer that is mostly reassuring alleviates guilt and is thus psychologically liberating. Working at one's faith now means being open to sympathetic encouragement whatever the source may be. If we think about Suellen Park, we realize that her inspiration comes from a wide range of sources and experiences, even though she lives primarily in the world of evangelical Christianity. She does not look to Zen because she has no exposure to it, but she receives counsel from her friends who go to different churches; she listens to religious radio and to inspirational tapes, reads religious books, sends her children to Catholic school, and participates in a small group at her church. These activities allow her to regard all people as God's children, to have a universalistic notion of their goodness, and to regard her Christianity simply as a technique that some people can use to live better lives; it is not so much gospel truth as gospel technology.

Utilitarian justifications of discipline that focus on its capacity to pro-duce results, to keep one's spirits high, and to make one feel better about life must be understood in relation to the broader changes taking place in Americans' outlook on the nature of reality itself. When this reality is a sacred dwelling, it is inherently meaningful and thus capable of legiti-mating the activities that customarily take place within it. Heaven, one can imagine, is a place where saints sing praises not only continuously but also enthusiastically. But when realities have to be negotiated, the ef-fort required seems more strenuous. The cloak that once sat lightly on our shoulders, as Max Weber observed, feels more like a cage—and this is true even for those who voluntarily seek to lead disciplined lives.[22] Ac-tivities are carried out not simply because they are customary but be-cause some specific justification for them can be provided. Prayers that calm doubts and reassure people that what they are doing is worthwhile are especially valuable under these circumstances. It is hard enough to

conjure up the discipline required to achieve even these results; heeding
the call for a great revival of discipline may be all but impossible.

CONSERVATIVE ACTIVISM

Religious leaders who advanced a conservative moral agenda, such as
Falwell and Robertson, attracted a great deal of media attention in the
1980s, especially when they called on legislative bodies to impose a kind
of moral discipline that people themselves seemed incapable of pursuing
voluntarily. Capitalizing on Americans' sense of spiritual homelessness,
they argued for a return to absolute moral principles, deep faith, and personal discipline in matters of the spirit. "The church should be a disciplined, charging army," Falwell intoned, working to "encounter the en-
emy face-to-face and . . . move them into the household of God."[23]
Other leaders viewed the 1980s as a time when the moral excesses of the
1960s could be reversed by reasserting traditional values, including closeness to God and a disciplined respect for moral authority. Economist
George Gilder, describing the 1980s as a decade of "relentless discipline,"
wrote that the 1960s had been plagued by a pseudomorality of "crippling creeds" that came close to destroying the United States. It was time,
he argued, to forget the lax, undisciplined complainers of the 1960s, a
time for mothers to discipline their sons and daughters, a time to bring
back the Christian virtues on which civilization itself depended.[24]

For the minority who took up this call, the politics of morality came
to be a way of fighting back and of rebuilding the castle of God. Those
who rejected the social experimentation of the 1960s needed a cause of
their own, a way to correct the damage others had done. The fight against
abortion gave them a moral crusade to believe in. In addition to its substantive focus, it also took on symbolic significance. A man who said he
had been uncomfortable with sixties' style sexual morality commented,
"It was a demonstration of the decay of our culture. The fact that we are
aborting children. We're semi-active in supporting antiabortion activities even now. We had a girl in our home for a while, a pregnant girl who
wasn't married. And we marched down at Center Hospital and protested
Abortion Now on a scheduled basis through our church, through our
congregation. But to me, it was both a signal of the decay of our culture
and also kind of a call to arms, really, to become more involved in our
culture because the decay, I guess, was becoming obvious enough that it
just cried for some action."

Yet, given the way spiritual discipline was popularly understood, it is easy to see why moral conservatives had more success in bringing their message to the media and to a few activists than they did in effecting widespread changes in the ways Americans related to God. If spiritual discipline meant controlling one's passions and rolling with the punches, it carried a mind-your-own-business mentality as well. Americans who thought it important to live morally themselves remained skeptical of political leaders who "made hay," as one man put it, of every cause they could lay their hands on. Spiritual discipline to the majority of Americans meant witnessing in love and obeying moral principles more than it meant taking to the air waves in a holy war against abortion or on behalf of Christians' rights.

For many, the deeply personal character of spirituality meant, at a minimum, that one tried to control one's own behavior, but they did not favor efforts to extend this control to others. Many of the people we talked to said they disagreed with the conservative political movements of the 1980s because it did not seem right to them to bring about moral change by political means. Some of them explained that the whole idea of morality is that you have both the freedom and the responsibility to discipline your own behavior. Those who emphasized spiritual discipline said their faith in God was a way of fortifying themselves to do what was right.

A woman who attends church regularly and who is trying to teach her two children strict moral values illustrates this view when she explains that she has two objections to how religious groups have been attempting to influence public morality since the 1980s. One is that she feels they are inflexible and intolerant in dealing with other groups. She feels it should be possible to hold high moral principles yourself without being critical of others who may disagree. Her other objection is to the use of politics to enforce moral codes. She wants to be moral herself, not have someone else's view of morality imposed on her.

Resistance to conservative religious movements on grounds of separation of church and state is also rooted in the view that spiritual discipline means taking responsibility for one's own relationship to God and thus requires the freedom to think about God in any way one pleases. A Catholic woman who agrees with her church's stance against abortion illustrates this connection as she explains her views about separation of church and state: "I think you can believe very much in God and try to live by the laws of God, but it should not be intermingled with your government because I feel there's always a danger of leaders or people elected, or however they get in positions in governments, trying to equate their power with God, such as Adolf Hitler. In Germany during the time of Hitler, you were really supposed to take your children for a state ceremony when they were born, and if you took them to a church ceremony for baptism, it's like the state ceremony was more important. I guess because of that danger, I strongly believe in the separation of church and state. When the fundamentalists tried to worm their way into the political scene and became successful, I was terrified. I was terrified and I was so turned off to our government at that time. I was scared because I think all the fundamentalism is dangerous. I really do."

Interestingly enough, a similar logic is evident among those who have chosen to be active in religiously based political movements. They, too, have adopted a language of individual rights rooted in the idea that believers need to exercise their religious freedom. The man who participated in antiabortion protests explains, "I think that if you believe deeply in something, you have to stand up for it. While church and government should remain separate, there is a place where your spiritual and religious beliefs have to influence how you behave politically. If the government decided to make a law that it was all right to kill people under certain circumstances, would you not have a moral obligation to object to such a law, if your religious belief was that it was not right to kill people? I think so. Now if those people who become involved in politics become corrupted by it, then they will not be good representatives of religiously oriented people. Anyone has a right to become involved in politics. And we're certainly better off if those people involved have a sense of fairness and honesty. That should be consistent with a Christian faith, so why shouldn't they participate in the government process?"

Thus, the idea that spiritual discipline is basically personal does not necessarily lead people to retreat entirely from public life, as some observers have suggested, but it does suggest an emphasis on the individual, on personal freedom, and on rights and responsibilities. In the United States, this emphasis causes many people to worry about organized efforts that may curb individual freedom, even in the name of moral discipline. They may sympathize with the rhetoric of leaders who decry moral decay, but their support for these leaders is soft when it comes to heavy-handed efforts to legislate morality.

The pragmatic meanings of personal discipline also carry into views of legislative and political action. Pragmatism means that discipline should work, helping one to accomplish personal goals rather than putting pressure on oneself to conform to absolute standards of behavior. Religiously or morally, the absolute becomes a somewhat distant, yet commonsensical orientation that provides considerable latitude in how one actually behaves. Even the leaders of conservative movements have often expressed this view of what it means to be disciplined. Perhaps choosing one or two concrete policy issues on which to focus, they have a view of the absolute that nevertheless allows room for compromise and negotiation. Falwell, for example, once explained to a reporter that "we work hard," but he also emphasized the need to be pragmatic and to roll with the punches, observing that "we do the best we can. We negotiate."[25]

THE GOOD LIFE IN AN UNCERTAIN WORLD

The way in which Americans came to understand spiritual discipline in the 1980s scarcely deterred them from many of the secular pursuits in which they were so actively engaged. In some ascetic understandings, personal discipline has meant cutting back, being content with less, and, in many of its traditional interpretations, spiritual discipline has been associated with an ascetic life dedicated to communion with God rather than worldly pursuits. Kathleen Norris has written that asceticism is "a way of surrendering to reduced circumstances in a manner that enhances the whole person."[26] For most Americans, however, asceticism is a way of controlling one's impulses long enough to get what one wants, not an act of radical defiance against advertising, consumption, and the demands of careers. To be disciplined means taking care of things for God, and God wants you to work hard and do well. Making money, providing good educations for one's children, and participating fully in the recreational pleasures of an advanced industrial society are all compatible with spiritual discipline. Prayer need not take much time away from these pursuits; even to see it as an escape from them is inaccurate. Prayer is a way of seeking emotional strength to go about one's business. The plea "Lord, do not lighten our burdens, only make our backs strong to carry them" still applies.

For all the emphasis placed on discipline in the 1980s, research shows that Americans who favored it—and even those who followed it in their religious lives—did not abandon the commitment to freedom that had emerged in the 1960s or find ways to escape the uncertainties of life in the 1980s. They did adopt positions on specific issues, such as sexuality and abortion, that were widely publicized as "moral concerns." But otherwise the desire for discipline appears to have had little impact on the way most Americans led their lives. Thus, despite all the attention premarital sex received, especially from religious conservatives, the portion of Americans who believed that it was wrong did not change substantially during the 1980s. The same was true of attitudes toward extramarital sex. The percentage of parents who used corporal punishment as a way of disciplining their children actually dropped substantially.[27] Other measures also showed little change. Misbehavior among students, cheating on tax returns, and relativistic views of morality all remained about the same.[28] And in public life, despite Reagan's emphasis on religion and moral responsibility, critics pointed out that the White House itself had presided over a deregulation of morality in the personal conduct of its top officials, in its involvement in the Iran-Contra scandal, and in its handling of the savings and loan scandal.[29]

On the whole, the new interest in spiritual discipline did make organized religion somewhat more respectable than it was in the 1960s, thereby producing new vitality in some churches and synagogues. But the religious revival that clergy hoped for failed largely to materialize. In fact, church membership continued to decline, falling from 69 percent of the adult population in 1980 to 65 percent in 1988, and weekly church attendance hovered around 40 percent throughout the period. There *was* a slight upturn in per capita giving (measured in constant dollars) between 1980 and 1986. But when compared with family disposable income, giving decreased.[30]

It was also doubtful that organized religion was holding its own in comparison with other ways to spend time and money or to pursue happiness.[31] John Lennon's 1966 boast—"We're more popular than Jesus now"—may have been presumptuous; yet the entertainment industry was clearly giving organized religion a run for its money. In 1985, for example, organized religion was a $38 billion industry, but consumer electronics, motion picture theaters, records, and books were a $50 billion industry in the same year. Sporting equipment alone constituted a $27 billion industry that year. And commercial advertising accounted for another $100 billion of the U.S. economy.[32] Organized religion did not fare well in the public's confidence either. During the 1970s, attitudes had fluctuated, but after 1978 they became steadily more negative: between 1978 and 1988, the proportion of Americans expressing a "great deal" of confidence in organized religion declined from 34 percent to only 17 percent.[33]

Broadly speaking, the religious mood was one of continuing and, for a majority of Americans, casual interest in spirituality. Most were serious enough about spirituality to take comfort in beliefs about the existence of God and a life after death. Many participated faithfully in their churches. But serious commitment to spiritual discipline itself seems to have been characteristic of relatively few. Indeed, many of the people we talked to openly admitted that leading a spiritually disciplined life was either too difficult or took too much time. For instance, a Catholic woman who believes that spirituality should be the center of her life muses that it would be nice to sit her family down, pray with them, and read a few Bible verses together. "Religious people do that," she notes. But she adds, "I think it would be awkward." Another woman, noting that spiritual discipline used to mean "mortifying the flesh," often through extended fasting and other ascetic practices during the Lenten season, observes that in recent years it has amounted to little more than giving up token pleasures, such as chocolate, French fries, or ice cream sundaes. Similarly, a man in his thirties who considers himself an evangelical and who can recite passages he's been reading lately in the Bible admits that his life is an emotional roller coaster. He thinks he is doing his best however. He says he used to tie himself in knots trying to do what was right, but now that he is a Christian he agonizes less because he figures God loves him no matter what he does. A Protestant clergyman who had recently been reading books on the topic explains that spiritual discipline, such as prayer or fasting, is something people should do for their own good, and then only if they feel like it.

For these people, spiritual discipline is an activity that has to fit easily into the busy schedule of everyday life. Like other disciplines, it needed to be pursued, if it was practiced at all, in a way that did not interfere with being an average person. Contrary to the maxim "No pain, no gain," many Americans seem in fact to be skeptical of anything that has to be achieved at too great a cost. They criticize people who deliberately subject themselves to pain as being masochists or as suffering from a hero complex. In our interviews people dismissed the discipline required to be a long-distance runner on the grounds that running is just a way of getting an endorphin high. We also heard people say that making extreme sacrifices to help the poor is probably just a way to compensate for some deficit in one's personality.[34]

On balance, then, the desire for discipline that occupied public attention in the 1980s appears to have been neither as consequential as its advocates hoped nor as worrisome as its critics feared. Americans did not flock to the religious leaders who called for a return to rigid moral absolutes, nor did the people who sympathized with these pleas discover that it was possible to reorient their lives around simple moral rules.

Many people were working harder than ever before, struggling to earn a living for their families, and trying to teach their children what was right. Yet there was little evidence of people engaging in spiritual disciplines that called them to sacrifice the standard of living to which they had grown accustomed or even to devote significant portions of their week to seeking a deeper relationship with God. Pursuing a disciplined spiritual life meant, at most, rediscovering the soft technology of uttering a brief prayer before going to bed. Indeed, spiritual discipline depended almost entirely on individual intuition and, in the absence of organizations to mentor or monitor it, amounted to little more than keeping one's feelings in check and having faith that one's intuitions were right.

These understandings of spiritual discipline were loose enough to help most Americans adapt to the complex world in which they lived. To be in favor of a disciplined life was to avoid the moral chaos that one read about in the newspapers and to give up the wild-eyed restlessness of the 1960s. It was possible to find discipline in one's faith by affirming that goodness existed, even if one did not have a clear sense of how this goodness might impinge on one's life-style. The discipline of the 1980s was thus not that far removed from the new freedoms of the 1960s. Personal integrity, liberty, and negotiating one's own sense of how to live were still an important part of what it meant to lead a spiritual life.

Of course, the point of spiritual discipline is not to encase the soul in rigid rules but to give it room to maneuver and to grow. When it is rightly understood, the sacred is always too powerful to be tamed by simple formulas and techniques. But spirituality also requires practice, a serious engagement with the sacred that moves one beyond the realities of everyday life.

To have achieved the personal and social transformation that many observers (on the left as well as on the right) were calling for in the 1980s would have required greater dedication and more sacrifice than was popularly associated with the idea of discipline. "Most of us are not naturally or instinctively humble or contrite, and we have little practice in being still or waiting on the Lord," observed theologian Hugh Kerr shortly before his death in 1992. "Discipline, exercises, regimens of various sorts put us in the mood to receive the injunction that a spirit-filled and spirit-led life requires us 'to do justly, and to love mercy, and to walk humbly with [our] God.'"[35]

CHAPTER Five

Angel Awakenings

"I really don't know if I can talk about this," Heather Maxwell falters, slightly embarrassed, then proceeds. "A couple of years ago I was on this camping trip with several of my friends. All the snow was melting, and the river was raging. I found this really great place where you could crawl out on a rock in the middle of the river. You had to crawl over a tree to get to it, and it was quite dangerous. I crawled out first and yelled for my two friends to join me. They came out too, and it was just so invigorating that I stood up. All of a sudden I started to slip. I knew I was going to fall into the river and drown. I was slipping backwards. But then something just seemed to be pushing me forward. Neither one of my friends say they touched me."

Sara Kahn, a woman in her early thirties, traces her spiritual journey to a mysterious event that happened one night when she was four. Lying in bed, she observed a hole in her ceiling. A ladder appeared, and a man wearing a bowler hat and top coat, whom she assumed to be English, descended. He turned briefly, looked at her, and then left the room. Sara remembers that she didn't know what to make of the event at the time. She told her parents, who insisted that she had been dreaming. But Sara believes she was awake.

The more Sara has thought about this event the more she is convinced that it was a signal from "the other side." She doesn't think she would have recognized the man's clothing as that of someone from England unless she had been to England. Since she was never outside the United States as a child, she thinks she probably lived in England in a previous life. She thinks the man was her "spirit God," who had been sent to show her something. Despite the skepticism that this story evokes from her friends, it convinces her that she is in essence a spiritual being.

Experiences like this provide another way of assessing the changes that have been taking place in U.S. spirituality. Although the sacred has often been encountered through such mysterious events, the late 1980s and early 1990s came to be characterized by an exceptional interest in such experiences. According to polls, as many as three Americans in four believed in angels, substantially more than did so a decade earlier. Spirit guides, channeling, encounters with angels, and near-death experiences moved from tabloid journalism into mainstream culture. Bestseller lists typically included prominent titles on such topics. As one pundit quipped, drawing on the titles of several popular books, "In best-seller heaven, there are angels (hark, a whole host of them) jamming the roads less traveled with soul mates embracing the light in their search for the celestine prophecy."[1]

This apparently growing interest in miracle and mystery merits special attention as an indication of how spirituality has been changing. Critics attribute this interest to Americans' desire to make sense of a world that is increasingly dangerous and chaotic. Sympathetic discussions suggest that Americans are simply getting in touch with their spiritual needs and point out that such experiences have been recorded throughout the centuries. Both perspectives hold value. But it is important to ask what is distinctive about this interest in miracle and mystery.

I want to suggest that experiences of miracle and mystery not only are prominent but also take the special forms that they do in contemporary culture for several reasons. For one, there is a legacy of spirituality within congregations and families that supplies the underlying models for these experiences. As people like Heather Maxwell and Sara Kahn describe their encounters, it often appears that these experiences are entirely without precedent in their lives. Yet close attention to people's spiritual journeys shows that such experiences are rooted both in the spiritual dwellings they have known as children and in the spiritual seeking they have done as adults. Another reason why many Americans consider these experiences to be especially meaningful is that such encounters are relatively fluid, personalized, ephemeral, and amorphous, all of which fits with the complex, homeless world in which spirituality is currently sought. These experiences also exhibit some of the traits associated with people who are "newly arrived"—what might be termed an *arriviste* quality that is symptomatic of an increasingly secular culture in which there are few safe places and little discipline for spiritual seeking. Miraculous experiences help to reassure people that there is more to life than meets the eye, but people who live in an otherwise secular society are often unsure what to make of these experiences. It will be helpful to consider the following example.

"THEN THE CANDLE BLEW OUT"

Caryl O'Shea, who is in her thirties, wants to be a writer and in her spare time is working on a true crime book about a murder that took place in a haunted house. But for the time being she works as an assistant advertising production manager for a company that publishes computer magazines, and her book is on indefinite hold. She and her husband are leaving in a year to work abroad, and they spend most of their spare time preparing for that. Caryl has been learning how to teach English as a second language, passing her first aid requirements, and doing volunteer work.

The granddaughter of Irish immigrants, Caryl was raised in an intense—but fully acculturated—Catholic environment. As a child, she was taken regularly by her mother to mass and was sent to catechism class. Her father seldom attended, but Caryl simply assumed he was too busy. He was a lawyer and liked to have a little time around the house to himself on Sunday mornings. Only much later did Caryl learn that he did not believe in God. Caryl's mother said the rosary and attended mass but did not go to confession and did not take communion, which bothered Caryl considerably. Her mother was beautiful, and Caryl thought perhaps she had cheated on her father at some point in their marriage and for this reason avoided going to confession and taking communion. Caryl also remembers that her parents had a statue of the Virgin Mary in their bedroom. Caryl's older sister always insisted that the statue had "special powers."

When Caryl was in high school, she went through what she describes as her "born-again phase." For about a year, she attended prayer meetings with a group of people who were mostly her own age and who came from both Catholic and Protestant backgrounds. The group had a "communal feeling" that appealed to her. "It didn't feel like anyone was really pushing me to do anything; it was just all these really warm people who would get around and talk about their religious experiences and read from the Bible; it just seemed like a really nice thing." The group talked a lot about the Holy Spirit, and some of the members spoke in tongues when they were filled with the Holy Spirit. Caryl thinks she spoke in tongues, too, but isn't completely sure. All she knows is that God was a big part of her life for a while.

Her born-again phase ended gradually during her senior year in high school. Caryl started thinking about going away to college and began wondering whether her born-again life-style would be appropriate for college. "I wondered how feeling so religious and being so under God was going to fit into my college life because I really wanted to go to college and be accepted by people, not to be seen as an outcast, which I guess I thought I would have been seen as." About the same time, she also started having serious doubts about the Catholic church. "I started feeling that the sexism involved in the Church is just too much for me. There are so many sexist things in the Bible, and just surrounding the church in general, and it really bothered me. I really was very much a feminist, so it put me in a conflict. And nobody could explain why, why these things are still going on. And if this church was so great, then why weren't women on an equal ground to men. And since I didn't have any answers for it, I just dropped it altogether."

In fact, Caryl quit attending church and for the next six or seven years thought of herself as an atheist. Only in the last couple of years has she started rethinking her spirituality. One day she was walking through an art museum looking at some of her favorite paintings when she suddenly realized that she was terribly upset about her life. "I was crying hysterically, and nobody really seemed to notice," she recalls. "All these things started flooding into my mind about myself—not necessarily good things. It was all there all the time, but for some reason I was just open enough to it to think about some of these things." Caryl considers this event an important turning point in her spiritual journey.

At present, she no longer thinks of herself as someone who does not believe in God. She still has trouble saying she actually believes in *God* because of the connotations this term has for her. "God is considered by Catholics as a male," she explains, "and this one supreme being somehow controls things." Caryl says she prefers a different view. "Why does God have to be that?" she asks. "Why can't God just be some supreme power, not necessarily a person, just something that sort of is in everything. I mean, if it was one person, how could all these horrible things be going on in the world? I mean, why wouldn't that one supreme being say, 'No, I'm not going to let that woman get raped or that person get murdered'? So I think my idea about what God is is changing, and that's making me wonder, well maybe I do believe in God then."

Caryl's current view of God is simply that some higher power exists that cannot be fully understood and that acts on people from an entirely different plane of reality. This view is consistent with her reluctance to be part of the church and with her commitment to her career, her marriage, and her efforts to help others. It is also consistent with an important part of her past.

When Caryl was thirteen, someone told her that if you stared into your own eyes in the mirror long enough, strange things would happen. Caryl went home and tried it. She got ready for bed, turned off all the lights, set a candle on the dresser, and stared into the mirror. "All of a sudden," she remembers, "I felt a presence in the room, and my face changed in the mirror. It changed to what I would describe as a dying old man that was terrifying. Then the candle blew out." She continues, "I felt this presence around me in the room. And I didn't have any clothes on, and somehow I managed to get the courage to stand up and turn on the light and look around. I didn't see anything there, so I turned the light back off, and I lay down on my bed. I felt something lie down on top of me. And eventually I just felt it sort of vanish." Afterward, Caryl felt safe and calm. She points to it as a time that convinced her "there might be something else."

Since that moment, she has remained convinced that there may be more to life than meets the eye. Her older sister earns a living as a psychic—telling fortunes, channeling psychic energy, and performing seances. Caryl thinks her sister probably goes a bit far. But hearing her sister's stories is another reason Caryl entertains the possibility of a supernatural realm. For instance, her sister claims to have gotten interested in psychic powers in the first place because of a miraculous healing. Caryl admits that the healing seemed miraculous to her too.

Caryl O'Shea is too young to have participated directly in the new religious movements that sprang up during the 1960s. But like many of the people we talked to, she is indirectly a product of these times. Her older sister became a "hippie," Caryl says, and participated both in the drug culture and in some of the alternative religions of the sixties. Caryl is somewhat wistful as she talks about her sister's experiences. Caryl herself participated vicariously in the hippie culture, especially when she helped put on the musical *Hair* in high school. She also sees the Vietnam war as a turning point in American history. Sometimes she looks into the eyes of people she knows who fought in that war, and she realizes that something awful must have happened.

Reagan was elected president when Caryl was sixteen. She did not support him and she found herself feeling increasingly at odds with the conservatism of the times. Even during her born-again phase, she did not agree with the church's stance on sexuality. "There were so many things I didn't agree with," she muses. "I just ignored them. I just decided, well, I'm my own person, I have my own ideas, and even though I follow a lot of what the church preaches, I just have to have my own ideas. I mean, just to give you an example, when I was in high school, I had a very serious boyfriend that was older than me, and so I was having sex with him, even when I was going to these prayer meetings; but I thought, 'Well, I love him. Why shouldn't I be making love to him?' I mean, it wasn't like I was just sleeping with anyone in high school. It wasn't like that. He was a special person to me that I planned on marrying, even though I didn't."

Caryl also found herself at odds with the church on abortion. "Thankfully," she says, "I've never had to have an abortion, but certainly a lot of my friends have." She remembers taking a girlfriend to have an abortion and recalls having to walk through a "crowd of pro-lifers who were screaming horrible things at both of us." Caryl thinks it is stupid to be irresponsible about sex and birth control, but she is also convinced that the situation was worse when abortion was illegal. She thinks the prolifers should do more to adopt unwanted children and be more willing to provide information about birth control.

More than anything else, though, it was the feminist movement that caused Caryl to distance herself from the church. Her feelings about the church's paternalism toward women were compounded by a growing sense that her mother had given an interesting career as an artist to marry her father and had become a "sheltered little wife" who was afraid to venture out of the house without her father there to protect her. Caryl's sisters were feminists, and most of her friends in high school were too. "It's made me very determined about equal rights in the workplace," she says. As she has witnessed gender discrimination herself, the feminist movement has given her courage to speak up.

In considering why she behaves as she does, Caryl says she has been speaking up for herself her whole life. Her parents taught her to think for herself, and her sisters encouraged her to take risks sooner than other girls her age. Perhaps because she has known this degree of freedom, she does not feel that she is opening out or experiencing the thrill of liberation the way some of the other people we talked to did. Her life was already open. What animates her sense of spirituality, therefore, is the quest for those rare moments when the sacred breaks through and fills her with awe. She is attracted to the idea that there is a kind of animal spirit inside her waiting to break through and to empower her. She is especially attracted to the idea that there are other realities waiting to be discovered.

DAYS OF MIRACLES

On September 13, 1863, a group of clergymen visited Abraham Lincoln to advise him on issuing a declaration of emancipation. Lincoln expressed his desire for some divine revelation telling him what to do. But he concluded the conversation by stating, "These are not, however, the days of miracles."[2] Lincoln was perhaps reacting to the wave of spiritualism that had been spreading across the nation since 1848 and that would soon reach the White House itself. Preferring to take counsel in reason and from the "facts of the case," Lincoln might well be surprised to know how enamored his fellow Americans are with reports of miracles more than a century later. He might be amused by the Paul Simon song that intones, "These *are* the days of miracle and wonder." But Lincoln's rejection of miracles does suggest the need to understand why Americans' interest in the miraculous has remained so strong. By the 1890s, spiritualism had been roundly condemned by scientists and church leaders alike. A century later, the mysterious has become a growth industry.

One manifestation of this growth is the enormous interest in angels. In only three years, Sophy Burnham's *A Book of Angels* sold 450,000 copies. So many readers wrote letters to the author reporting their encounters with angels that her edited anthology of these letters (*Angel Letters*) sold another 175,000 copies. Joan Wester Anderson's book, *Where Angels Walk*, proved even more successful, selling more than a million copies. At least twenty other popular books on angels appeared about the same time (some bookstores devoted whole sections to these books), including such titles as *Ask Your Angels, Touched by Angels*, and *The President's Angel*, with sales of many individual titles exceeding one hundred thousand copies.[3]

As if to capitalize on the popular interest, in 1993 First Lady Hillary Rodham Clinton decorated the White House Christmas tree entirely in angels, declaring "this is the year of the angels," and First Daughter Chelsea Clinton was said to wear an angel pin to school on test days. Overall, the number of books on angels (according to the Library of Congress) rose from 20 published between 1971 and 1975, to 31 between 1976 and 1980, 34 between 1981 and 1985, 57 between 1986 and 1990, and 110 between 1991 and 1995. During the last of these periods, total sales of angel books were estimated to exceed five million copies.[4]

In our interviews, approximately one person in five mentioned that angels had been a significant part of his or her spiritual journey, without prompting or being asked any direct questions about angels. Had we probed, the proportion would have undoubtedly been higher. The comments ranged from simple affirmations of belief in the existence of angels to reports of visitations and encounters. One of the most dramatic stories was told by a fifty-eight-year-old woman whose teenage daughter had tried to commit suicide. After four days and nights sitting at her daughter's bedside in the hospital, the woman came home exhausted. That night an angel appeared to her. "At the foot of the bed stood this magnificent creature of God and said not to be afraid, that my daughter would make it and that God would heal her. I knew that she wouldn't die. I knew it." This woman has taken to collecting pictures and figurines of angels. She now has more than a hundred of them. "I love angels," she says. "I believe there's one who looks after each of us. I believe that God assigns each of us an angel. And I believe we're angels. I believe all of us are. I believe we're angels on earth. People tell me I have long arms. I really think of them as my wings!"

Another woman we talked to gets in touch with angels by inviting friends to her house for "guided meditations." They sit in a circle, talk, relax, and then try to transcend their "ego minds" by focusing their thoughts on the universe. "I'm a part of the universe," she explains. "I know that there are angels or guides around me. I feel them. I wish I could feel God in me every second of the day. I feel God when I'm out of my ego mind. Then I just know that everything I need to be doing will come to me."

National studies suggest that at least a third of the public claims to have had a personal encounter with an angel, that the number of Americans who believe in angels is much higher, and that the number probably increased during the 1980s and early 1990s. A 1994 poll conducted by *Time* magazine, for example, found that 69 percent of Americans believed in angels. Of those who believed, slightly more than half (55 percent) said they thought angels were "higher spiritual beings created by

God with special powers to act as His agents on earth," while 18 percent thought angels were "an important religious idea but merely symbolic," and 15 percent thought they were "spirits of people who have
died" (the remainder were unsure).[5] In a poll conducted by CBS News,
67 percent of the public said they believed in angels, and 32 percent said
they had personally "felt an angelic presence" in their life. Among all
those who believed in angels, 80 percent thought they personally had a
guardian angel.[6] Other surveys conducted between 1992 and 1994 estimated the percentage of Americans who believed in angels to be between
67 and 76. In comparison, a survey conducted in 1980 found that only
50 percent believed in angels then.[7]

Millions of Americans also reportedly believe in miracles. They have
come close to dying and have experienced the presence of some divine
force, or they have experienced the presence of God in their lives in some
other way. One study found that 75 percent of Americans claim to
have had "an experience that [they] thought brought [them] closer to
God."[8] A Gallup Poll found that eight million Americans have had some
sort of near-death experience in which they glimpsed a reality beyond the
present one.[9] In another study, 83 percent agreed that miracles are performed even today by the power of God, and another poll reported that
68 percent of Americans definitely or probably believed in miracles.[10]

In these studies, women are generally more likely than men to believe
in miracles. People with lower levels of education are somewhat more
likely to believe than people with higher levels. Church-goers are more
inclined to believe than nonattendees. And older people are more likely
to believe than younger people. Nevertheless, there is fairly widespread
belief in the possibility of miracles in all sectors of the population. Except among people with graduate degrees (where only 18 percent definitely believe in miracles), among those with no religious preference, and
among Jews, there is a broad propensity to entertain the thought that
miracles can take place. Even among people who seldom or never attend
religious services, a majority think miracles probably happen.[11]

Fewer Americans believe in other manifestations of the supernatural
or mysterious, but the numbers are still significant. Channeling—the effort to allow a spiritual being to temporarily assume control of a human
body during a trace—is one such practice. Talk-shows, New Age periodicals, and psychic bookstores provide graphic tales of such experiences. One survey found that 11 percent of Americans believed in channeling, 67 percent were sure they did not believe in it, and the remaining
22 percent were unsure. Two percent of the public claimed to have been
personally involved with channeling.[12]

Extraterrestrial beings, haunted houses, and clairvoyance fall into the same category. Most Americans do not believe in these phenomena. Yet there is a large enough minority who *do* that books, television shows, psychic boutiques, and the like abound. According to one survey, 27 percent of Americans believe that extraterrestrial beings have visited the earth, 29 percent believe that houses can be haunted, and 26 percent believe in clairvoyance. The same survey found that 14 percent of Americans have consulted a fortune-teller or psychic; 6 percent have consulted an astrologer.[13]

During the 1980s, the term *New Age* was used to describe alternative ways of encountering spirituality, such as channeling or using crystals; yet it should be clear from the figures just presented that Americans' fascination with miracles and spiritual experiences extends well beyond the New Age movement.[14] Indeed, one study found that only 15 percent of the public described themselves as holding some New Age beliefs, while another 12 percent expressed interest in learning more about New Age beliefs.[15] The broader interest in spiritual experiences was reflected in the fact that virtually all Americans continued to believe in God, and that 82 percent of them thought God "is everywhere and in everyone"—suggesting that it should be possible for people to experience miracles.[16] This interest was evident too in the fact that in spring 1994 half the top nonfiction bestsellers focused on spiritual themes.[17] It was also evident in Americans' interest in prayer, in the fact that most Americans claimed to pray often, and in the frequency with which stories about miraculous answers to prayer appeared in the national media.

This interest in miraculous and mysterious experiences can be attributed to a number of factors, not least of which are the promotional efforts of booksellers and journalists' eye for stories about the unusual. Yet one of the factors that most observers emphasize is the uncertainty of the times, including uncertainty about what to believe. Ironically, Americans' interest in angels is probably symptomatic of the growing uncertainty many people feel about the existence and presence of God. Were God as much a part of their local geography as in the past, they could simply experience the sacred in ordinary objects and activities. It has become harder to know God in recent decades, and thus it is necessary to emphasize brief encounters with the ecumenical intermediary deities that are known as angels. Author and priest Andrew Greeley suggests, "We live in a problematic and dangerous universe [and] we feel that God is a great distance from us. Angels . . . have the appeal of beings who will take care of us."[18] In a similar vein, Barnard professor Randall Balmer writes that "the fascination with angels almost certainly stems from the sense that we live in a difficult and dangerous world." With fear of physical harm added to Americans' existential uncertainties, Balmer asks, "Who wouldn't want some sort of supernatural protection while walking down the hallways of a public high school? A guardian angel would come in handy."[19]

Uncertainty is generally understood as a psychological state that can cause people to seize hold of some encounter with the supernatural as a way of gaining assurance that life has meaning or that divine help is available. There is some truth in this understanding, but it needs to be amplified in order to see clearly how social conditions have contributed to the interest in miracles and mystery. Uncertainty can lead people to find comfort in many other ways—for example, by working harder, overeating, or joining a support group.

The reason people find solace in supernatural experiences is generally that they have had some religious training that predisposes them to do so. In describing their experiences, however, most people emphasize the miraculous nature of these events by denying that there were any such predisposing circumstances. Indeed, the experiences are often depicted as being entirely unexpected and inexplicable. And yet it is important to consider how prior religious practices provide models for these miraculous experiences.

These prior religious practices need not be those of a particular person, for there is much in American culture generally that predisposes people to accept the legitimacy of miraculous events. Certainly literature is one source of such predisposing potential. Of angels, Ralph Waldo Emerson wrote, "It seems as if heaven has sent its insane angels into our world as to an asylum, and here they will break out in their native music and utter at intervals the words they have heard in heaven; then the mad fit returns and they mope and wallow like dogs."[20] From a different quarter, Jack Kerouac described angels as "potent and inconceivable radiances," "the magic mothswarm of heaven."[21] Recent popularizers of angels often legitimate their stories by repeating accounts of angel appearances from a wide variety of historical material and from literature, as have popularizers of near-death experiences, channeling, spirit guides, and so on.

But the practices that predispose individuals most powerfully to believe in miraculous encounters are generally embedded in the religious histories of their immediate family. This connection is perhaps obvious, but it is easy to overlook. Because it is practiced individually and in diverse ways, the new spirituality of the nineties is often characterized as a populist movement having little connection with organized religion, even with the organized religious involvements of people's families. For instance, Eugene Taylor, director of the Cambridge Institute of Psychology and Religion, writes that the new spirituality's "motive power is not coming from mainstream institutionalized science, *religion*, or education." Rather, he asserts, "it is a popular phenomenon of epic proportions."[22] Yet such assertions miss the extent to which popular spirituality is rooted in experiences shaped by institutional religion.

For example, Betty Eadie, author of the bestseller *Embraced by the Light*, attended Catholic school, went to a boarding school run by Wesleyan Methodists, and grew up attending Lutheran, Baptist, and Salvation Army services. By the time of her first encounter with an angel, she was well-schooled in the existence of a God who watched her and intervened in human affairs.[23] Eileen Elias Freeman, editor of *The Angel Watch Journal* and author of the best-selling book *Touched by Angels*, associates her first encounter with an angel with the deep anxieties she experienced as a five-year-old when her grandmother died. Yet the event was significant to her because she had been sent regularly to Sunday school, because her grandmother was a pious Christian, and because Freeman later cultivated her understanding of spirituality through church-going and by majoring in religion in college.[24]

In our interviews, we found that people who had encountered an angel or had some other mysterious experience as an adult were consistently predisposed by their religious upbringing to entertain such possibilities. Heather Maxwell's father was a Dutch Calvinist who, in her words, believed in fire and brimstone, and she attended a Catholic elementary school where she loved to sit in the chapel and feel close to God. Caryl O'Shea was keenly interested in her parents' religious behavior when she was a child, and although she claims not to have understood what they believed, she went to church with her mother regularly, saw her mother pray the rosary every day, and knew that the most powerful object in their house was a statue of the Virgin Mary. The woman who saw an angel after her daughter tried to commit suicide was raised by a Presbyterian mother and a Catholic father who, because they disagreed with each other about religion, taught her that she should make up her own mind about God. She also prayed every night with her mother, learned Bible verses, and can still sing some of the hymns she heard her mother singing as she cooked dinner.

From statistical studies, it is possible to see that early religious training increases the likelihood of adults' believing in or experiencing a wide variety of mysterious phenomena. For example, in one national study, 59 percent of those who had received religious training as children said they had been "aware of, or influenced by, a presence or a power—whether [they] called it God or not—which [was] different from [their] everyday self," whereas only 36 percent of those who had not received religious training agreed with this statement. It is also possible to see that coming to believe—from whatever source—in one kind of nonordinary reality makes it more likely that people will believe in other such phenomena.[25]

And it should not be assumed that the effect of religious practices is limited to those raised in the most devout or observant homes. Indeed, people who have grown up with doubts about what they believed or about what their parents believed are sometimes the most likely to seize on brief encounters with the sacred as having special significance.

The importance of doubt can be understood by thinking about the implicit conversations people engage in with their past. During times of doubt—and when individuals are experiencing genuine crises in their lives—the silence that normally surrounds the sacred is broken. God may not speak to them in an audible voice. But their friends and family may. People who otherwise feel that the sacred is too private to discuss with anyone else suddenly violate their self-imposed taboo in an effort to give advice or comfort. People may not accept this advice, but they are still likely to be thankful for it. And they are likely to feel that these are special moments because they sense that the sacred dimension that was once present and that has been silenced is now temporarily evident again. When friends and family talk about the sacred, people are likely to realize that these acquaintances are expressing a hidden dimension of themselves and thus feel that they are relating to each other at a deep level.

Adam Westfield, the man who said his family had become "weary" of its religious history by the time he was a child, offers a compelling example of why a brief word about the sacred can carry special meaning. As a child, he remembers, his father said a little prayer with him each night after his mother tucked him into bed. But decades went by and Adam never heard his father say anything more about religion or his personal struggles with spirituality. Then, a few years ago, Adam's father was dying, and Adam himself was going through a difficult divorce. Adam remembers sitting beside his father's bed one night and talking with him about the divorce. "There was a lot of pressure for me to move out of my house," he says, "and I didn't want to move out." His friends and his lawyer were counseling him not to move out. Adam brought the issue up with his father. "My father said, 'Don't fight back. It's pagan-ism.' And I thought, 'I believe that. That's right.' It was probably the only overtly Christian thing he ever said to me." Adam muses, "I don't know; in legal terms he was certainly wrong, but in faith terms and in family love terms he was right. I was deeply impressed with that."

A conversation like this is rare. The fact that it stands out, one might say, is because life for many Americans is so thoroughly secular that they seldom allow the sacred to enter their language. Yet a conversation like this takes on great significance in their thinking because it suggests to them that some lost dimension from their past is still there, hidden be-neath the veneer of secular life. They understand that the faith of their grandparents or parents may not have disappeared entirely, only gone underground.

It can also be seen in this example that the language of "privacy" pro-vides a way of understanding this peculiar kind of underground spiritu-ality. Some scholars argue that a distinctive characteristic of contempo-rary religion is its penchant for privacy: people keep their beliefs to themselves, perhaps fearing to express them in a secular environment, or they are reluctant to impose their views on other people. Not sur-prisingly, other scholars disagree with this interpretation, arguing instead that it is meaningless to draw distinctions between what is private and what is public.[26]

But this quibbling can be avoided if it is recognized that "privacy" itself is a rhetorical device, a construct, a symbol that people deploy strategically to help them make sense of their world. If they want to believe that they still have some of the religious vigor of the past, even though they seldom see evidence of it, they can invoke "privacy" to explain how this is possible. When asked about his parents' spirituality, for instance, Adam Westfield says he is sure they believed in God, prayed, and took their faith seriously, even though they never said anything about it to him. He explains this seeming incongruity this way: "I think their brand of being New Englanders would have thought that [faith] was something that was very private, so private that if you'd asked them about it, they might have said, 'Oh, I don't know.'"

This comment attributes privacy to New England. But the larger point is that the meaning of talk about privacy can be grasped only in relation to Americans' sense that some element of transcendence has been lost. To put it differently, privacy is the answer to the question that lurks in people's minds as they reflect on their past. They wonder where the sacred has gone and find an answer by saying that it has become private. The language of privacy tells people that maybe something is still alive— that maybe the sacred has not been irretrievably lost after all.

We can now return to the question of how the interest in miracles reflects changes in social circumstances. The primary way lies in the fact that religious organizations no longer hold a monopoly over authoritative interpretations of these experiences. Much of the popular interest in angels, near-death experiences, and the like has been kindled by journalists, writers, physicians, psychics, and holistic health advocates rather than by the clergy. Indeed, there is a marked contrast between the popular literature that has been produced in recent years and the literature about angels and other mysterious beings that was published within religious circles a decade or two ago. The earlier literature quoted biblical stories about angels, placed them within a theological framework, and interpreted them in terms of Christian teachings about Jesus, God, evil, demonic possession, and the need for salvation.[27] Few of these books attracted wide audiences. The more recent literature suggests that angels are rather ill-disposed toward institutional religion, that they transcend religious and theological distinctions, and that they simply appear to good-hearted people who need them.

A similar shift is evident in the way ideas about prayer are communicated: people who attend religious services regularly pray more often than those who do not; yet most references in the mass media now occur in some context other than a discussion of organized religion. In fact, in one database of newspaper, magazine, and television journalism, "prayer" appeared more than fifty-five thousand times within a two year period—and only twenty-five hundred of these mentions occurred in articles referring to religious organizations.

Other examples suggest that organized religion is unable to control how many Americans understand the sacred: most Americans say they pray generally to God or a supreme being rather than specifically to Jesus or Christ, most pray for themselves rather than seeking to worship through their prayers, only half of adult Americans know that Genesis is the first book in the Bible and only a third know that Jesus delivered the Sermon on the Mount, only 39 percent of teenagers believe the Bible is completely true (compared with 62 percent who held this belief in 1961), and more people perceive religion to be declining in influence than perceive its influence to be increasing.[28]

Many Americans are tired of being exposed to different faiths and trying to find rational arguments to defend one faith against another.

They believe such arguments are dead ends, yet they remain convinced that some element of mystery in life requires them to have faith. An older man who was raised in two different Protestant denominations, married a Catholic, and watched as one of his sons converted to Islam explains his beliefs in these terms: "I have a feeling that God is with us all of the time. I can't explain some of the things that happen. So, being a realist, it's like there's somebody up there that's doing this stuff." He adds, "I've had many arguments in years gone by about religion. But it's like there's a point where you've got to admit there's something else involved here." It just makes sense to him that angels and other spirit beings exist, even though he is doubtful that organized religion can help him understand them.

For other people, it is not that interest—or even participation—in organized religion has declined but that many other interests have been added; they may regard some of these interests as legitimate ways to pursue spirituality rather than considering them pagan, secular, or profane. For instance, gardening is a weekend activity that now involves more Americans on a regular basis than going to church. One woman remembers that her mother was often critical of neighbors who had flower gardens because they did not spend as much time as they might have doing church work. She herself feels just as close to God in her garden as she does in church. For other people, camping and hiking are activities that help them experience the sacred. Participation in these activities doubled between 1965 and 1982. And there was a threefold increase in the numbers who took nature walks and who went backpacking. Although most probably did so for recreation, many of the people we talked to said that getting away was also an important way to communicate with the sacred.[29]

Research also suggests that Americans may be drawn to the miraculous because it makes them feel good rather than filling them with awe or fear. Most of the beings that people report encountering are friendly and do their bidding. They are no longer fearsome, evil forces needing respect or divine magistrates jealously seeking human allegiance. The people who have these experiences also tend to believe that the forces governing the universe are benign and that human nature is basically good.[30]

Yet another reason for the popularity of miraculous experiences is that it is sometimes in the interest of nonreligious professionals to emphasize them as an alternative to organized religion. Psychologist Bruce Greyson, a student of near-death experiences, writes, "Because much of society has lost faith in traditional religion, we need another source to give us values and tell us what virtue is. Most near-death experiencers become less conventionally religious and espouse a universal spirituality, saying things like, 'I'm aware of God in everything. I don't feel the need for a particular church. Now I know that I'm part of something greater than myself.'"[31] Greyson may be overgeneralizing, but his statement does point to the appeal of universalistic, nonjudgmental beings in a society that has difficulty convincing itself that absolute truth can be known. As another example, television producer Norman Lear argues that "the spiritual life of the human species occupies a much larger, more heterogeneous realm than any one organized religion can lay claim to." Thus, in his view, television, other media, business, and private individuals need to help break down the barriers to spirituality imposed by "religionists" and encourage people to get in touch with their own mysterious, invisible, inner life, which is the best feature of humanity.[32] Among the people we interviewed, Sara Kahn draws one of the sharpest distinctions between spirituality and organized religion. Organized religion repulses her because of people like Falwell who are telling others what to believe. For her, spirituality is something that you can only experience. She invokes the following analogy: "It's like having an orgasm. You can't describe it to someone else. You can say, 'It feels great.' But the description is inadequate. Spirituality is also something that each person has to experience for themselves."

With religious organizations less in control of spirituality, the interpretation of miraculous experiences necessarily bears the imprint of popular culture itself. Thus, there is a wide range of understandings of what these experiences mean, just as there is diversity in musical tastes and in entertainment preferences. The emphasis on self-gratification in the culture at large is also evident in the ways miraculous experiences are interpreted. They cater to the interests of persons reporting them, and they provide spiritual comfort without making demands on people's time or commitments.

A common thread running through these various experiences is that they put the individual in direct contact with something that cannot be understood within normal, everyday experience. Whether it is direct contact with God or simply a breach in ordinary laws of gravity, such an experience points toward realities that remain mysterious yet are also powerful and in virtually all instances are benevolent. Although many popular treatments of angels and of warm, enveloping visions of light also mention dark spirits, ghosts, and demonic beings, the malevolent forces receive far less attention. Miraculous experiences seldom frighten and scarcely ever punish. Ghosts and goblins may roam the streets on Halloween, but people are less likely to believe in them than in the more benevolent spirits. The same surveys that estimate belief in angels at three-quarters of the public, for instance, place belief in ghosts at approximately one-third of Americans. Even fewer—about 14 percent—believe in witches.[33] And whereas one person in three claims to have encountered an angel personally, only one in ten believes he or she has seen a ghost.[34]

Author Eileen Elias Freeman provides a telling example of how interpretations of mysterious events may reflect self-interest or the need to feel secure. As a student in New York City, she was entering the apartment of her boyfriend one evening when something warned her of danger in the building. Having had an encounter with an angel as a child, she immediately assumed this might be another angelic intervention. But her response was dictated by her interpretation of the event, not by a clear message from the angel. She immediately ran and later, upon learning that someone had been murdered in the building, concluded that the angel had been sent to spare her life.[35] Yet she could have summoned assistance or yelled to see whether someone was in danger. She apparently entertained no questions about why the angel had not warned the murder victim. Indeed, she leaves readers wondering why she made no effort even to find out whether her boyfriend was all right. In short, an angel may or may not have spoken to her, but how she responded and most of how she interpreted the event were her own doing.

Not without reason have religious leaders, journalists, and even some advocates of new forms of spirituality been critical of the interest in miracles, referring to it as "cocktail spirituality" and arguing that it fosters a "do-it-yourself morality" that is too self-centered to promote a commitment to the common good. The message of angels and spirit guides is, one critic writes, that "you will receive whatever you want" and that "you should be independent and look inside yourself for answers."[36] Similarly, Howard Rheingold, author of a book on virtual reality, argues that angels and other supernatural beings are attractive because they bolster Americans' confidence that a higher, more meaningful reality exists than the technological one we have created for ourselves; yet he writes that much of the current interest in spirituality is leaving "a trail of noisy, tin-can foolishness."[37]

Leaders of organized religion, while recognizing teachings about angels within their own traditions, point out that the current interest is more consistent with consumer culture than with theology. Anglican theologian Tom Harpur asserts, "There's a lot of attempts at quick fixes and spiritual junk food."[38] Another writer, arguing that people have turned elsewhere for ideas about the sacred because the clergy are not speaking clearly enough, observes that "awesome, frightening creatures have been taken out of the Bible and turned into cuddly little things that sit on coffee tables and perpetually smile at us, . . . a picture of modern American theology for the masses."[39]

In similar fashion, television producer Katherine Smalley laments the "acquisitive spirituality" and the "spiritual thrill-seeking" she observes, noting that true saints were people "who laid their lives on the line every day." Psychologists and therapists also voice criticisms, worrying, as one puts it, that people "think you can go to a workshop and that's what will save you." Even writers sympathetic to these spiritual quests are sometimes critical. For instance, Steven Kerzner, executive producer of *New Age Journal,* worries that an "absence of rules" leads to abuse, especially among people who are already vulnerable.[40]

Even if such criticisms are overstated, miraculous encounters, especially with angels, have clearly come to be presented in ways that fit comfortably with contemporary values. As depicted in popular books and in our interviews, angels never scold. They give unconditional love. They have a good sense of humor. They also protect people, giving something to hope for or depend on when life seems like too much to handle on one's own. They appeal to populist or democratic strands in American culture: their existence cannot be proved or disproved by science, and thus experts may not have much to say about them; they appear to common people and, indeed, are thought to be ridiculed by people with education and in positions of authority. They are also personal, serving, as one writer notes, as "Ethereal Secret Service agents" who protect people from danger. Yet they are often anonymous beings who make no demands and require no continuing relationship.[41] Moreover, they are uninterested in theological arguments, preferring just to perform random acts of kindness; indeed, they can conveniently be found in all religious traditions and even in the experiences of atheists and agnostics. Above all, they make for great stories and can be a source of fame and wealth if one chooses to write about them.

But if seekers of the light are often finding little more than spirituality lite, the fault is not entirely theirs. Spirituality has become big business, and big business finds many of its best markets by putting things in small, easy-to-consume packages. Few of the many angel books are long or difficult to read. They have wide margins, attractive pictures, and colorful stories. They are more likely to prick one's wallet than one's conscience. Seekers can also pay handsome fees to attend lectures given by well-known authors. Yet they expose themselves to fire walkers and mystics with little more than their admission fee at stake. Through the recording industry, Gregorian chants can be heard by millions; no knowledge of Gregory or of chanting is required. Such marketing spreads spirituality to the masses, just as missionaries did in centuries past. But the medium also shapes the message. Angel books seldom instruct readers that it may be hard work to lead a truly spiritual life. Their message is only to do what one was doing anyway and hope that an angel will land on one's shoulder.

The extension of market forces into new areas often subverts established values. Missionaries and traders undermine the cherished traditions of colonized peoples. Newspapers and consumer products can be the bearers of revolutionary ideas. Marketed miracles are no different. To titillate viewers, an otherwise serious public television series pieces together snippets of Hebrew prophecy and Native American tradition. The integrity of both cultures is breached. Seekers who have tried to live faithfully within particular religious traditions know the value of these traditions. But contemporary viewers are more likely to conclude that spirituality is a sexy item that can be understood by dabbling.

NEGOTIATING WITH THE SACRED

To hear some tell it, the interest in miracles and mystery nevertheless arises primarily from a profound epistemological transformation in Western thought. As one author states, "[The new spirituality] is the engine of a whole paradigm shift in society with the power to heal the mind-body split that has dominated Western thinking for centuries."[42] Such conclusions are drawn by elites, such as psychiatrists, Zen masters, and full-time devotees of new spiritual practices. For these elites, the current interest in spirituality often generates thinking that does challenge Cartesian philosophy or Freudian psychology. Yet, for most Americans, the interest in spirituality has much less dramatic intellectual implications. Indeed, their spirituality bears scrutiny precisely because it accommodates so well the demands of an overwhelmingly secular society.

One of the curious aspects of the current interest in miracles, demons, ghosts, angels, and other supernatural phenomena, in fact, is how this interest can be reconciled with the highly advanced scientific knowledge that also characterizes American culture. Some exposure to science is virtually inescapable for anyone who has finished high school or attended college; yet belief in some kinds of paranormal phenomena is, if anything, more common among younger, better educated people than among older or less educated people. The explanation is that most people live from day to day, focusing on the realities of daily life, rather than thinking about scientific images of the universe. Consequently, the relationship that needs to be understood is that between the supernatural and everyday life, more so than between the supernatural and science.

In one sense, the present interest in supernatural phenomena is difficult to reconcile with people's everyday lives. These lives focus on the here and now. People are interested in things that work and that can be understood; Americans rely heavily on technology and pride themselves on being able to manipulate the natural world—if not each other as well. Everyday life is fairly routine, a busy whirlwind of obligations that leaves open little time—or space—for the supernatural. As writer Lee Smith observes, "I can't be transported. I have to go to the grocery store. I can't have a religious experience; I have to be back by three."[43]

The routineness of everyday life, however, is precisely why current understandings of the supernatural fit so well with it. One experience of the supernatural will do. Just one. People can look back to one moment when, as teenagers, they experienced something so unexplainable that it had to be proof of a reality beyond the present world. Perhaps they had another confirming experience five or ten years later. Almost by definition, these events stand out because they are dramatic or exceptional. People do not expect earthquakes—or miracles—every day. Moreover, these experiences not only reinforce belief that the supernatural exists but also persuade people that the supernatural cannot in any way be understood and, therefore, it need not take much of their time. The supernatural remains a mysterious force, not something that is revealed in an authoritative text or institution.

The spiritual realm is thus a reality that people can muse about in everyday life, but its location remains on the periphery of their daily routines. It diverts little of their attention. It does not require them to set aside portions of their day to pray, worship, read sacred texts, reflect on ways to deepen their relationship with God, or be of service to others. Caryl O'Shea provides an unwitting metaphor of this removal of the sacred from everyday life when she talks about what it will be like after she and her husband relocate in another country. She says she is not sure what to expect, but she does imagine that it will be a rich time for her spiritually. As she fantasizes about it, she sees herself "dealing with all my religious issues while I am sitting in the jungle somewhere." The sacred is thus remote, just as it is in most of her daily life, a kind of fantasy that is easier to place in the exotic future than to grapple with in real time. In fact, she also states, "Right now my life is really hectic and I don't have time to think about God and religion."

Another arresting example comes from Tim Forsythe, a pilot in the Air Force Reserve who earns a living as a special education teacher. His spirituality expresses itself in much the same way as Caryl O'Shea's. Tim, who is in his mid-thirties, was raised by his mother; he describes her as a "barbiturate addict and an alcoholic." As a child, he found religion too confusing to sort out. Part of the problem was that his mother considered herself a German Jewish Catholic, his adopted father was a Protestant, and his biological father was a "recovering Catholic atheist Unitarian." Tim's mother took him to mass periodically and sent him to Catholic school—an experience that Tim says mostly made him "hate nuns." One day Tim was walking home from school and saw a puppy get run over by a milk truck. Tim decided at that moment that God could not possibly exist, and he became "a full-time, seven-day-a-week atheist." By the time he was sixteen, Tim was heavily into drugs, stealing from neighbors' houses to support his habit, and his mother and stepfather had expelled him from their home.

That year, two experiences convinced Tim to entertain the possibility that God—or something supernatural—did exist. One was his first LSD trip. At first nothing happened, so Tim took a larger amount of the drug and suddenly found himself floating twenty-five feet above the street and looking down on himself. The experience was so vivid that Tim is sure it was his soul that was literally floating above his body. The other experience was in the county morgue, where Tim was working. One night as Tim was finishing up the paperwork on a body, he saw a bluish-white light rise from the body bag and disappear into the ceiling. These experiences have convinced Tim that humans have souls and that there has to be a spiritual realm in the universe.

Like Caryl O'Shea, Tim Forsythe points to these few, highly dramatic experiences as evidence that some other reality exists. He has a few other stories as well. When his mother died, he went to a psychic and was reassured that she had found peace with God. Tim's spiritual practices, in fact, consist of visiting psychics on rare occasions when he is especially troubled, of reading books or articles about spirituality from time to time, and of having conversations with his friends about the strange, mysterious things that happen to them. Lately, he has been "big into angels" and has read all the popular books that have come out about them. This interest is part of his attraction to the unknown.

Tim says he believes in the efficacy of prayer; yet he does not pray. He remains skeptical about any single religious tradition and has no desire to pursue any particular spiritual discipline. After his experience at the morgue he read avidly in a number of religious traditions. He was convinced that these traditions were inspired by people's belief in the sacred and that they were conveying good moral principles. But he also doubts that any of these traditions is a valid revelation of the sacred. "There's a lot of crap in all the quote-unquote holy scriptures," he asserts. "They weren't written by God, they were written by people. People are (a) fallible and (b) usually pretty stupid. And even if they were originally messages from God, it's almost like playing a game of telephone. I mean, even if you're given the most divine message, a human being will probably mess it up a lot, especially over the years."

Although this may be an extreme example, it is not dissimilar from the way many people talk about spirituality when they are candid. With no particular community or set of teachings that they consider authoritative, they have to negotiate their own understanding and experiences of the sacred. As situations change, it becomes necessary to renegotiate their views, perhaps to make sense of new books that their friends are reading or to understand a conversation with someone who holds quite different views. Of course, stories about encounters with miracle and mystery make for good reading and good conversation. They are dramatic, puzzling, suggestive. Yet they are completely personal, meaning that one can accept them or treat them with mild skepticism but not have to decide whether they are universally valid. One's own stories can be understood in the same way: as interesting episodes that other people cannot challenge and that one can continually reinterpret in the light of new experiences. The sacred moments of which they speak do not require much more than a willingness to entertain the possibility that ordinary reality is not all that exists.

It is also important to understand that dabbling of the kind illustrated by Caryl O'Shea and Tim Forsythe is not limited to people who have moved out of the safe havens of their churches or synagogues. Church members, too, have a notable tendency to dabble with spirituality of many kinds, including ones that are not entirely compatible with established doctrine. For example, in one national study 24 percent of church members read their horoscope at least once a week, 22 percent said they believed in astrology, 20 percent believed in reincarnation, 12 percent had consulted a fortune-teller, 11 percent believed in channeling, and 8 percent thought they had lived a previous life in another body. Indeed, a majority of church members (55 percent) held at least one of these beliefs.[44]

Organized religion has always had difficulty keeping heterodox beliefs from attracting the faithful. But the ease with which church members can pick up ideas about everything from spirit guides to sacred crystals has never been greater. Dabbling with the sacred in a variety of ways may not be inimical to cultivating a deep relationship with the divine or letting that relationship have a profound impact on one's life. Nevertheless, the culture of people in religious congregations may not be very different from that of the wider society if it provides only momentary encounters with sacred beings who make no demands of their own. One critic puts it well when he writes that Americans are "turning to the 'middle beings' instead of working on the more difficult relationships, namely with God and with our neighbors."[45]

PARVENU SPIRITUALITY

We come finally to one of the more puzzling aspects of the current interest in miracles and mystery: life in the United States at the end of the twentieth century is in many ways thoroughly secular, organized around technology, rationality, and the surface appearances of everyday life; indeed, many people live primarily in secular contexts and attach little importance to spirituality; yet spirituality in the forms we have considered seems to flourish in these secular contexts. How is this possible?

Believers would probably answer this question by saying that there is just no getting around the divine realities of life. No matter how hard people try to live without God, the argument goes, God persists and keeps reminding people of their need for God. Social scientists have put a different spin on this argument but suggest something similar. In social science jargon, everyday life is a "constructed reality" that people live in most of the time but cannot live in all of the time. There are dangerous gaps, such as tragedies and catastrophes, and so people invent statements about the sacred as a way to make themselves feel better about these gaps. Either argument works reasonably well to explain why atheists pray in foxholes. Still, it seems obvious that these arguments do not provide the entire explanation, especially because most of the recent interest in the miraculous has had little to do with atheists or foxholes.

To be precise, two things are missing. One is an adequate understanding of the interplay between everyday life and spirituality. The standard arguments create a place at the edges of everyday life for spirituality. Yet most people—including ones who lead quite secular lives—also
talk about spirituality within their everyday lives more than might be
imagined. It is necessary to make sense of the specific ways they do so.
The other missing ingredient is an adequate understanding of the interplay between everyday life and secularity. In other words, everyday life
is not a reality that people simply take for granted or regard neutrally;
instead, it is a reality that is considered "secular." Why? And with what
consequences?

An answer to these questions can be drawn from the main argument
on which the previous chapters have focused. I want to suggest that the
peculiar interplay of spirituality and secularity in everyday life can be
understood only by paying attention to the implicit conversation people
engage in with their past—a conversation that frequently includes an as-
sumption about the declining importance of the sacred. Although many
people live in a world that is almost totally secular, Americans generally
regard themselves as relative newcomers to such a world.[46] They believe
that religion is declining, that it is excluded increasingly from public life,
and that young people are not receiving proper religious training. Many
people have a vague sense that this exclusion of the sacred has not always been the case and that there may be pitfalls to this way of living.
In fact, because of their upbringing or the reading they have done, they
believe that in the world of their grandparents (or their parents), religion
played a more serious role. Without necessarily wanting to live in that
world, they nevertheless worry that something important has been lost.
As a way of dealing with this concern, many people sacralize small aspects of everyday life, reading spiritual significance into them and do so
in a way that gives these sacred moments greater meaning than they
may realize. Despite the rational, scientific world in which people live
(some might say *because of* this world), people are often startled by the
miraculous and are likely to muse about its significance more than people who lived in societies where such experiences were commonplace.

Hannah Arendt observed in *The Human Condition* that "a notice-
able increase in superstition and gullibility" is invariably a sign of "alienation from the world."[47] Although her words may not be entirely appropriate, this observation is helpful in the present context because she
is suggesting that experiences of miracle and mystery do not arise simply from prescientific or nonrational sources, such as folk beliefs or the

popular religious sentiments of traditional peoples. Rather, such experiences come to have significance (standing out in a way that they might not in such traditional settings) when the *polis*, or the body politic, in which common sense is rooted, no longer carries authority. In terms of the present argument, alienation of this kind is symptomatic of the homelessness that people experience when their sacred habitat can no longer be taken for granted. The common-sense spirituality of that world does not provide compelling understandings of reality but neither do the secular interpretations provided by science or by public institutions (as evidenced in the widespread contemporary mistrust of such institutions). Accounts of encounters with angels and spirit guides are thus ways of saying that one is unpersuaded by prevailing understandings of reality— indeed, that one has received a kind of *gnosis*, or privileged knowledge to which most people (especially the leaders of established institutions) have not had access.

Put differently, Americans are particularly fascinated with miraculous manifestations of the sacred because they are uncertain whether the sacred has really gone away. They talk about everyday life as secular because they sense that it contrasts in some important way with a more sacralized way of living. Some people take pride in the fact that they are able to live secularly; others worry more about the inherent dangers of secularity. In either case, there is a kind of "gullibility," as Arendt says, regarding accounts of sacred experiences because religious authorities no longer are able to control the conditions under which these encounters occur and the common-sense world of secularity is not fully believable either. Like other occupiers of in-between statuses, Americans are, therefore, in an important sense parvenus seeking to make peace with the secular world in which they find themselves. They struggle with how to think about the sacred, vacillating between long stretches in their lives when they pretty much live as if the sacred did not matter at all and extraordinary moments when some unexplained experience with "the other side" takes on special significance.

The parvenu mentality is generally depicted as being unstable, uncertain, and inauthentic. Parvenus desperately want to fit in and to be accepted. Historically, the American middle class has often been subject to this desire. Its critics, at least, argue that it is shallow and inauthentic, compared with working-class people, on the one hand, or true aristocrats, on the other hand. Some aspects of contemporary spirituality also reflect this eagerness to fit in. Religious experiences that somehow link people to the seemingly more authentic help. Sometimes, these experiences provide a way of fitting in with tradition and with minority peoples, both of which are assumed to have depth and authenticity. White, middle-class Americans may believe that African Americans have always understood spirituality better than they have and that Asian religions are also better because they were never seduced by Western positivism. Part of the appeal of a bestseller such as *Embraced by the Light,* for example, is that its author is half Sioux and thus is expected to have access to more authentic insights about spirituality than European Americans have. More generally, leaders of the new spirituality who are themselves white, middle-class Americans must be demographically correct: they are preferably baby boomers who can claim to have experienced the angst of the 1960s; they must have dabbled widely with gurus and shamans, perhaps experimented with drugs, and undergone therapy; it is preferable if they are women, have suffered from divorce or abuse, and have had significant exposure to feminist spirituality; and it is best if they have rejected organized religion, had a near-death experience, and recovered miraculously from some injury or illness—all of which gives their readers a vicarious sense of spiritual authenticity.

In their desire to fit in, parvenus are also inveterate name droppers. Their books and articles are vetted by doctors, psychiatrists, scientists, musicians, and best-selling authors, despite claiming to be about the experiences of common people and presenting ideas that experts ridicule. For instance, popular treatments of spirituality regale readers with Madonna's quest for the sacred, with actor Richard Gere's association with Tibetan Buddhists, and with singer Don Henley's nature mysticism.

Parvenus also insist that they can perform their new roles easily, making up with enthusiasm what they lack in training or sophistication. Advocates of the new spirituality not only distance themselves from organized religion; they often take an in-your-face attitude toward it. Eadie describes how the nuns at Catholic boarding school punished her and taught her that God was angry with her because she was wicked. Her direct encounters with angels, bright lights, and other manifestations of the sacred demonstrate that she has just as much right to speak about God as the nuns did. Parvenu spirituality thus presents itself as an alternative to the quest for strict moral discipline that has also been increasingly evident. Of course, parvenus are detested by those who have achieved status the hard way—by growing up with it and by paying the price of conformity over long years of practice. But parvenus themselves revel in the freedom of their newfound status, believing they can combine the best of several worlds.

In fairness, the parvenu mentality is not always comfortable. It brings a certain sense of awkwardness and embarrassment, both because parvenus sometimes try too hard to gain acceptance for their views and because they deliberately signal their alienation from the common-sense world. In a society where it is more acceptable to be spiritual than pious, parvenus of the sacred sometimes brandish their secularity to show that they are still normal, fun-loving people. A published account of a wealthy engineer who becomes a devotee at a Kripalu Yoga ashram illustrates this point. He happens onto the ashram by taking a wrong turn on the way home from a concert. Hearing chanting inside, he expostulates, "What the hell is this?" Quite without meaning to, he is drawn into the ashram by some mysterious force. By this account, he retains his image as a thoroughly secular American who is not easily duped by the sacred.[48] Parvenus are also great salespeople, extolling their new position as the solution to everyone's ills.

The present interest in angels, near-death experiences, and the like is an affirmation in its own way that life is sacred and that it should be experienced with reverence. Yet it should not be forgotten that all experience—even of the sacred—is filtered through the distinctive lens of the cultural milieu in which it occurs. People see dimly, as through a glass darkly, because their thoughts are shaped by what they see on television, by what they have learned in school, and by what their families have taught them.

In the United States, the norms of secularism are largely taken for granted. Although blatant defenses of atheism are seldom articulated, there is little in the official wisdom of public institutions that validates the sacred except as personal conviction or as quaint tradition. Such norms do not prevent spirituality from expressing itself. But they do influence how it is expressed. As reluctant occupants of a secular land, Americans cultivate a spirituality that embodies all the tensions and contradictions of the newly arrived. They often protest too much, claiming great significance for mysterious experiences that might not have been considered special in different contexts.

CHAPTER Six

Spirituality of the Inner Self

$\mathscr{A}$nother important development that came to characterize Americans' quest for spirituality in the late 1980s and 1990s was a renewed interest in the inner self as a way of relating to the sacred. This quest was evident in the popularity of workshops, retreats, support groups, and books that attempted to link concepts of spirituality with the inner self. Thomas Moore's 1992 bestseller *Care of the Soul*, which went through nineteen printings in its first year, was one example.[1] John Bradshaw's *Homecoming*, Gerald May's *Addiction and Grace*, J. Keith Miller's *Hunger for Healing*, and M. Scott Peck's perennial bestseller, *The Road Less Traveled*, were part of the same interest.[2] These authors encouraged readers to take responsibility for their feelings and to remake themselves in a way that would allow them to be happy despite the complexities of contemporary life. Readers were offered a beguiling mixture of therapeutic, recovery, and religious advice that would help create the kind of self needed to seek spirituality despite growing uncertainties about the nature of the sacred. To understand the importance of this quest in the 1990s, it is necessary to begin with two examples.

RECOVERY OF THE INNER SELF

When Beth Holwith was a little girl, she traveled about once a month to visit her grandmother who lived on the other side of the city. Beth did not especially like her grandmother. The woman, Beth says, was an introvert who said little and who seemed not to like children very much. But she was also a devout Catholic who said her prayers daily and attended services regularly. "I was afraid of her," Beth remembers; "she was very stern." What Beth liked about these visits was her Aunt Kit's taking her on outings to shop and to buy ice cream. Aunt Kit was her father's sister—the one who never married and who took care of their mother during her declining years. On Sunday afternoons and on some weekdays during the summer, Aunt Kit picked up Beth and her cousin Mindy (who was about the same age) and drove them to Grandma's house. It was, Beth says, Aunt Kit's way of having children. But Beth also remembers that the way Aunt Kit treated her would now be considered sexual abuse.

Like many victims of sexual abuse, Beth blocked these experiences from her conscious thoughts for many years. It was not until her thirties that she started remembering them. Even now, a decade later, she has trouble talking about Aunt Kit. Having discussed her visits to her grandmother and Aunt Kit, for instance, she later names her father, his brother, and two other sisters, insisting that there were four in the family. Only with prompting does she recall Aunt Kit as the fifth. At another point, talking about the aunts and uncles whom she enjoyed visiting, she avoids mentioning Aunt Kit.

The way Beth came to realize what happened to her as a child was by attending a retreat on "discovering your inner child." She says she had no idea what the problem was: she just felt a deep need for healing. "A lot of the time," she says, "I just suffered with this sense of not being worthwhile and of feeling unworthy." There was an abiding sense of shame, as if she had done something wrong. She had been deeply religious as a child and had always been taught that God loved her. So she did not feel unworthy of God's love or even distant from God. She simply felt that something was askew inside herself.

Beth thinks part of the problem was that her religious upbringing—indeed, her entire ethnic tradition—paid scant attention to people's feelings. It was okay to be "close to God," especially in an intellectual sense, but strong emotions were taboo. Her parents seldom expressed anger (the only time she remembers her father being angry with her ended with him laughing it off and saying he'd been silly). She idolized her parents but also recognizes that she was not particularly close to them. Her mother, she felt, was more responsive to her brothers than to her. Beth says she did feel shame but assumed it was just "a natural thing," prompted by her brothers' teasing her, and that it was not important. She thinks now that her spirituality could not grow until she came to a better understanding of her feelings.

The retreat helped Beth look at her emotions and in the process to embark on a journey of self-discovery. It was not an isolated event. For several years prior to the retreat she had participated in the charismatic movement. She learned from the people she met to feel the presence of God more acutely in her life and to express her own emotions more openly. Rather than thinking of God as a being outside herself, she came to believe that God was inside her. Indeed, she experienced a religious conversion that made her faith come alive and spread through all the crevices of her daily activities. She felt especially close to God when she looked inside herself and found warm, reassuring feelings there. The retreat she attended gave her a special opportunity to look directly at her sense that something was wrong.

Beth says it was the Lord who told her to go on the retreat and that it was the Lord who helped her remember what had happened. "All of a sudden," she says, "all the memories flowed back." She now understood clearly the source of her shame. She understood something else as well: why she had married an abusive husband. She had never been able to understand why she had been attracted to an abusive man, especially because she was sure her father had not abused her. Now she had an answer. "It took a long time," Beth explains, "but I started walking away at that moment." Her husband, she says, picked up on her shame, accentuating it by telling her she was ugly and an unfit mother. She knew he was wrong, but now she was starting to have the strength to say so. Several years later she divorced her husband.

"I did a lot of crying," Beth explains, "but it was a release for me. I could start to feel feelings. I'd never felt any before. I couldn't really tell you how I felt." She says she had been taught to get a grip on life and to get on with things, always fitting in and playing a role. "If life is tough, just make the best of it." Recovery has thus been a matter of coming to terms with her whole outlook on life, not just with having been abused. Beth has spent a great deal of time focusing on her inner self, trying to understand what is going on inside her, and developing an appreciation of her emotions. She says her spirituality has become stronger as a result. She realizes that her relationship with God is a foundation, a source of inner strength. "It's what has kept me sane," she asserts.

Another person who illustrates the complex relationship between spirituality and the inner self is Tom Rivers, a man in his forties who works as a building inspector. His father was an ex-Navy man who drank too much, suffered from clinical manic depression, underwent shock treatments, and died while Tom was still in his teens. Tom's mother was married three times and bore eight children. Both parents were devout Catholics.

Tom was the "good son" who wanted to please his parents. Having been involved in church activities from childhood, he decided to enter a Jesuit boarding school that would prepare him for the priesthood. By the time he was nineteen, Tom was an antiwar activist whose Catholic training had served mostly to spark his interest in Buddhism and humanistic psychology. He was having serious doubts about becoming a priest. Erich Fromm's book *The Art of Loving* inspired him to major in psychology when he went away to college.

In addition to Fromm, Rollo May and Viktor Frankl became Tom's intellectual heroes. He also read Hermann Hesse's *Siddhartha* with interest and several of Alan Watts's books about Zen, especially *The Spirit of Zen*. The high points of his college years included participating in a three-day seminar at which Watts was the main speaker. Another high point was spending a year in Spain. This experience convinced him that he believed most of what he did only because of the culture in which he had been raised.

To find out who he really was, Tom became involved in macrobiotics. Through meditation, fasting, and eating a strict diet consisting mostly of brown rice, he lost weight to the point that he was almost "skin and bones." During one vacation, he tried to water ski and found he was too weak to hold onto the rope. But the diet also quieted his churning thoughts and deepened his interest in spirituality. After his sophomore year, he dropped out of college, intermittently took part in antiwar protests, and spent the rest of his time living on a farm with seven other people who were pursuing spirituality through macrobiotics.

During the next three years Tom briefly became a disciple of a fellow resident of the farm who invented a new religion based on ancient teachings about the healing power of the sun. For a few months he also followed the teachings of a visitor to the farm who claimed that he was the father of the second messiah. When this man left, Tom and the other residents decided to move to Illinois to participate in a commune there. Meanwhile, Tom and one of the women in the group got married and gave birth to a son who was mentally retarded. Within a year they were expelled from the Illinois commune for reasons that are still unclear to Tom.

At this point, Tom put his quest for spirituality on the back burner. He and his wife were on their own now. They rented a place in the country where they could grow their own food, and Tom earned a living working fourteen-hour days as a carpenter. Their "spare time" was devoted almost entirely to taking their son to clinics and helping him function more effectively mentally. Tom occasionally read books about spirituality, but he was no longer part of a group. He believes the time was one of spiritual rumination.

For the next few years, Tom's thinking about spirituality focused mainly on questions about who he was and what he wanted in life. He began to concentrate increasingly on his inner feelings. Some of these were "lower feelings," he says, such as feelings about pleasure and security. He felt that he was largely in command of these feelings. His focus was more on higher feelings about himself as a whole person. He also believed it was possible to transcend these feelings, perhaps in moments of ecstasy.

Tom's present understanding of spirituality is a synthesis of these earlier views about his inner self and some new teachings that he has gleaned from books about alternative healing practices, counseling, and recovery from addictions. He believes his inner self consists of three parts: a lower self composed of his body, physical needs, and emotions; a middle self composed of his mind; and a higher self that is his soul. The goal of his spirituality is to relate his soul more directly to God. But he believes most people mistakenly seek this relationship by trying to pray directly to God with their mind. The better way, he says, is to pray through your lower self—"getting your body, your senses, your inner child in touch with God."

What is notable about the spiritual journey in which Tom has been engaged since high school is not only the many kinds of spirituality that he has explored but also the extent to which these explorations have resulted in an emphasis on his inner self. Like Beth Holwith, he does not locate God entirely in his own being. But he has an elaborate language with which to describe his inner being. This language encourages his spiritual seeking to focus inward. He spends a great deal of time thinking about his inner self, meditating, reading books about psychology and spirituality, and trying to understand himself better.

THE CHANGING NATURE OF THE SELF

Making sense of the way in which spirituality and the inner self have come together in recent years requires returning briefly to the contrast between dwelling and seeking. A spirituality of dwelling demands that the self learn to be at home, fitting in, cultivating interests, and playing

one's roles responsibly; it may generate questions about personal authenticity, but it emphasizes being a respectable member of one's community. Had Beth Holwith and Tom Rivers remained in the religious communities in which they were born, they might not have focused as much
attention as they have on their inner selves. A spirituality of seeking, such
as Beth and Tom exemplify, requires a great deal more than accepting the
identities and roles that one's community assigns. Decisions must be made
about one's spirituality: how to pursue it, what to believe, where to find
helpful information. The self must be refashioned in a way that gives it
the authority to make these decisions. People like Beth Holwith and Tom
Rivers live, as it were, in the interstices between institutions; they have
been jarred out of socially acceptable ways of living and thus cannot create a self by playing the roles prescribed by social institutions. If their
lives are to have coherence, it must be of their own making. They require
knowledge of who they are, of where they have been, and of what they
want in life. Being exposed to trauma that could not be understood in
terms of traditional beliefs, as in Beth's case, or being exposed to many
different beliefs, as in Tom's case, they have found it hard to make sense
of their spirituality through religious teachings or doctrines. Philosopher
Carol Ochs expresses the same idea when she writes that her spirituality
"did not present a doctrine about who I am, but . . . initiated, instead, a
process by which I could transform and claim my self."[3] But this process
is not one that individuals simply choose for themselves. It reflects changing understandings of the self in the wider culture.

Some of these changes are evident in the ways public debates about
the self have been framed. In the 1950s, social observers worried that
the rugged, inner-directed individualist of the past was becoming a soft,
other-directed suburban bureaucrat who survived by fitting in and by
doing whatever he or she was told. The self seemed mostly to be a conformist. The 1960s witnessed widespread rebellion against the other-
directed self that observers had identified as the fifties' norm. People
went off on a proverbial quest for themselves, tuning out and turning
on, and doing their own thing. The 1970s became known as the Me
Decade, and the 1980s as the Decade of Greed, both apparently taking
the narcissism of the 1960s to its logical extreme. Despite efforts to rediscover and redefine standards of moral discipline, the 1990s came to
be known as an era of addictions. Self-help groups emerged to help
Americans recover from their addictions. Yet it was unclear whether
these groups represented a return to more communal notions of
responsibility or were simply an extension of the therapeutic motif.

Spirituality has not been all that the debate over the self is about, but it has always been an important dimension of this debate. Support groups such as Alcoholics Anonymous counsel members to take responsibility for their addictions but to do so by granting that they cannot control their lives and need to acknowledge their dependence on a higher power.[4] Best-selling books encourage readers to heal their wounded psyches by meditating and by taking seriously the idea of a soul. Critics ask whether any of these developments truly reflects a deep understanding of spirituality or whether they are popular psychology in new garb.

After World War II, scholarly discussions of the self came to view it in relation to a complicated, diffuse, and problematic social environment, but attention to the inner being was overshadowed by other concerns. With few exceptions, theories of the self emphasized personality formation, attitudes, and value orientations, all of which depended greatly on the social influences to which a person was exposed.[5] Indeed, these ways of describing the self fit comfortably with prevailing conceptions of communities, congregations, and homes as sacred space. Healthy values were cultivated in all these places. Families and schools, neighbors and peers were assumed to exercise a positive influence on the self. By conforming to the norms of these places, one internalized strong values and developed an integrated personality. Beth Holwith illustrates these assumptions when she describes the core values her parents taught her as, above all, a deep respect for the teachings of her school and her church.[6]

Implicitly, it was assumed that basic values, once nurtured, would serve the individual in other settings as well, especially when orderly patterns of personality development could be identified and when social settings reinforced these patterns. "Stabilities in the organization of behavior and of self-regard," counseled a widely read article, "are inextricably dependent upon stabilities of social structure."[7] Little attention was paid to the possibility that individuals might have to undergo a major retooling of their selves in order to survive new situations.[8]

The 1960s witnessed new thinking about the self, shaped by new experiences and opportunities but also reacting to the ways the self had been described during the 1950s.[9] A host of new hyphenated self words started to appear in popular discourse: self-acceptance, self-emancipation, self-esteem, self-fulfillment, self-identity, self-realization.[10] The term that most aptly characterized the new mood, however, was *self-expression*. If the previous decade had emphasized conformity and adjustment, the alternative was to express oneself. The self came increasingly to be those traits that defined one's individual uniqueness, rather than the needs, dispositions, and values that humans shared nearly every-where. Inward feelings started to become increasingly important.[11]

A woman whose quest to "find herself" began in the late 1960s illustrates how a growing uneasiness with given social experiences led to psychotherapy and then to an interest in the inner self. "I hated the kind of life I was leading, even though I always worked hard," she remem-bers. "I was working during the day, going to school at night, and would go out with friends at night." She felt that something was missing in her life. She turned to drinking heavily but still felt that she did not have an adequate understanding of who she was and what she wanted. "One day I couldn't stand it any more, so I went into psychotherapy. That was the beginning of my journey. I was in psychotherapy for four years and then for four more years I read like crazy about psychology, religion, philos-ophy, and self-improvement—a little bit of everything." Gradually, her reading convinced her that the answers lay within her self: "There is something so big inside of you and it is so powerful that you have to find it. That was *it* for me."

For many people, the deeper spiritual context in which such explo-rations were being carried out consisted of a growing uneasiness about objective knowledge itself. When there is assurance that an objective re-ality exists, either in nature or in the supernatural realm, then attention can be devoted to understanding this external reality. But when doubt arises as to the objectivity of this reality, attention shifts inward toward the subjective realm of perceptions and experiences. "Neither the Bible nor the prophets—neither Freud nor research—neither the revelations of God nor man," asserted psychologist Carl Rogers, "can take prece-dence over my own direct experience."[12]

In the shift away from objective truth, the self becomes problematic because its reality also comes into doubt. Nevertheless, the self's impor-tance is elevated because it is the locus of questions about meaning. Ultimately, all that exists is what one is able to experience. Thus, the height of spiritual existence becomes the process of journeying, seeking, perceiving, and experiencing. "Nothing out there, just our quest" is all that remains. "Our engagement . . . remains, even though we don't know who we are, don't know where we're going, don't know where we're coming from."[13]

During the 1960s new understandings of spirituality were also being discussed in syncretic terms, drawing insights from existentialism, phe-nomenology, the so-called wisdom literature in Christianity and Judaism, other world religions, as well as Freudian and Jungian psychology.[14]

Many of the major religious figures of the late 1960s and 1970s (including Thomas Altizer, Daniel Berrigan, Hans Küng, Thomas Merton, and D.T. Suzuki, as well as other Catholic, Presbyterian, Reformed, Unitarian, and Congregational thinkers) wrote books on Christian-Buddhist dialogue.[15] Buddhism offered a way of circumventing the harshest arguments advanced by existentialist and nihilist philosophy; it gave hope that in nothingness meaning could still be found, rather than despair alone. It is thus hardly surprising that Tom Rivers became interested in Buddhism while attending a Jesuit school.

By the late 1970s, it was evident that the inner self was complex territory waiting to be explored. Book sales provided a revealing indicator of Americans' growing interest in questions of the self. According to a national survey conducted in 1978, approximately a quarter of the reading public listed self-help and psychology as their favorite category of nonfiction books—about the same proportion as those listing religious books.[16] But the self was a black box in which half-remembered childhood influences were tucked away, and subsequent observers would perceive it in quite different ways: one perspective would view it as Pandora's box, yielding unwanted and unresolvable problems if its lid were opened; another perspective saw the self as a treasure chest from which true happiness, if not salvation itself, could be retrieved.

THE SELF AS PROBLEM

Observers who believed that Americans were focusing too much attention on the self argued that therapy, Alcoholics Anonymous, and popular psychology fundamentally contradicted a deepening understanding of spirituality. Some worried that people who were interested in self-expression were not interested enough in social problems or were too individualistic to be guided by the counsel of religious communities. They encouraged people to become involved in congregations or in social movements that would focus less attention on themselves and more on others. Other leaders feared that Americans were finding God too much inside themselves, rather than looking to religious traditions or theological arguments for authoritative statements about spirituality.[17]

Critics of the self would probably admire Mardell Jamison because she tried to find spirituality within herself but discovered that she needs to be involved in a community. She was raised in the Congregational church, but found its teachings "too watery" in the 1950s to provide her with answers to the important questions in life. For a time, she devoted herself wholeheartedly to her husband and her three children but gradually realized that she had an unfulfilled desire for spirituality. When she started looking, she found an abundance of spiritual resources: churches and synagogues, witches, sorcerers, astrologers, and practitioners of black and white magic. Mardell consulted them all. "I became a workshop-aholic," she laughs, "and I developed a wonderful library of books about spirituality." Eventually she assimilated so much information that she realized she was saturated. At this point, she felt that she could simply look inside herself. "I didn't have to go to 'places' to find the essence of spirituality. It was there inside me. I had my own sacred refuge. It was *my* truth. And each person has to find his or her own truths." She still has her own sacred refuge, but she is increasingly convinced of the importance of being with others as well. She has found community in a group of women her own age. "We're sharing our humanity," she explains. "We're just into loving and revering our humanness." She can do some of this loving herself, but the sharing helps her focus intentionally on life. "Before, I was just living in a comatose state, living very unconsciously. Now, as I talk of living, I'm also living much more consciously."

Much of the concern about an inward-looking spirituality focuses on Americans' withdrawal from public life and their seeming apathy toward social problems. The call to quit focusing on one's inner self is thus linked to the hope that Americans will get involved in politics, in volunteering, or in working for social justice.[18] But it is evident in cases like that of Mardell Jamison that finding community may not have the results such observers hope it will.

Mardell feels herself linked with humanity in general and with her women's group in particular, but she has not become involved in politics, and she is still intensely interested in her own personal journey, even when she has to look inside herself for answers. Her group helps quiet her doubts about the watery beliefs she was raised with and prevents her from having to attend every workshop in town to find spirituality. Lacking confidence that any belief system can adequately express religious truth, she has found what anthropologist Clifford Geertz calls "local knowledge" within the conversations of her own community.[19] She can disclaim any certainty about absolute truth but feel comforted in her personal convictions by the affirmation received in her group.

Another woman we talked to, a few years younger than Mardell Jamison, illustrates how religious communities can encourage an inward-looking spirituality among people who are no longer satisfied with the creedal teachings of religious tradition. She was raised in the South and went to church and Sunday school regularly until she was fourteen. Feeling that the church was "trying to put me in a box and nail the lid down," she dropped out during high school but participated in a religious group oriented toward social action in college. After she started working, she joined a predominately black church, attracted by its gospel choir. She, a white woman, enjoys the people and has continued to attend because "there's no requirement of accepting a stated definition of God." She favors an emotional orientation that allows her to approach God "through my gut" and thus is glad that the church does not impose any specific beliefs on her.

This woman is not unlike many Americans who have turned to the local realities of their congregations or have participated in other subcultures that reject universalistic conceptions of truth. For some, feminist critiques of prevailing theories of society have helped them reject these theories; others point to the diverse subcultures of ethnic and racial groups as evidence that all knowledge must be local.[20] The critics of self have thus been vindicated to the extent that Americans have been rediscovering their need for community. But it is not clear that this quest has done much to temper Americans' interest in themselves. Even within congregations, self-reliance and personalized views of truth are widely in evidence.[21]

THE SELF AS ANSWER

Against the idea that too much emphasis on self is a problem, many people have come to the view that they can cultivate deeper spirituality only by gaining a better understanding of themselves. In this view, the self is territory rich in potential and simply waiting to be cultivated. From therapists to writers interested in addictions and from theologians to New Age devotees, the self has been reconceptualized to offer personal power and to serve as the key to spiritual wisdom. In the process, spirituality has often been redefined to focus on empowerment and inward discovery. For example, there has been a renewed emphasis in some Christian circles on the idea that Christianity—the example of "the Christ"—helps people to discover latent powers within themselves. The key is not so much to depend on Christ as a redemptive force that exists independently of oneself but to allow Christ's example and teachings to awaken one's own capacities. Rather than trusting in Christ, the believer learns from Christ to trust the power that lies within.

Viewing the self as answer is in many ways an extension of efforts in the 1960s to encourage self-expression. Yet thinking on this subject in recent years has had much room in which to contribute new insights. As shown previously, the self of the 1950s was often little concerned with deep personal trauma or with learning by paying attention to feelings (despite the growth of popular psychology during that period). The late 1960s encouraged exploration of the inner self but often did so with little sense of what might be found in that quest. For this reason, critics of the expressive self had an easy target on which to focus; yet their own inattention to the need for self-understanding and their emphasis on community and social responsibility left many unanswered questions.

Social resources have been increasingly available for people who want to develop their spirituality by exploring their inner selves. Middle-class people especially have the educational backgrounds to read and understand "how-to" books written by psychologists, therapists, and spiritual advisers, not to mention the wherewithal to participate in psychotherapy or to attend expensive seminars. Family life, jobs, and neighborhoods may be sufficiently uncertain that people turn to these sources for advice about sexual abuse, marital problems, loneliness, and addictions. Religious traditions still encourage people to engage in self-improvement projects, and the widening venues in which spirituality is discussed make it possible to pursue self-understanding in a variety of ways.[22]

Alcoholics Anonymous (AA) and related twelve-step groups, such as Al-Anon and Adult Children of Alcoholics, have offered one of the clearest ways for pursuing self-understanding. Founded in 1935, AA combines religious ideas, group support, and personal accountability to provide a method of combating alcoholism.[23] By the 1950s, AA groups had spread to most cities, and during the next three decades they provided a model for thousands of other self-help groups, including ones for narcotics and nicotine addicts, teenagers with special needs, gamblers, persons struggling with obesity or eating disorders, and families of addicts. The recovery movement continued to grow rapidly during the 1980s and reached a plateau in the early 1990s. Its growth was facilitated by health insurance that permitted many corporate employees to attend rehabilitation clinics where treatment often included reading free books about self-help and recovery. In addition, therapists encouraged clients to attend twelve-step groups, and religious congregations provided free meeting space, hotlines, and information about meetings.

By the early 1990s, books on "recovery" from alcohol, drug, and other addictions were estimated to be earning approximately half a

billion dollars annually; the number of bookstores specializing in recovery titles had risen from one in 1984 to 550 in 1991; and AA groups
alone were estimated to number more than sixty thousand worldwide.[24]
According to a national survey conducted in 1991, approximately 4 percent of the population claimed to be regular participants in an "anonymous" group of one kind or another.[25]

The twelve steps of AA emphasize personal introspection as well as
candor about one's failings and accomplishments as the path to recovery from addictions. In Step One the participant acknowledges that life
has become unmanageable, Step Four requires making "a searching and
fearless moral inventory" of oneself, Step Ten involves an on-going commitment to making a personal inventory, Step Eleven suggests prayer and
meditation as a way of contacting God or a higher power, and Step
Twelve invokes the possibility of a spiritual awakening.[26] Twelve-step
language is thus concerned with finding truth through increased awareness of the self, yet it recognizes with critics of the self that unrestrained
desires for fulfillment are likely to be unhealthy—indeed, the source of
addiction—and that introspection is likely to be ineffective unless individuals participate in a supportive community.[27]

For self to be the answer to spiritual longings, AA advocates insist
that introspection focus not only on surface desires and experiences but
also on the deeper hunger for spirituality that is presumed to lie within
each person. Psychologist Gerald May writes that "all human beings
have an inborn desire for God," which forms the basis for human love
as well as the quest for personal fulfillment and the capacity to exercise
moral responsibility.[28] The problem, May suggests, is that people lose
awareness of their desire for God and thus turn their energies in directions doomed to be unfulfilling. The way to overcome addictions, which
May regards simply as attachments to wrongful desires, is to regain one's
awareness of grace—the "active expression of God's love," which is a
mystery and can only be known through experience and imagery.[29] For
May, stripping away the attachments that give meaning to the self in
everyday life is much like the Buddhist emphasis on peeling layers of the
onion until one discovers nothingness at the core and in the aridity of
that experience recognizes the sacred.

The recovery movement that grew from AA and similar groups during the 1980s also emphasizes introspection and personal responsibility
but often focuses less on submission to a higher power and more on cultivating trust in oneself. Melody Beattie, author of the bestseller *Codependent No More*, argues that the purpose of taking an inventory of
oneself should be "to switch from a shame-based system to a system of

loving and accepting ourselves—as is."[30] In this view, the self is an answer to its own problems in two respects: people take responsibility for their own happiness by looking at their lives and choosing to give themselves new messages, and they accomplish this transformation by identifying a core self that is unconditionally acceptable.

Beattie insists that "mistakes are what we do, not who we are."[31] The true self, from her perspective, is human and therefore fallible; yet because this is the way we inevitably are, we can call ourselves "perfect," thereby defining imperfection out of existence and thus learning to cherish ourselves. In the process, people who learn to love themselves also become more autonomous, not in the sense of being socially isolated but in being able to resist the self-defining messages they receive from other people. Being "codependent no more" means focusing more attention on one's own needs and feeling less compulsive about serving others. Writers like Beattie acknowledge that their message appeals to the selfish side of Americans' character but argue that their emphasis on self-acceptance is a way of moving this selfishness to a more desirable level. "We can accept ourselves—all of us," she argues. "Assert ourselves. We can be trusted. Respect ourselves. Be true to ourselves. Honor ourselves, for that is where our magic lies."[32]

For Beth Holwith, this message of self-acceptance contributed most to her process of recovery. A long-time and regular participant in twelve-step groups, she explains, "I felt such shame about myself for so many years. The twelve-step program helped me to deal with and name it, because I couldn't even name it before. So it was a freeing of those bondages of self-doubt and shame." Another woman remarks that recovery "is not like going to church and being a good girl [but] is loving the fact that you make mistakes, get bloody noses, and say bad words twelve times a day." As she puts it, self-acceptance means "loving our wonderful humanness."

For people who believe that increased emphasis on the self is the answer to their spiritual problems, taking responsibility for themselves is often an important way to gain the authority they need to make decisions about their lives. Taking responsibility helps them to move beyond introspection alone to achieving an appreciation of the small meanings inherent in daily activities. For all its emphasis on a higher power, recovery language in its various dialects focuses especially on the present moment, emphasizing the need to take one step at a time and to find balance rather than engaging in extreme behavior.

People who attend recovery groups generally acknowledge that their main purpose in becoming involved is to improve themselves. As they focus on themselves, they also sometimes worry about becoming too involved with the expectations of other group members. One man who has participated in twelve-step groups for a number of years expresses this sentiment well when he remarks, "We were holding hands and chanting. I thought, my God, bring on the baby so we can drink its blood; they were like a cult. Everybody, these strangers, were walking up to me and hugging me and saying, 'Here's my phone number; here, let's call each other.' I don't know. I'm like a cat. Let me alone."

More broadly, focusing on one's inner self provides a way of coping with the complexities of social life. People who remake their own identities can sometimes gain emotional distance from their parents, especially if relationships with parents have been dysfunctional (as with Beth Holwith and Tom Rivers). The same may be true of relationships with spouses, children, neighbors, and fellow employees: learning to be responsible for oneself means that others, too, must take charge of their lives. If circumstances are unpredictable and if there are few rules on which to rely, then it is helpful for people to respond in their own ways and to tolerate other ways of responding.

A woman in her forties who has been involved with twelve-step groups and therapy for more than a decade illustrates how a focus on the inner self can lead to a greater sense of responsibility despite complex circumstances. She describes her spiritual journey almost entirely in terms of the "recovery work" she has been doing. She remembers that she rejected God and the church when she was a teenager because "they weren't cool." She then embarked on a "hippie life-style" that included taking LSD and experimenting with other mind-altering drugs. She thought of God during these years as a last resort who would bail her out if she got into serious trouble. After graduating from college, she lived with a man who abused her psychologically. When she discovered that he was married, her self-esteem "dropped through the floor." Eventually she sought help from a therapist who convinced her to attend as many as four or five twelve-step groups a week.

The twelve-step groups reinforced her earlier beliefs that God was a force capable of protecting her. But she also started to conceive of this force as a power inside herself. Thinking in this way helped her to realize that she needed to take responsibility for herself, rather than expecting God to bail her out. In order to gain the inner strength to take such responsibility she worked for several years with another therapist who was also interested in spirituality. She now feels that she has an "inner wisdom"—a divine force inside her—that helps her to live more effectively than she did before. She says she feels lonely sometimes, taking so much responsibility for herself. But the inner spirit affirms her and gives her the power she needs to make decisions about how to live. She is unsure whether this spirit is God or whether it comes from her own efforts to summon up some inner strength.[33]

FROM SELF TO SOUL?

The blending of language from psychology, therapy, and recovery literature with the language of religion makes it difficult to determine whether spirituality of the inner self is similar to traditional religion or a radical departure from it. The subtle mixing of language is especially evident in popular books that have played a large role in defining spirituality in the 1990s. It is also evident in the ways people like Beth Holwith and Tom Rivers try to distinguish their spirituality from other ways of understanding the self.

Moore's *Care of the Soul* provides an instructive example of how therapeutic and spiritual language come together. It builds on Jungian psychology, the interest in Buddhism in the sixties and early seventies, and pastoral counselors' mixing of religion and psychotherapy.[34] Still, it represents a new direction in popular treatments of the self. With few exceptions, mainstream psychologists and therapists during the sixties and seventies avoided words with obvious religious connotations, such as *soul,* preferring to use clinical and scientific terminology in their descriptions of the self. Their ability to do so testified to the legitimacy of secular thought and to a continuing respect for the distinctiveness of religious language. As spirituality moved increasingly into nonreligious circles, its appearance in therapeutic discussions of the self, such as Moore's, was probably to be expected.

Moore insists that a precise definition of the soul cannot be given, thereby permitting it to be used almost interchangeably with "self."[35] Indeed, he suggests only that the soul "has to do with genuineness and depth."[36] Having soul is to be spirited, as in showing a zest for living, perhaps by sharing a good joke or enjoying one's food highly seasoned; conversely, to say that one's soul is lost is to suggest that one is suffering from confusion, anxiety, or boredom. The traditional connotations of soul found in religious teachings are nearly absent in Moore's work. "I do not use the word here," he states, "as an object of religious belief or as something to do with immortality."[37] The soul does not connote survival beyond bodily death or eventual union with God in paradise;

instead, Moore's focus is on moments of sacredness in everyday experience. Absent, too, is the idea that the soul must be (or can be) saved from evil, through either an act of religious commitment or gnostic insight. People should learn to be content with themselves, Moore counsels, because "dropping the salvational fantasy frees us up to the possibility of self-knowledge and self-acceptance."[38]

Moore is hardly alone in this emphasis. Uma Silbey, the author of another popular book on spirituality, makes a similar case for the here and now, arguing that spirituality should not take time away from everyday living.[39] Although these writers entertain possibilities of some transcendent or heavenly existence (citing near-death experiences as evidence), they speak mostly to the concerns that dominate ordinary life. The key to spiritual enlightenment, says Silbey, is "to have your entire awareness centered right here where you are instead of thinking about yesterday or tomorrow."[40] Everyday life is thus sanctified to the point that spiritual seekers must find transcendence in each of its minute activities.

The large questions of good and evil, suffering and salvation, and life and death can thus be refocused to have meaning chiefly in relation to the individual's personal struggles. For example, one of the women we talked to who was deeply influenced by writers like Moore described evil this way. "Evil exists, absolutely. It is a denial of the higher self. It comes from making choices that are motivated by fear. It means not taking responsibility to act in a loving way."

The authority of formal religion is sometimes explicitly challenged too. Moore contends that spirituality rooted in religious traditions but without proper grounding in psychological insights is actually dangerous, "leading to all kinds of compulsive and even violent behavior."[41] Similarly, Peck asserts that everyone has religion because religion is simply one's understanding of life, and he says we should not think that religion must include "a belief in God or some ritualistic practice or membership in a worshiping group."[42]

Such views of the soul are also an attempt to resacralize the self, making the individual explicitly holy, as it were, rather than assuming that the self is an autonomous entity that may simply be predisposed to believe in a deity that is also a separate entity. This shift in perspective is accomplished through slight but significant twists of conventional religious formulations. For example, Moore interprets the birth of Jesus as a "motif of the divine child [that] is common to many religions" and explains that this motif suggests not only the childhood of God but also "the divinity of childhood."[43] People who seek new awareness of their inner child are thus getting in touch with divinity within themselves. Or, as Tom Rivers asserts, "Jesus, God the Son, is what? He's your body, he's your inner child."

Although the self is resacralized, it is perhaps curiously not the inner self that is particularly sacred; indeed, with the exception of some references to the inner child and to deeper dimensions of the self, the distinction drawn in literature from the 1960s and 1970s between a core self and a surface self is now minimized.[44] Robert Sardello, founder of the School of Spiritual Psychology, explains that the soul is most clearly evident in its activities. Sardello specifically distances himself from Freudian conceptions of the inner self, insisting that the soul "is an activity that seeks to be fully conscious and not remain trapped behind the scenes, in the dark, labeled as the unconscious."[45] Metaphorically, the child who dirties his pants has replaced the wounded child who lies buried within and who needs special coddling.[46] The relevant self is one whose problems never go away, who eats and sleeps, works, maintains a busy family schedule, shops, and goes to the movies. This self is sacred because all these activities carry meaning and connect the person to humanity and to nature, not because a unitary self exists that is somehow more real than its surface appearances.[47] The purpose of self-reflection is thus to affirm the givenness of ordinary experience rather than to escape it by retreating into a purer state of introspective consciousness. Everyday life ceases to be an alienating experience from which one must flee; instead, its details are inscribed with meaning and with moral worth.

In one respect, the rediscovery of the soul is thus an effort to recapture the sense of being at home in the universe—indeed, of having heaven on earth—that was prominent in the 1950s. Popular writers and a large share of their audience are typically baby boomers whose childhood religious experience is rooted in that era. Making the sacred a part of everyday experience is to resacralize one's home as well as one's self. Suggesting that trees, cars, animals, hills, and buildings all have souls, Moore writes that feeling a connection with these things is necessary in order to overcome the "homelessness we feel in our hearts."[48]

Tom Rivers shares this view. Although he does not often think in precisely these terms, he acknowledges that making spiritual connections with trees, people, and other aspects of his everyday world helps him feel spiritually at home. As he puts it, "When you feel connected, then you feel at home. When you're in touch and you're feeling that spirit, then the respect you're giving is coming back to you. What you give, you get; so if you're giving out that respect, it's coming back. You feel at home."

The most important implication of these views of the soul, however, is that spirituality must be found within ordinary life and is thus as varied and as unpredictable as everyday experience and as individuals themselves. Spirituality is not to be found in special places, certainly not in churches or synagogues, and perhaps not on the therapist's couch either. To the extent that therapeutic wisdom or the teachings of esoteric scholars are accorded special authority, they are drawn on to show that spirituality is more banal than generally supposed. The potential for spiritual insight is everywhere; it must, however, be sought. Indeed, the process of seeking—the journey—now becomes more important than the destination. Life is to be lived, not expended in efforts to achieve, and the self is what one experiences, not a bundle of predispositions waiting to be propelled into action. Care, in the sense of attending to the self in its daily journey, becomes the key word, rather than the various cures suggested by medicine or traditional religion.

In the popular literature, these views are generally presented as unconventional perspectives that run counter to the dominant thrust of U.S. culture. They do in fact differ from religious teachings that privilege what happens in congregations, and they contrast with goal-oriented, success-driven behavior that is encouraged by business, television, and the schools. Nevertheless, the road less traveled is, as pundits note, a veritable four-lane highway of book buyers, retreat-goers, and spiritual seekers. The reason is perhaps, as historian Laurence Moore has observed, that the way to be "in" in U.S. religion has always been to pose as an outsider (apparently satiating some perverse psychological need to feel different, even though everyone is the same in this respect).[49] But there is also a deeper reason for the popularity of current writings about the soul: their perspective on spirituality fits quite well with current conditions. The self has been refashioned to adapt to present experience.

The key to understanding this refashioning lies in the ambivalent relationship between the self as transcendent, unified being—the soul—and the self that attends fully to the reality of each momentary experience. Although there have always been religious arguments favoring this view, it is a special kind of self that can accomplish it. Following psychologist James Hillman, Moore uses the phrase "psychological polytheism" to capture the kind of self that has many different claims made on it and that is able to find small truths in many places, rather than deriving answers from a single source.[50] He argues that psychological polytheism is more than a feature of contemporary life; it is a better way to live because it creates flexibility, keeps life interesting, and encourages us to accept different life-styles and peoples. The gods and goddesses of the Greek pantheon, he suggests, are perhaps easier for us to understand than the monotheistic God of Judaism and Christianity because they fight among themselves and express many different views of morality. Hillman, too, celebrates the decentered individuality he finds in polytheism, championing the "messy confusion" of "the current delight in superstitions, astrology, witchery, and oracles."[51] It is best in his view to quit searching for ultimate wholeness and to let ourselves wear the many robes we are asked to wear in everyday life.

Despite its awkwardness, the idea of psychological polytheism is helpful for understanding the kind of self that fits with contemporary experience.[52] Americans have generally espoused faith in a monotheistic God but in practice have not been immune to polytheistic beliefs, as the popularity of guardian angels—or reverence for parks and trees or the mascots of athletic teams—illustrates. In psychological polytheism something sacred can be seen in each event or object that a person encounters. Moore's claim that trees and automobiles have souls is an example. Without necessarily equating these souls with their own or with their sense of a supreme monotheistic God at the center of the universe, many Americans would probably agree that there is a kind of living power in trees and automobiles that merits respect. For example, Tom Rivers asserts, "There is no one God. But there is a spirit that moves through all things. There's an energy and there's spiritual laws that determine how that energy moves." He believes the purpose of life is to be happy, and that the way to happiness is recognizing how the spirit energy that he calls God is present in all things. If he is feeling depressed or frustrated ("blocked"), he tries to move past this feeling by paying attention to the spirit of God in the things around him. "Like, I'll see a tree, and I try to give it respect. Giving respect often helps me break into a more spiritual mood."

Insofar as he sees spiritual energy in the things around him, Tom's view of God comes close to being polytheistic. There is an underlying unity in God that Tom describes as energy and, in some ways, as a kind of natural law. But he also favors religious ideas that distinguish among various gods or spirits. He says the reason he prays sometimes is to keep "the spirits" from being angry with him. He also believes in spiritual beings. "There's spirit helpers. When people die, I don't know if you've ever had a relative die and had them communicate with you, but maybe you've felt this communication. So you know that, 'Gee, seems to be an afterlife and he seems to have communicated.' I've had that happen a couple times. People may be channeling information from spirits."

Lynda Sexson, author of *Ordinarily Sacred,* tells a story, which makes a similar point, about a man who kept a cabinet full of his deceased wife's personal effects as a way of retaining part of her spirit. The cabinet held special meaning for him; part of his own self was located there as well.[53] Sardello emphasizes the same idea. He suggests that the self should be interpreted broadly enough to include our understanding of the world, rather than only what is located within our own bodies. He writes that "the sense of who we are incorporates all of the world, which at the same time means that where we find our individual soul is in all of the world."[54]

We might call this the *dispersed self* to distinguish it from other conceptions of the self.[55] The dispersed self is one whose being is defined in a wide variety of encounters and experiences, including moments of interaction with sacred objects, such as trees and automobiles. Broadly speaking, it is a dispersion of experiences, themselves widely separated in space and time, with different people, and of varying significance. Although the self is always more than these experiences, it must be understood to reside in them as well and thus to be as scattered as they are. Pieces of the self inhere in these experiences, so much so that in common language we speak of defining moments. We recognize that we are not the same person we were a few years ago, and we lament the loss of part of our self when a loved one dies.

To say that a self can be dispersed may strike a dissonant chord because we generally emphasize what is sometimes called a *unitary self*— one that has spatial integrity and temporal continuity. Yet the unitary self is a fragile concept reinforced by modern emphases on the connection between body and self and by such social constructs as the doctrine of "one person, one vote."[56] Throughout much of history, in fact, questions have been entertained about the possibilities of self-dispersion, and in other cultures arguments have been made about discontinuities arising from lapses of consciousness or the scattering of self-fragments in different thoughts and sensations.[57] For instance, Navajos believe that part of their spirit resides in their land, remaining there even when they are located elsewhere; Americans of European descent speak similarly of pouring themselves into their work or of feeling that their heart goes with a friend or a child who is far away.[58] Increasingly, the scattered lives that we lead reinforce this conception of the self. Roles and relationships that are constantly in flux are especially conducive to thinking of our selves in this way. As William Barrett, author of *Death of the Soul,* writes, "Our modern civilization brings with it an immense dispersion of human energies, in the course of which many of us may find it hard to keep our own individual being from getting dispersed."[59]

Larry Dossey, author of *Recovering the Soul,* also captures the idea of a dispersed self when he writes of the "nonlocal" nature of the mind. The soul, he contends, "displays its nonlocal character in a million ways, showing us that it is free in space and time, that it bridges consciousness between persons, and that it does not die with the body."[60] The dispersed self should not be thought of simply as a multifaceted self with a unified inner core that presents itself differently in different situations. The dispersed self goes beyond the idea of malleability, which implies a unity of being that is simply able to adapt to new circumstances. The dispersed self is more nearly separable from its past and from other roles it plays, focusing its full attention, as Silbey suggests, on the present moment. Not all of the self is necessarily present in that moment, yet the moment is taken seriously enough that it is indeed a powerful, self-defining experience. The self is thus dispersed among the diverse encounters that define it.[61]

A dispersed self has obvious advantages for coping with a complex, changing, and unpredictable environment.[62] This view of the self legitimates paying close attention to the details of each moment and then shedding these details so that the next encounter can be approached freshly. A person need not worry about playing roles that may inhibit the true self because the true self is whatever is present at the moment. But a dispersed self still requires some sense of unity, and this unity is provided by the concept of soul. As a more transcendent self, whether regarded only as a perspective or as something of substance, the soul provides a loose framework in which the momentary selves can come together.[63]

Tom Rivers's dispersed self has been integrated by developing an inner being similar to Moore's idea of a soul. Rivers's personal development was shaped by the tensions in his family: his father's illness and death, his mother's multiple marriages, his siblings and half-siblings, the church, psychology, drugs, and political activism. He has lived in four regions of the country and has been influenced deeply by the several communes of which he has been a member. He has changed career plans at least five times and worked for a number of different employers. His views about spirituality are drawn from Christianity, Buddhism, the charismatic leaders he has known personally, the books he has read, and the seminars he has attended. He continues to absorb new teachings, attaching himself temporarily to a new guru, listening to self-help tapes, and attending retreats. He describes himself as a "spiritual junkie" whose views are eclectic; "I'm all over the place," he admits. One way a focus on his inner self has helped him is by encouraging detachment from many of the social roles he has pursued. At one seminar, for instance, he concentrated on breathing deeply and consciously detaching from his concerns about work and family. Another role that his inner self plays is to provide common ground for the many beliefs and philosophies to which he ascribes. He translates them all into teachings about how to get in touch with his inward being.

The dispersed self may conjure up images of personal fragmentation and even of a nihilistic attitude toward life.[64] But Moore and company have in mind the stabilizing experiences of everyday life, in addition to the unity that comes from an emphasis on the inner self.[65] As one woman we interviewed (the daughter of a therapist) explains, "Spirituality is a practice of everyday things and everyday life; it's not limited to ritual times; it calls me to honor everything that is before me." She says, "Everything is a spiritual activity," whether it involves mumbling a prayer or picking up a piece of litter.

Tom Rivers's example of "giving respect" to trees is another illustration of how ordinary experience is sacralized. He says it makes him feel at peace with himself and with the things around him when he tries to "make connections" with them in this way. He admits it is often difficult to give other people respect because he is a judgmental person and people often irritate him. But trees are different. "It's really easy to look at a tree and go, 'Wow. Nice. Beautiful. I like your leaves.' As soon as you start doing that, and you make that connection, whew, the energy starts going and you can feel the energy and you feel the connection. Pretty soon if you get good at that, you can do that for people too."

The one difficulty with a form of spirituality that focuses this much attention on ordinary objects and events is that it may reaffirm the status quo rather than challenging people to improve their lives or even to entertain hopes that life can be better than it is. To argue, as Moore does, that there is nothing wrong with narcissism and to suggest that jealousy and envy are simply "healing passions" runs contrary to traditions that have recognized the need for people to rise above their passions and to rein in their interests in themselves in order to live in harmony with others and to realize their dreams for a better world.

The way saints and mystics have combated the tendency to live too much at ease with existing conditions is by recognizing that human life includes suffering that cries out for amelioration. Care of the soul, when properly understood, would require both an awareness of one's own failings and attentiveness to how these failings hurt other people and, collectively, to the need to care for social institutions and the physical environment.[66] Tom Rivers's comments suggest some of this awareness—especially his admission that it is hard to respect the foibles of other people.

The dispersed self whose being is most fully present in the ordinary experiences of daily life exists, therefore, in precarious tension with the coherent self symbolized in the concept of soul. For the soul to be compelling, it must be rooted in authoritative traditions that in fact transcend the person and point to larger realities in which the person is embedded. Only then is it possible for immediate moments to be truly instances of eternity, rather than fragmented, self-indulgent experiences that do not add up to a meaningful life. Linking those traditions requires effort that is likely to compete with the business of daily life. It also requires self-interpretation and thus may depend on specialists whose knowledge of spiritual traditions is greater than that of the average individual.

Clergy, therapists, popular writers, academics, and even talk-show hosts are poised to provide these interpretations of spiritual tradition. One can, as many Americans do, draw from the arguments of these various authorities with utter gullibility, silencing doubts about all such authorities by questioning none of them. A more diligent response is to engage in critical reflection, realizing fully that authority in the contemporary world is never absolute but also knowing that there is deep wisdom to be gained from many authoritative traditions.

SPIRITUALITY AND THE SELF

Where, then, have we come? Certainly the last decade of the twentieth century cannot be assumed to have provided the final word on spirituality and the self. But even a brief review of these topics demonstrates that the self's relationship with spirituality is far more complex than many of its critics have acknowledged. To say that Americans have become narcissistic in their spiritual orientations and to argue that they need to overcome this obsession by participating in congregations and by doing volunteer work is a gross oversimplification of the situation, just as it is to suggest that modern therapy has somehow subverted our understanding of true spirituality.

The relatively stable dispositions and personality traits that were prominent in popular psychological theories during the 1950s have given way to a variety of therapeutic and recovery models oriented toward probing and redefining the inner self. During the 1960s a new concern was evident in popular psychology for understanding the inner self, yet this understanding appears in retrospect to have been relatively shallow. It focused chiefly on expressing some inner potential that had been repressed by hostile social conditions. This emphasis on self-expression became the occasion for criticisms about the dangers of too much expressiveness and for counsel about the value of submission to the more orderly patterns of established communities and institutions.

But many of these criticisms were overshadowed by other perspectives that urged participation in intentional communities, such as twelve-step groups, or that relied on therapeutic advice to encourage people to take responsibility for their own identities and personal happiness. Much of this emphasis has included an acknowledgment of the value of spirituality, but it has also been eclectic in how it has defined spirituality. It has been especially interested in helping people adapt to the demands of everyday life.

These changes can be understood in terms of unresolved tensions within dominant conceptions of spirituality and the self. If the popular therapies of the 1950s helped Americans adjust to circumstances, the understandings of the self that they reinforced nevertheless had unsettling consequences. People like Beth Holwith who valued "school" learned that "IQ" was an important part of their personal make-up, that experts could measure this trait, and that other tests were available for assessing "aptitudes" and "preferences." They learned that certain traits were rewarded and that it was often necessary to leave friends and family behind in the quest for these rewards. In the process, they became estranged from the neighborhoods and families in which they had been reared and lost the rich spiritual meanings that were attached to these contexts.[67]

The quest to overcome estrangement has been an important part of many Americans' search for a spirituality that gives them a new sense of self. The popularity of Rogerian therapy in the fifties and sixties is partly understandable in these terms: it tried to humanize the therapist-client relationship. The inward turn of the late sixties and seventies was in some ways as concerned with reclaiming the richness of spiritual traditions as it was with sheer self-expression. The criticisms of rampant individualism in the 1980s recognized that moral conviction was born in intimate relationships and not in psychological laboratories. The work of twelve-step and inner-child specialists has emphasized, too, that people need to rediscover their spiritual roots.

Yet many of these theoretical understandings of the self have ignored the fact that personal life continues to be lived in everyday worlds that may be regimented and alienating. The recent emphasis on souls and dispersed selves is an effort to redeem these everyday worlds rather than providing an escape from them.[68] Its rejection of salvational language is as much a denial of the hope that everyday life can be transformed as it is a rejection of traditional religious language. Like Rogerian therapy, it is skeptical of techniques, even when they are self-imposed. Its answer to the sameness and impersonality of everyday life is to argue that the details of daily existence are more varied than often supposed. Its emphasis on the present moment shifts attention away from comparisons with other people and places. The dispersed self is not regarded as a floundering entity in search of its hidden being but one that draws strength from the varied situations in which it exists.

The diverse ways self and spirituality come together are still in flux, but it should not be surprising that there is an affinity between them. Those who attribute the inward turn to Americans' growing desire for a sense of the sacred are right in one respect: the collapse of a sacred canopy under which to live in spiritual security has awakened a compulsion for faith of a new kind, a faith that requires inner knowledge and that must be renewed and renegotiated with life experience. Perhaps Carl Jung put it best when he wrote, "A 'complete' life does not consist in a theoretical completeness, but in the fact that one accepts, without reservation, the particular fatal tissue in which one finds oneself."[69]

CHAPTER *Seven*

The Practice of Spirituality

*I*n this final chapter I consider the possibility of an alternative to the dwelling-oriented and seeking oriented spiritualities on which the preceding chapters have focused—specifically, the idea of a practice-oriented spirituality, to which I alluded in Chapter 1. If the foregoing interpretation is correct, dwelling-oriented spirituality has become increasingly difficult to sustain because complex social realities leave many Americans with a sense of spiritual homelessness. Seeking-oriented spirituality requires individuals to negotiate their own understandings and experiences of the sacred. It has become increasingly common because it provides freedom to maneuver among the uncertainties of contemporary life and capitalizes on the availability of a wide variety of sources for piecing together idiosyncratic conceptions of spirituality. Yet, if a spirituality of seeking is suited to the complexities of American society, it nevertheless results in a transient spiritual existence characterized more often by dabbling than by depth. Identifying another kind of spirituality is thus an important task.

To locate the idea of a practice-oriented spirituality, let me also refer briefly to two ways in which scholars have written about U.S. religion in recent years. One views contemporary spirituality as, in essence, communal, requiring individuals to be "in community" for their faith to be meaningful at all; the other depicts spirituality as increasingly private, invisible, and ephemeral, so that if it has meaning at all, its meaning may be too amorphous to observe or understand. In the communal view, the vitality of congregations is often pointed to as evidence of true religious commitment. In the private view, individual beliefs are deemed to be more important, but it is unclear how vital these beliefs are, especially when people are unable to talk about them openly.[1]

Neither of these views is adequate: spirituality is not just communal or else trivial. It can also be quite serious, practiced deliberately by individuals who draw on resources from other individuals and from organizations and yet who are not fully submerged in any one community. To say that spirituality is practiced means that people engage intentionally in activities that deepen their relationship to the sacred. Often they do so over long periods of time and devote significant amounts of energy to these activities. In most cases, prayer and devotional reading are important; and, in many cases, these activities are life-transforming, causing people to engage in service to others and to lead their lives in a worshipful manner.

A practice-oriented spirituality has been part of all religious traditions. Drawing inspiration from sacred texts and from the lives of saints and other religious leaders, clergy have encouraged the faithful not only to attend public worship services but also to devote time to prayer, meditation, study of sacred texts, inspirational reading, and service. In Christianity, most church constitutions and catechisms refer to the value of private prayer and emphasize other acts of worship or religious observance in daily life.[2] Other religious traditions emphasize intentional daily practices aimed at transcending ordinary life and putting the believer in touch with the sacred. Indeed, it is well to recall William James's insistence on the centrality of prayer, broadly conceived, in all religions. "Religion is nothing," James wrote, "if it be not the vital act by which the entire mind seeks to save itself." Defining prayer as "no vain exercise of words, no mere repetition of certain sacred formulae, but the very movement itself of the soul, putting itself in a personal relation of contact with the mysterious power of which it feels the presence," James observed that "wherever this interior prayer is lacking, there is no religion; wherever, on the other hand, this prayer rises and stirs the soul, even in the absence of forms or of doctrines, we have living religion."[3]

In recent years, there has been a resurgence of interest in spiritual practices. In Christian settings classic works, such as those of Teresa of

Avila, John of the Cross, and Francis de Sales, are being reexamined.
Churches sponsor small groups aimed at teaching members how to pray
and read the Bible. Seminaries offer popular continuing-education
courses on these topics for laity as well as advanced professional degrees in spirituality and spiritual direction. Countless spiritual guides
and meditation books have appeared in the popular market.[4] In addition to such emphases within Christianity, many Americans are finding
guidance for their spiritual practices in Judaism, Buddhism, or Islam,
and in eclectic approaches.[5]

Broadly conceived, spiritual practice is a cluster of intentional activities concerned with relating to the sacred.[6] Although it may result
in extraordinary or miraculous experiences, it generally takes place
in ordinary life. In the sixteenth century Ignatius Loyola described it
as a "method of examination of conscience, of meditation, of contemplation, of vocal and mental prayer, and [a] way of preparing and
disposing the soul to rid itself of all inordinate attachments, and, after
their removal, of seeking and finding the will of God."[7] How these
activities are performed and understood has varied enormously in
different cultural and religious traditions. Practices are not performed
without rules, and they are not devoid of rewards (in other contexts,
one thinks of chess or medicine as practices). But most practices are
embedded in ordinary life, and their rules are generally difficult to
codify. A focus on practice helps orient our thinking to the fact that
spirituality also exists in the complex and fragmented arena of contemporary society.[8] Commuting, dual careers, and busy family schedules have added complexity to many people's lives, often making it hard
for them to find community (or to see the relevance of community),
but spiritual practice remains possible in the midst of these challenging
circumstances.

Many people already have some appreciation of the importance of
spiritual practices. We learn from the writings of such leaders as
Thomas Merton and Mother Teresa that spirituality deepens only as it
is practiced and that practice includes such activities as prayer, meditation, contemplation, and acts of service.[9] In ethics, scholars such as
Alasdair MacIntyre and Jeffrey Stout emphasize practice as the way
moral wisdom is imparted.[10] In the social sciences, theorists write that
practice is the way in which personal identity is created and describe it
as a way of understanding how beliefs and assumptions influence ordinary life.[11] Increasingly, we are coming to realize that our practical
knowledge is rooted more in stories and in partial understandings of

what we do than in abstract theoretical formulas.[12] Practices are the ways practical knowledge and skills are developed.[13]

WORKING TOWARD AN INTENTIONAL SPIRITUAL PRACTICE

Two examples provide a way to grasp the distinguishing characteristics of a practice-oriented spirituality. Coleman McGregor is a pharmacist in his fifties. As a child Coleman attended the Methodist church regularly with his parents. When he was fourteen, he went with his father one Sunday afternoon to a "fire-and-brimstone" service at a different church that was up the block from their house. "I came away thinking, 'I really want to be in touch with this God, whatever this God is,'" Coleman remembers. He also had more questions than he had answers. "I was really kind of overwhelmed. I remember trying to pray and thinking, 'Well, this isn't working, and so much for that.'" As he matured, Coleman's questions about God persisted. He didn't understand who God was or how he could relate to God, but he kept thinking about God. He also observed people to see how they related to God. "Some of the people were strange," he remembers. "I couldn't put my finger on it exactly, but there was something different about them. They didn't fit in with the rest of the world. I was attracted to them. I wondered what made them different."

During his late twenties and thirties, Coleman and his wife settled into a suburban Methodist church where they made friends, took their three sons to Sunday school, and participated in small fellowship groups. But Coleman still had questions. "How does all this connect? What does the institution have to do with one's personal experience of God?" He says he "just couldn't get it." There was a "gap" inside him that he could not fill. As he looks back on these years, he believes the problem was that he was looking too much for security in the congregation and in his fellowship group, rather than developing his relationship to God. "We were not drawing on the love of God. We were drawing on our own little fellowship, our little group. We just wanted to keep our little group going."

Coleman began seeking actively for answers to his questions. He remembers visiting pastors and talking to people who came into his drugstore. He would ask, "How does spiritual growth take place? What is prayer? What happens when you go to prayer?" He says few people understood why he was asking these questions. They would respond, "Well, what do you mean? You just pray." But Coleman suspected that praying might be little more than "shouting into an empty room." He wanted to know how prayer works. "I couldn't find anybody who could tell me that."

One day, almost by accident, Coleman's eyes fell on an advertisement for a seminar at a retreat center. "It talked about hearing God's word, listening for God's voice, engaging one's deeper interior life and engaging that with God and having God engage that with you." It sounded like what he was looking for. Still, the words seemed trite. He didn't know what it might mean to hear God's word, other than just reading it and thinking about it. He decided to attend the seminar. Coleman arrived at the retreat center expecting the familiar bustle of visiting, singing, listening to lectures, and talking that he had experienced at church conferences. What he found was a man "sitting there cross-legged, staring at the door." He was meditating, but Coleman didn't know what he was doing. "So I came in and sat down. Pretty soon the room was full. I'm looking at my watch, it's time to start and nothing's going on. Five after, ten after, the leader's still staring at the door. I'm thinking, 'He's waiting for someone, there's a co-leader that's supposed to be coming.' Nobody's saying anything, and I'm waiting and waiting and waiting. About twenty after I begin to think everybody in the room is deathly ill because it's deathly quiet. It felt sick because it was so quiet. I'm thinking, 'My gosh, what in the world is going on here?' I'm looking at people like, 'Does this seem strange to you? Or is it just me?' and I'm realizing it's just me."

During the first break, another participant explained to him what was happening. She said that most of the other people at the seminar were involved in "spiritual direction"; they met individually with someone trained in giving guidance about how to deepen one's relationship to God. She offered to put Coleman in touch with a spiritual director. A few days later, Coleman drove to a large Jesuit retreat center about forty-five minutes from where he lived and met with a man who devoted his life to prayer, meditation, seeking spiritual wisdom, teaching, and serving others. Coleman has continued to meet with a spiritual director at least once a month for the past ten years. Regular devotional practice has become the key to his spiritual development.

In this example spiritual practice is situated exclusively within the Christian tradition. Coleman has continued to be regularly involved in his local Methodist church. Indeed, he might appear to a casual observer to fit the "community" model of religion that so many advocates of congregations have emphasized. Yet his own account suggests that the core of his spirituality is not his congregation but the activities in which he engages to deepen his own relationship with God.

The second example provides a sharp contrast. Avery Fielding is a massage therapist who is about twenty years younger than Coleman McGregor. She lives with a man whom she describes as her "significant other" and is expecting their first child. Unlike Coleman McGregor, she has long since abandoned the church in which she was raised. Whereas his spiritual seeking took the form of consulting with pastors and priests, hers has taken her far outside the Christian tradition. When asked her religious preference, she asserts that she follows her own personal religion. She notes that she emphasizes spirituality more than any formal religious tradition. She could easily be an example of the privatized spirituality that many observers of U.S. religion have criticized. Yet her story shows that she is not as isolated as these observers might suppose and that her spiritual life has developed because of the regular time and effort she devotes to a set of spiritual practices.

Avery's father became a Catholic when he was in the military as a young man, but then he became angry with the church and quit attending. Her mother did not attend either. When Avery was little, they sent her to a Lutheran church that was within walking distance of their home. She went to church services and Sunday school every week, including three years of catechismal instruction when she was in fifth, sixth, and seventh grade. Avery hated every minute of it. But she was also intrigued with what she was hearing about God and with the way she was experiencing the world. "I had a lot of dreams where I would be flying," she recalls. She also had waking experiences that seemed to defy physical limits. In retrospect, she thinks she had a budding understanding "that there was a oneness with everything, whether it was the tree or it was a bug on the ground; there was no separation, there was no right or wrong, there was no better or less than."

She got the sense from her parents that all these experiences were strictly in her imagination. When she tried to talk about them at church, people looked at her as if she were from a different planet. So she quit talking about them and became increasingly alienated from the church. "Everything was based on fear, and it was just uncomfortable for me," she says. The only outlet she could find was talking to her grandmother, who was not involved in church but was quite interested in spirituality. She encouraged Avery to believe that there was more to life than simply seeking pleasure or focusing on a material existence.

When Avery was in high school she began reading books about metaphysics, yoga, the occult, and spirituality. Her interest in these subjects continued when she got married and opened a shop specializing in her own handcrafted women's clothing. She remembers going to work each day, saying to herself, "Something is wrong with this picture." She was interested in spirituality, and she was having experiences with the sacred that she could not understand. She was also gravely concerned about her teenage brother, who had a lingering illness. Avery spent a great deal of time with him, observing his body weaken but also seeing his spirit grow stronger. When he died at age seventeen, she decided she wanted to devote herself full time to helping people.

She abruptly liquidated her shop, earned a certificate in massage therapy, took a job at a psychiatric hospital, and over the next three years gained experience by working at several clinics. Toward the end of this time she and her husband divorced, and Avery decided to start her own clinic. These changes precipitated a great deal of inner turmoil, forcing her to focus deliberately on her own spiritual needs. Indeed, she suffered an emotional crisis that put her close to death.

The crisis came when she was in her mid-twenties. She was separated from her husband, working at a chiropractic clinic, and beginning to realize that she had been physically abused as a child. Having taken a few days off to think about her life, she returned to work only to be injured by the chiropractor (he damaged a nerve in her arm) so that she could not continue working. Her life seemed hopeless. She quit eating. She remembers crawling into bed one night thinking she might not wake up because she was too weak to stand up. That night she dreamed of a golden tunnel of light, and a voice encouraged her not to die. At that moment, as she recalls, "this light that I was seeing went right through me. It was like a laser beam that just flooded through my whole body, and then it was just radiating and it was warm and it was a wonderful feeling. It was absolutely wonderful. I don't know how long it lasted. It seemed like it was forever, and yet it was probably only five or ten minutes in actual linear time." Avery got up and made herself dinner. A friend telephoned, and she told him what had happened. As she looks back on this experience, she says her life has never been the same since. "It gave me the strength to go on; there was a tremendous amount of healing in it. It hits you on such a deep level. It's just like there's a knowing there."

She admits she still does not understand what happened, whether she was simply so weak that she began hallucinating or whether some supernatural force entered her body. What she does understand is that she was able to surrender to the pain she was experiencing. "It was like I was just letting go. There was a surrender on such a deep level. I guess that's a part of healing in life, being able to let go. You think you're doing it, and yet there's always a deeper and deeper level of surrender."

It took Avery several months to recover physically because her kidneys had begun to shut down, her pulse was high, her blood pressure was weak, and she was badly in need of nutritious food. When she was better, she started attending weekend retreats at a center that specialized in spirituality. The eclectic mixture of beliefs and practices (what some would call New Age) helped Avery recover the will to live and find enough emotional peace that she could start putting her life back together.

Rather than simply looking back on her near-death experience as a special moment, Avery has continued to cultivate her spirituality intentionally through prayer and meditation. For the past four years she has worked intensely on herself. She describes her spiritual journey as one of "really becoming aware of what is real for me and what is not real, looking at parts of my personality that needed refinement or harmonizing or balancing, letting go of the judgments, letting go of the criticism, letting go of the expectations, all the things that I had been taught in the early years of my life. There's like a whole other level of understanding. I shifted from having a whole thought system based on fear to a thought system based on love. It's learning how to look at life differently. I may not be able to change what I see, but being able to see it differently helps me to respond to it much differently." As she has started to spend time practicing her spirituality, she has experienced what she can only describe as a personal transformation. It has been like "waking up from a long sleep and starting to see new possibilities," she explains. "I began seeing other ways of living, other ways of approaching life, other ways of being." She summarizes the role of spirituality in her life by characterizing it as "a blueprint for my living." Spirituality is "the way I live my life, the way I relate with people, the way I choose to see the world."

In both these examples, the decision to seriously pursue a deep form of spirituality was not one that came easily. Coleman McGregor did not wake up one morning and decide he wanted to be more spiritual, nor did Avery Fielding. Coleman's decision to work with a spiritual director followed years of searching, questioning, and feeling dissatisfied with his relationship to God. Avery's realization of needing to surrender to some "knowing" reality that was larger than herself came after years of unhappiness that almost resulted in her death. Neither of them found much help in the congregations with which they were most familiar. The people they met there seemed not to understand the personal anguish they were experiencing, let alone their desperate longing for a genuine relationship with God. Both felt compelled to seek in wider venues for answers to their spiritual questions.

But both embarked on a serious spiritual journey that has required them to engage deliberately in efforts to understand themselves better, to relate consciously and regularly with what they would describe as a sacred being or transcendent reality, and to work on themselves so that they can live in a way that is true to the ideals they believe to be associated with spirituality. Both spend a significant amount of time each day working on their spiritual development.

What Coleman McGregor has learned in his ten years of spiritual direction illustrates the importance of spiritual practice being intentional. His spiritual director has encouraged him to become conscious of his intentions—his desires. "Tell me about those inner longings, those pullings, what's going on inside you," his spiritual director says. As he meditates on these questions from day to day, Coleman comes to have an understanding of where God is located in relation to his other desires. The news is not always good. The commandment "Thou shalt have no other Gods before me" has come to have new meaning. Coleman realizes clearly that he does have other gods, other desires. "I often follow some kind of vanity," he explains, "like riches and honors and pride."

In this process Coleman has come to think differently about the evil in the world and inside himself. "Sin is not just about being a good boy or not being a good boy." The more important questions, he now realizes, are "What are the fundamental tenets that are causing me to behave this way? What is kind of pulling me? How are my fears blocking my way to God? How can I talk to God about them?" Talking to God is a way of expressing these fears, a way of giving voice to the intentions that he often does not want to recognize. "In talking to God, I become more self-disclosing to myself, first of all, and then certainly with God."

Intentionality also means being deliberate about communicating with God. Coleman readily admits that it is often difficult to focus his attention on God, especially when he is trying to meet deadlines or thinking about family issues. Indeed, he recalls that he engaged in daily prayer and meditation and met with his spiritual director for about two full years before he felt as though he was making any progress. Still, he believes firmly that times when there seems to be little progress are among the most productive of all. Just realizing that the questions he was asking were legitimate, he says, has been helpful. When he talked with pastors and people at church, they often told him he should not have any questions. He now believes that God is sufficiently beyond human comprehension that such questions are inescapable.

Intentional spiritual practices are, as this example suggests, generally ones that take a significant amount of time and energy. Not that doing church work or reading books about angels can be done without investing time and energy. But people who are seriously committed to cultivating their devotional life allocate this time explicitly to focusing on their relationship to God. Just as they would not expect to learn chess by thinking about it occasionally as they drove to work, so they do not expect to deepen their relationship with God without spending time focusing specifically on this relationship. In Coleman McGregor's case, a few minutes spent in prayer each day and a monthly trip to the retreat center eventually became a full weekend of silence and meditation, then a series of eight-day silent retreats, and finally a thirty-day silent retreat.

On a daily basis, Coleman pursues his relationship with God differently at different times, depending on his needs and interests. But he tries to clear some time from his busy schedule each day to pray and to think at a deep level about his life. He has been following what are known as Ignatian spiritual exercises. These require him to pray for an hour a day and spend fifteen minutes getting ready to pray and about fifteen to twenty minutes of quiet time after praying. He also spends twenty to forty-five minutes writing in his journal about what happens while he is praying.

But his times of communicating with God take different forms. "What I've come to grips with is that my devotional life will take a lot of different shapes and forms," he asserts. Because he believes that God "is in all things" and because he spends weekends attending spiritual retreats and devotes time to prayer and meditation, he is able to identify a devotional dimension in all his relationships with people, in his work, and in nature. At other times his spiritual practices take specific form because he is working on a special aspect of his relationship to God. The process involves "a lot of meditative and contemplative time," he explains, including "being still, doing some reading, studying some Scripture, reading the spiritual exercises, being involved in the spiritual exercises, and meditating on what is being said." After following this regimen for a while, he finds he needs a change: "pulling away and moving to places where there's more of an openness, a spaciousness."

Avery Fielding is also quite intentional about her spiritual practices. Nearly every morning she spends anywhere from half an hour to an hour and a half meditating. She prefers to meditate first thing in the morning because she is relaxed and not yet thinking about the details of her work. Typically she begins by reading from a devotional guide, which helps quiet her and prompts her to think about the broad aspects of her life and her relationship with the sacred. She does not follow a set routine or employ special breathing techniques. Indeed, she is somewhat at a loss for words in trying to describe exactly what she does when she meditates. But she does know that meditation works for her because it forces her to sit and reflect on the deep issues of her life for a significant period each day. She does not spend the time thinking about how to get her work done. Nor does she focus on a prepackaged plan for spiritual growth. She tries to pay close attention to her body and her emotions as well as her thoughts. The issue one day may be overcoming her lingering doubts about the purpose of life; another day, it may be trying to relate in a loving manner to her clients or relatives; on other days it may be attempting to relate directly with divine power. She firmly believes that this time is essential for her spiritual development. Without it, she becomes absorbed in the details of life to the point that she neglects dealing with the larger issues.

CHARACTERISTICS OF SPIRITUAL PRACTICE

These examples suggest that a practice-oriented spirituality requires devoting a significant amount of time and effort to praying, meditating, examining deep desires, and focusing attention in a worshipful manner on one's relationship to God. The practice of spirituality is thus quite different from simply taking the existence of God for granted. It assumes that developing a spiritual life requires deliberate effort, just as other practices do. Practicing architecture requires deciding both to learn it and to do it on any given day. Developing expertise at chess is considered a practice because master chess players have had to learn the rules of the game, develop skills, make a decision to focus on it rather than spending their time doing something else, and then play the game in order to get anything out of doing so; they do not simply believe that the game exists. Similarly, spiritual practice involves intentional ways of seeking contact with the divine and of relating one's life to the divine.[14]

One writer, who likens spirituality to learning how to play baseball or to drive an automobile, observes, "How do you learn? By practice."[15] He suggests, too, that the kind of practice he has in mind is seldom easy. A business executive in his late thirties who has been practicing Lakota sweat-lodge methods of praying for several years puts it well when he observes, "It's really difficult to pray when you're drinking a beer, watching TV. The thing about Lakota practices is that they are very hard. The four-day vision quests, the sweat lodges, the sun dances are difficult. Preparing for them takes a lot. Trying to be obedient is difficult. But the thing about difficulty is that you pray much better when things are difficult." This is not to deny that practices eventually become habitual and thus may be engaged in without the same degree of conscious deliberation or effort that it took to develop them. Unlike a set of techniques that may not have been internalized, practices tend to become sufficiently part of the practitioner's personal identity that it is unnecessary to think about each step. As Reynolds Price observes, "Most practitioners of any art or any skill are fish in water. They basically don't do . . . a lot of thinking about 'where are my gills right now? Are my fins in the right place?'"[16]

Coleman McGregor draws a similar distinction between practice and merely following techniques. Pastors he talked to sometimes tried to give him tips on "how to pray," such as "do this and then do that." There was too much emphasis on "what I do" and not enough of a focus on "who I am," he thinks. He also makes this point in reference to his understanding of Ignatian spirituality. The basic idea, he says, is to become aware of one's deepest objectives or goals in life—the goals that influence how one lives—and then to meditate deeply on whether these goals and the activities related to them are moving one closer to God or further away. Doing so is not a matter of "getting out your pencil and making a list," he says, but of developing one's inner sense of who God is to the point where one is able to be discerning.

In fact, the key word for many of the people we talked to is *discernment*. Like someone who has mastered a complex set of skills, they no longer think much about specific rules or techniques. They have internalized these rules to the point that they can play the game well—perhaps even improving on how it is played and understood. The role of the inner self is often mentioned in this regard because spirituality is now connected with who one is, not simply with roles that one may play. But people do not mean to suggest that spirituality becomes a matter primarily of paying attention to their feelings. If it were, then it would be guided so much by their moods that they would mistrust it or sense that it lacked coherence. Coleman provides an interesting analogy. Denying that his spirituality has much to do with his feelings at all, he says that feelings are "like being inside one of these giant commercial dryers where you see the clothes go up and drop and go up and drop." His feelings can go around and around, too, but he is not sure it is valid to draw conclusions from whether they are up or down at a particular moment.

The people we talked to also emphasize that spiritual practice is *rewarding*. Despite the hard work and frustration involved, they are convinced that there is no better way to live. Indeed, they emphasize that spiritual practice is its own reward, that it is of intrinsic worth and should not be thought of merely as a method of achieving some other objective, such as success in one's career or happiness in one's marriage.[17] James provides an apt description of these intrinsic rewards: "the feelings, acts, and experiences of [individuals] in their solitude, so far as they apprehend themselves to stand in relation to whatever they may consider the divine."[18] And these intrinsic rewards—the experience of grace, to use the Christian term—in turn motivate and further commitment to the practice.[19]

Coleman McGregor illustrates this point. He believes that individuals can come to understand God as they spend time trying to communicate with God. This knowledge and experience of God is for him intrinsically satisfying. "God is self-disclosing God's self in scripture," he says. "You can celebrate that. You can expand it, like a relationship. Sometimes we have our relationship with God just one way. But we can have it in a bigger way." To say that spiritual practice is rewarding does not mean it is always pleasant. Coleman likens his relationship with God to that with his wife. "Sometimes we hear things from our spouses that we don't want to hear. They may say, 'There's some hard things we need to do together here.' I think God does that with us. And we only can hear those things when we, A, know we're loved, and, B, once we've built some relationship and we trust it." Coleman also asserts that spiritual practice should not be used as a remedy for problems that are better treated in other ways. Those who are deeply depressed, he says, probably cannot concentrate on God, so they may need to see a therapist to help them with their depression. One time at a retreat he had lunch with a man who kept complaining about how jittery he was. Coleman suspected that the jitteriness had to do with the fact that the man drank five cups of coffee while they were talking and it was not a problem that could be remedied by spiritual practice.

Avery Fielding's experience is similar. Her life is much improved because of her spiritual practice: her health is better, her outlook is more positive, she enjoys her work more. But these results are not why she pursues spirituality. In fact, some aspects of her life have not improved or have become harder; for example, her relationship with her significant other's parents is problematic, and she struggles with painful feelings that are sparked by the personal issues she is addressing. Her real reason for pursuing spirituality is that she feels she has to. She believes she has a spiritual dimension, as does all of reality. So she is true to that reality by attending to it. When asked why she meditates, she reflects this understanding of spirituality, saying, "It's just my yearning to have a deeper relationship with God." Sometimes she feels nothing; she meditates anyway. Other times she experiences a state of being that affirms her conviction that this is the way to live: "I get a sense of peace and of balance; I get to communicate internally with God; I can actually feel the oneness."

People with deep devotional practices run the gamut from being significantly involved in local congregations to not being involved at all. Some accept guidance for their spiritual development from groups, seminars, and study materials that stem from a single denominational or confessional tradition. Others piece together their spiritual practices by reflecting creatively about who they are and how they can best deepen their relationship with God. At both extremes, their practices are facilitated by institutions that make these resources available: colleges and seminaries that provide training to religious professionals, congregations and religious orders that pay the salaries of these professionals, retreat centers that provide places to meet, publishing companies, internet sites, and so on.

Because of this embeddedness in institutions, spiritual practices are inevitably *social*. Even someone who meditates alone is in this sense engaging in a social activity. This person's style of meditation probably follows some tradition; it was passed on from mentor to pupil. The person may attend classes, read books, and discuss spirituality with people who practice in similar ways. Such people may not be immersed in a single religious congregation, but they are linked generally to a variety of communities through their spiritual pursuits, their work, family, and friends. Practitioners also vary in how "communal" their spirituality is. Some believe it is essential to spend a lot of time interacting with other people; others have personalities that require them to withdraw from social interaction in order to read, think, work, or communicate with nature. In either case, the center of their spirituality is neither a group nor themselves but their relationship with God.

In the United States, spiritual practices are so often connected to religious traditions that they are typically facilitated by people's involvement in congregations or fellowship groups and by their interaction with trained religious professionals. Nevertheless, as we have seen, many people find it useful to draw a distinction between spirituality and religion. As one of the people we interviewed explains, "Religion is something outside of yourself. There's somebody in the pulpit telling you things, but I needed to know from the inside." In this person's view, spirituality is more the essence of one's relationship to God, relating the individual deeply to the sacred, whereas religion is a more impersonal set of social arrangements.

Religious institutions and spiritual practices are not always as much at odds with each other as this person's comment suggests. A person wishing to read the writings of a desert monk is aided by the fact that a religious publishing company has printed the monk's works or is encouraged to do so by hearing the monk quoted during the Sunday homily. Nevertheless, some tension between religious institutions and spiritual practices is often present.[20] As writer Wendell Berry observes, religion as an institution is "a hodgepodge of funds, properties, projects, and offices, all urgently requiring economic support"; maintaining these activities may be contrary to some of the principles of religion itself. Berry further observes, "The building fund can be preserved by crude applications of money, but the fowls of the air and the lilies of the field can be preserved only by . . . the *practice* of a proper love and respect for them as the creatures of God."[21]

One way of relating spiritual practices to religious institutions is illustrated by Coleman McGregor. He still attends worship services almost every Sunday. He also attends retreats at facilities that are supported by religious orders, and he receives spiritual counseling from full-time religious professionals. Nevertheless, he makes an important observation about religious institutions: "I value the institution, but as my relationship with God has become more important subjectively and objectively, I've been drawn more into that and drawn less into the institution." As a specific example, he mentions that as he started to spend more time attending seminars on spiritual formation at retreat centers, he felt a need to withdraw from the circle of people he knew at his church. "I needed to break out of that little circle," he recalls. "I needed that so badly, I was dying. I was dying just being caught in this little tiny group. I knew it was not good for me; it was strangling me, but I didn't know why. I didn't know what it was. I mean, they're nice people, they're good people, they're doing good things, but I'm dying." Coleman gradually came to realize that he felt this way because the group focused its attention too much on its members and not enough on their relationship to God.

The connections between Avery Fielding's spiritual practice and religious institutions illustrate a different pattern. Certainly she has broken ties with religious organizations. Yet she is by no means without social ties, and she does not make up her ideas about spirituality from scratch. The church in which she was raised is more a part of her than she is ready to admit. She loves music and has an understanding of the relationship between music and spirituality that stems from playing the organ at church when she was in high school. Her belief in the existence of God and in the value of unconditional love is a reflection of what she was taught in catechism class. She learned how to meditate by attending a Unity congregation for several months and by participating in another spirituality group for two years. She attends retreats and reads books produced by people who are professionally interested in spirituality. Her spiritual work is indirectly supported by the holistic health movement, parts of which owe their existence to universities, medical schools, churches, and insurance companies. More immediately, she has surrounded herself with a free-floating congregation of friends and co-workers from whom she can receive support. She keeps in touch with some of the women who were in a feminist spirituality group with her a few years ago. She also has a network of people she has met at retreat centers and conferences whom she talks with frequently by telephone. All these people reinforce her spirituality. She practices alone and in her own way, but her spirituality is also shaped by these people.

To the extent that formal institutions inhibit spiritual practices, people like Coleman and Avery are likely to feel uncomfortable participating in them. But religious institutions can also be supportive, providing both the resources and the encouragement that people who are interested in spiritual practices desire. Unlike the small group that Coleman left when he started going to weekend retreats, a new one is beginning to provide this kind of support. The difference, he feels, is that the present group is more open to the various ways its members may be developing their relationship with God. "The people are really open to each other, they're open to themselves, they're open to questioning their own beliefs, their own understanding of things. They're open to their understanding of God. They're open to their experience of God. They're open to your experience of God. Someone may very well say in the group, 'Gee, that flies right in the face of what I believe, but tell me more about it. I want to hear more about what happened for you.'" Under these conditions, Coleman feels he has the freedom to grow, but he also has a community, which keeps him from feeling all alone in his spiritual journey.

People who are engaged in spiritual practices also emphasize what might be called the *moral dimension* of these practices. To say that something is "morally binding" means, in part, that it includes rules that constrain a person's behavior. Rather than behaving strictly in accordance with whims or desires, the person follows a set of rules and tries to do what is right. Some of these rules are built into the practice itself: following them is morally binding because they are accepted as the way to conduct the practice. For example, to practice hospitality, one must make a commitment to open one's home to people in a way that makes them feel welcome, perhaps by following certain rules of etiquette, even though doing so means sacrificing some of one's time and having to clean up and relax later.[22] In the same way, a spiritual practice exercises constraint over the way people can live. It constrains them both by providing daily activities in which to engage and by requiring them, as in Coleman McGregor's and Avery Fielding's experiences, to evaluate all their activities in relation to their growing understanding of the nature of God.

Constraint of this kind is part of what distinguishes a practice from the mere development of a technical skill. Spiritual practice always involves a certain degree of technical knowledge—knowing where sacred texts can be found, perhaps memorizing some of these texts, knowing what stores to shop at for books about yoga or Zen. But practices involve a shaping of the person as well—becoming habituated to the practice to the point that one can exercise wisdom when new situations necessitate making difficult judgments, learning how to get along with other practitioners, being willing to pay the costs that may be associated with one's principles, and knowing how to relate the practice responsibly to one's other obligations and areas of life. Insofar as one becomes habituated to it, a practice provides some of the security offered by the familiarity and legitimacy of a dwelling-oriented spirituality; yet practices are more portable than sacred places, permitting practitioners to perform them under more diverse circumstances.

To practice is to accept the standards of evaluation that are part of a practice, such as the rules by which the winner of a chess match is decided or the expectations that govern whether one player is considered better than another. These standards need not be accepted blindly. Practitioners are always challenging norms as well as conforming to them. Their practices may alter the rules or lead to the creation of a new game. But practitioners do recognize that there is a binding quality about these standards. They recognize, for instance, that other people (past and present) say that doing X is necessary for achieving Y. Practitioners may also recognize that if they make up their own rules, they will pay certain costs for doing so.

This moral aspect of practice-oriented spirituality most clearly distinguishes it from a spirituality of seeking. Negotiating and choosing emphasize little more than what is in one's self-interest or what works or feels right at the moment; people are too easily led by circumstances and emotions. Practice requires integrity, a commitment to the internal logic and rules of the practice itself; it generates a basis from which to make judgments that are internally consistent. Although a practice-oriented spirituality may not provide as clear-cut rules as a game of chess, it nevertheless imposes discipline on practitioners and demands their allegiance.

In Avery Fielding's case, the moral aspect of her spiritual practice is expressed most clearly in how she relates to other people. A skeptic might say that she is engrossed with herself. But her spirituality has not resulted in an "anything-goes" attitude toward life. She explains, "One of the things that I learned as a child was to be judgmental and critical. So through my own spirituality I have really worked hard at undoing that: to learn not to pass judgment on what I see because I don't see the whole picture, to not be critical of people or places or things but to see it from a more loving perspective. Spirituality really affects the way I interact with the world, the way I present myself in the world. It doesn't matter to me if somebody doesn't understand me or if somebody finds something that I do unacceptable."

How she expresses a "loving perspective" depends on her taking responsibility to do what to the best of her practice-informed judgment is morally right. Again, a skeptic might say that she can justify anything she chooses. What she understands is different. She understands moral responsibility in the first place to involve being willing to take a stand rather than simply doing what other people expect, including trying to understand them for who they are, rather than immediately jumping to critical conclusions. In the second place, moral responsibility requires searching her own soul to understand her biases and interests. Spiritual reflection is the process by which she examines her soul. It is also the occasion to remind herself of the higher principles or the larger perspective that spirituality entails. It reminds her that love is a principle that transcends the easiest or the quickest solutions.

Avery most clearly expresses her increased sense of moral responsibility when she contrasts her present view of herself with the "victim mentality" that she learned as a child. "I remember thinking, 'Well, if I do this or I do that, then God [will] punish me.' So if something happened, it must have been because God's angry with me. I try not to respond as a victim anymore. I look at what am I learning, what is this teaching me, and how do I respond with love. To me that is the core of existence, to learn unconditional love."

For Coleman McGregor, moral responsibility is also an important aspect of his spiritual practices. One connection is the responsibility he feels to develop his relationship to God. This kind of commitment is sometimes expressed in words like *duty* and *obligation*. It is, in his view, morally binding. He does not think of it particularly as a burden or as something he would rather not do but more as an inescapable aspect of being a child of God. To spend time deepening his relationship with God is for him quite different from shopping around for something that suits his fancy at the moment. The other sense of moral responsibility is to his loved ones. He recognizes that they are also children of God, and he wants to help them develop their relationship to God in whatever way they feel called to. For example, he tells how he and his wife began re-evaluating their relationship with each other; in the process he learned that she had a strong desire to go to graduate school and start a new career. Because of the self-evaluation he had been doing, Coleman was able to understand and support his wife's decision.

It is clear from these remarks that people who engage in spiritual practices are often quite reflective about what they are doing and why they are doing it. Although this may seem like an obvious point, it is worth emphasizing. Spiritual practice involves *deep reflection* about who one is. For many people, it results in a core narrative that provides coherence to their practice over time. They develop a story about their spiritual journey, and this story provides a way for them to understand their origins, how they have changed, the role that crisis events or significant others have played in their lives, and where they think they are headed.[23]

These narratives are often characterized by what literary critic Susanne Juhasz calls "dailiness," a pattern she says is especially evident in women's speech but that fits much of what men say about their spiritual practices as well. Dailiness emphasizes the circumstances of what happened, the discourse of "he said" and "she said" that supplies concrete interpretations of what happened, and the repetition involved in the process of living even more than the goals toward which living is directed. In spiritual practice, it connects meaning with personal experience and with sacred tradition.[24]

Coleman McGregor provides a good illustration of the self-interpretive process that is such an important part of many people's spiritual practice. As he started to meet with his spiritual director, his thinking about himself underwent a transformation. He began to formulate a new story about who he was. He recalls, "My spiritual life began to be more than, 'Oh, well, I'm called to be a pharmacist.' 'Well, yeah, you are one.' I mean, it was like, 'You're also called to be in a relationship with God. And what does that look like and how do you develop that friendship? And then how does God begin to disclose God's self to you? And how do you disclose yourself to God? And how does that relationship grow into more integrity, more honesty, more truth, more holiness?' So *that* was what I was looking for, and I began to know that deeply."

People who engage in an interpretive process of this kind say it is beneficial but also not particularly easy or enjoyable. People already have a self-identity that is familiar to them and with which they are at some level comfortable. To reshape one's conception of oneself is hard work. Coleman McGregor puts it well when he admits, "There was certainly a lot of fear about my own personal self-disclosure, even to myself." But he also asserts that it was "just incredibly important for me to be able to do that."

Self-interpretation is also about how one understands specific experiences, not just a wholesale understanding of who one is. Indeed, people often say the larger transformations have come from puzzling out the lessons of specific experiences. Coleman provides the following example. About fifteen years ago (when he was struggling to find a way to know God better), he attended a fundamentalist church in another state with some relatives, and at the end of the service the preacher asked those who wanted to know God better to raise their hand. Coleman raised his hand, assuming that surely everyone in the church would raise theirs too, and was surprised to find that his was the only hand raised. That afternoon the preacher came to visit. He explained to Coleman that he needed to repeat a prayer (printed on a card) that affirmed his faith in Jesus, otherwise he might have an accident driving home and it would be too late. Coleman refused. As he recalls this experience, however, his point is not to show that the preacher was misguided or that his own understanding of spirituality is superior. It is rather to indicate that he has tried to learn from this experience. Reflecting on it has forced him to clarify his own beliefs and to ask himself which ones are pulling him toward God and which are pulling him away.

Avery Fielding's spirituality is also so intensely concerned with her own struggles that it goes without saying that she is engaged in an act of self-interpretation. The point that her story illustrates best is that spirituality is life-transforming to the extent that she comes to make sense of her life in a different way. Repeatedly, she emphasizes that she is trying to learn a new approach to living and that her daily spiritual practices give her a different outlook on life. She does not deny that behavior is difficult to change, but she is often able to respond to events differently when she sees herself in a new way. For instance, when she asks herself what she can learn from a new challenge, rather than seeing it as a problem, she has the emotional strength and flexibility to meet the challenge.

An important aspect of self-interpretation is that it often involves grieving the past as well as trying to grow. Although people like Coleman McGregor and Avery Fielding feel their lives are better now than they were in the past, they do not tell stories that focus only on bad experiences then and good ones now. Rather, they have gained a new appreciation of the past, including the lessons learned or the love received but perhaps not appreciated at the time. They also recognize that giving up the past is painful. Coleman remembers a silent retreat in which he found himself overwhelmed with sadness. He realized that he was grieving the loss of his youth, his parents, and even some of the daily routines he had been following for much of his life. As he grieved them, he was able to sense clearly that God was with him and would sustain him.

The need to engage in self-interpretation is another reason that people who are engaged in spiritual practices sometimes band together with fellow practitioners: hearing the stories of others helps them to formulate their own stories.[25] They also insist, however, that self-interpretation can never be done by relying solely on other people. As we have seen, dwelling-oriented spirituality is generally rich with stories that legitimate corporate realities but not likely to generate deep introspection about one's own identity. Seeker-oriented spirituality focuses attention on the specifics of the moment but is likely to be insufficient without an interpretive framework that provides coherence to individual biographies. In contrast, practice-oriented spirituality must include considered self-reflection, examination of conscience, and scrutiny of personal habits. These must be performed with an appropriate balance of criticism and acceptance but with the goal of making sense of one's life in relation to one's understanding and experience of the sacred.

The people we talked to emphasize the value of rooting their spiritual practice in a specific *tradition*, too, rather than having to pursue their spiritual activities in a vacuum. They feel less alone because they know they are following practices that people have been engaged in for generations. MacIntyre puts it this way: "to enter into a practice is to enter into a relationship not only with its contemporary practitioners, but also with those who have preceded us in the practice, particularly those whose achievements extended the reach of the practice to its present point."[26] For some of the people we talked to, the tradition with which they associated was fairly short, embodied more in their own family, congregation, or community than in an entire history; others drew specifically on longstanding religious traditions.[27]

Coleman McGregor's spiritual practices are rooted specifically in the contemplative traditions of Christianity. He knows about the early Christians who lived in the desert so they could spend time in prayer and meditation, and he draws from the medieval mystics who wrote about their inner desire to experience God more fully. The method of praying that he has learned was developed by Ignatius of Loyola. More generally, he regards himself as a Christian and uses the biblical tradition as a language for understanding his relationship to God. When asked to summarize his beliefs, he puts them in his own language, yet he refers to ideas that would be familiar to other Christians. He asserts his belief in the existence of "a living God" who communicates through scripture. Following the creeds, he believes that there is evil in the world and that God is love.

In comparison, Avery Fielding's spirituality is less clearly connected to any tradition. She sometimes sounds as if she is groping for the right words to express herself, perhaps even making up words that seem devoid of traditional meaning. But she is not inarticulate and her spirituality does not lack concreteness. Rather, she has chosen to distance herself from specific religious traditions, especially the Christian tradition in which she was raised. To the extent that her spirituality is linked to a larger history, its connection is mainly negative. To say why she believes in a God of love, she identifies the God of her Lutheran upbringing as a God of fear. She does draw occasionally on the language of metaphysics, and yet she seems not to think of it as a tradition as much as an ideal that emphasizes love. Were she to embrace religious tradition, she might well be reluctant to identify herself with any single tradition.

Some of the other people we talked to were like Avery Fielding in having been exposed to several different traditions and not feeling fully at home in any one. For them, spiritual practices had become important because they could focus on worshipful activities that gave their lives stability even though they had unanswered theological questions. One woman in her thirties had been raised in India by parents who had been Hindus before they converted to Christianity; then, when she married, she converted back to Hinduism. She finds it interesting to compare the two religions. Both emphasize faith in God, she says, and both encourage forgiveness and compassion toward the poor. Beyond this, she is not sure what to make of the different teachings. Thus, she spends a significant amount of time in prayer each day, reminding herself to trust in God and asking God to be with her. After spending an hour in prayer each morning, she finds it easier to be thankful for God's blessings. As she engages in her daily tasks, she constantly reminds herself to put God first. "You devote your love to him," she says. "You concentrate with your prayers, put everything out of your mind, and you just concentrate on him. And I think he will answer your prayers." For her, religious tradition is not unimportant, but she has to negotiate between two traditions to understand the specific ways it is important.

Another woman, who was raised Jewish, is also reconsidering her relationship with her tradition. She is troubled by feelings that are almost instinctual to her that she is "one of the chosen," whereas other people are not. "I can get very hung up on the rightness of being Jewish," she explains. What bothers her most is the "dogma" that she associates with organized religion. In recent years she has been praying, practicing an Eastern form of meditation, and doing physical exercises that help to clear her mind. "I ask God to look inside me. I ask God to cleanse me and fill me," she says. In pursuing these practices, she has not abandoned her Judaism; indeed, she has become more observant. She also thinks she understands the core of her tradition better than she did before.

But the historical aspect of spiritual practice is not simply a set of writings that link people abstractly to some religious tradition. For most people, it is more tangibly expressed in the lives of particular individuals who have gone before them or who set an example by walking beside them. In Avery Fielding's case, her grandmother was such a person. Although Avery does not say much about the visits she paid to her grandmother while she was in high school, her grandmother helped her to see that she was not the first person in the world to be troubled by questions about the supernatural. In Coleman McGregor's case, the most tangible links to the Christian tradition as he now understands it are the various spiritual directors with whom he has met during the past ten years.

Indeed, Coleman's description of what a spiritual guide does provides a good illustration of how the past is mediated by someone who has been down a similar road. "A spiritual guide does not guide by telling someone how they should live their life," he explains. "If you wanted to go fishing in Wyoming and you looked for a guide, the guide would ask you first of all what you're fishing for. What's your desire? And then you'd say, 'My desire is, rather than going hunting, I want to go fishing.' And he'd say, 'Well, if you want to go fishing, this is where you'd have to go. Now, if you want to fish for trout, you would go here. Now if it's the spring of the year, you don't want to go here, you'd want to go some place where the pool's a little bit deeper. Come over here, the pool's deeper, because they go down deeper in the water that time of the year. When the water gets colder, there are springs here, so you'd want to fish here.' He doesn't fish for you, he simply tells you, 'Here's a place you can go. Why don't you try using this bait? Why don't you try using this lure?' A spiritual guide kind of walks with a person in their journey and says, 'Tell me what's going on, tell me what's happening in your life. Have you found God here? Have you tried praying this way?"

In this example, the guide is a person with experience and is thus a link to the past, and yet the past is open to interpretation and negotiation by the practitioner. To an important degree, a practice-oriented spirituality requires paying attention to some tradition or individual who has gone before, even more than a dwelling-oriented spirituality does, because there is a realization that tradition is not simply given, but interpreted, and that tradition is changeable rather than static. In comparison, seeker-oriented spirituality often tends toward a facile view of tradition, diminishing its importance in the interest of being unencumbered when one desires to move on.

A young Muslim woman from Tanzania provides a good illustration of this negotiated relationship between spiritual practice and tradition. As a recent immigrant, she retains some of the dwelling-oriented spirituality that comes from associating with people from her own background. But she also knows that she is living between worlds. Indeed, she is interested in exploring other religions, and she displays some of the characteristics of a seeker-oriented spirituality. What anchors her are her daily devotional practices. She prays, following the Muslim cycle of prayers, because it is a "must" in her life. She reflects on her whole day, thinking about what she has done wrong and asking forgiveness. "I feel in contact with God. If I don't pray, I feel that something is wrong." Having reminded herself that God "owns me," she remembers that all the world is subject to God. She is also trying to pass on her tradition by teaching Islamic history to immigrant girls.

Because their spiritual practices consist of specific activities, people who engage in these practices are also quick to emphasize how deeply *interlaced* these activities are with other parts of their lives. This, too, is an important consideration. To learn baseball, a person has to focus attention on the game itself. And the greatest enjoyment from baseball is likely to come from playing the game. But having played baseball, the ball player also finds the game interacting with other realms of life: the language of "hitting a home run" or "striking out" may be used at work; reading about the history of baseball may become a source of additional pleasure.

Coleman McGregor's understanding of spirituality suggests that it is richer when it is interlaced with other practices. He emphasizes the importance of having specific times when he intentionally tries to communicate with God, just as he does when he sits "knees to knees" with his wife and talks over some aspect of their relationship. But he insists that a deep relationship with God involves relating to God at other times and in other ways, just as with his wife. Lately, he has been thinking about how his relationship to God can be more a part of his life when he is playing or watching a beautiful sunset or appreciating a work of art. In these contexts he gains insights about the playful nature of God or the aesthetic dimension of God.

The way Avery Fielding's spiritual practice is interlaced with the rest of her life is evident in her remarks as well. At times each day she decides to focus her attention on her relationship to God. But she also insists that her spirituality is connected with all the rest of her life. She especially uses the language of holistic health to describe these connections. In this view the body and spirit are closely intertwined. Avery feels that physical pain can be a source of spiritual insight and that spiritual reflection can be a way to heal physical pain. Her massage therapy and her music are separate activities—practices—just as her times of meditation and prayer are. But each one complements the others.[28]

SPIRITUAL PRACTICE AND SERVICE

The interlacing of spiritual practice and service is a point of particular emphasis in many descriptions of spiritual practice. Although it is possible for people's spiritual practices to focus so much attention on themselves or on God that little energy is left for anything else, this possibility does not appear to be the typical result. Among the people we talked to, spending time cultivating their relationship with God seemed more often to free them from material concerns and other self-interested pursuits so that they could focus on the needs of others.

Avery Fielding's spiritual practices are directly related to her efforts to serve others. Although she could be earning more money in another line of work, her career as a massage therapist is part of a larger commitment to help people by applying holistic-health concepts that have been neglected in formalized medicine. Many of the people who come to her are suffering from severe stress, others are recovering from alcoholism, drug abuse, or trauma in their families. Avery is convinced that there is an integral relationship between the body and the spirit. In treating people she generally starts with massage because touching is a primordial form of communication. As people become aware of their bodies, they are often able to focus on their deepest desires. "[Massage] takes them into their core where they carry their beliefs," she says. "Sometimes they can discover what's keeping them from living a happy, fulfilling life. Other times people will get into parts of themselves where they go much [deeper] into their soul. Sometimes people have major breakthroughs." For example, she treated a man who was unable to walk properly because of a malfunctioning muscle in one leg. Physicians could find nothing wrong with the muscle, so they suggested he see someone who could treat it in a different way. Avery was able to help him discover some deep-seated fears that he was internalizing to the point that they were inhibiting the movement of his leg. In the process, he also started to broaden his understanding of himself as a spiritual being.

By cultivating her spirituality, Avery feels she is also able to perceive the spiritual dimension in the people she serves. Spirituality does not provide her with a secret remedy to their ills, let alone serve as a substitute for medicine when it is needed. She explains, "If it's an ache or pain or a tension, it's something that's restricting them, so what I do is help them try and identify where they're not being who they are, where their freedom of expression is limited. I hold them in a space of all potential and all possibility. I don't see it as a limitation; I see it as something that they need to learn from and something that can be cleared, not as something that is less than or crippling or unacceptable or judgmental." When she treats alcoholics, she tries to discourage them from identifying only with this condition. "You have a problem with alcoholism, yes," she says. "But I have trouble taking the words 'I am' and putting them with 'alcoholic' because you're identifying with that and you're limiting who you are. I mean, it's definitely affecting your personality, it's definitely a problem, and it's definitely a disease; but it's not all of who you are." "So," she says, "I always try to hold a higher picture for people; I hold a space to allow them to grow into or to expand into." The important point in this example is not the specific understanding of alcoholism or of health that Avery brings to her work. It is rather that her daily spiritual practice is directly linked to her desire and ability to help other people. Sometimes she meditates for a short period between seeing clients, often restricting herself to four clients a day so that she has time to do so. By meditating, she is able to remind herself of the reasons for going into this line of work and to remember her desire to express love toward her clients.

For Coleman McGregor, spiritual practice also deepens his commitment to helping others. For as long as he can remember, he has been drawn into charitable activities through his association with the church. But his devotion to God is changing how he understands these activities. "Working at soup kitchens and making baskets for the poor are all good projects," he asserts. "And I still struggle with this, but I think you need to do it out of the experience of being so deeply loved yourself that you want to give it back. When you are deeply loved by God, you want to return it." He elaborates, "I don't believe we are given what we have to hold to ourselves. I think part of what the circle of life is about is to share what you have, to give what you have, to be part of salvation history, to build a better world."

In Coleman's case, service is an outgrowth of his devotional life. In other cases, service itself is more at the core of a person's spiritual practice. Arthur Hoffman, who is in his twenties, illustrates this kind of spiritual practice. Reared in a Christian-Jewish family, he did not feel part of a religious community as a child. But in college he began reading and thinking about his Jewish heritage. One of the teachings that impressed him was the idea that God created the world incomplete. "It's up to us to finish the work of creation," he explains. One day he happened to walk past a campus ceremony devoted to remembering victims of the Holocaust. As he listened to the names being read, he overheard someone in the background saying that Los Angeles was burning in the aftermath of the Rodney King trial. Arthur's grief for the Holocaust victims turned to anger as he thought of the injustices in his own society. He vowed at that moment to devote his life to helping bring about social justice.

Since graduating he has been working for a community-development organization in East Harlem. When asked how spirituality relates to this work, he laughs, "The other day a bright light appeared and a host of angels said, 'Hey, you're doing a great job. Keep up the good work.'" As he shakes his head, he says, "No. We all wish it were that cut and dried. Let me tell you, it's not." But there is a deep connection between his service work and his spirituality. He nurtures his relationship to God by observing Hanukkah, Passover, Yom Kippur, and Rosh Hashanah, and by reading Jewish authors that help him to understand his own identity. He prays often but not according to a regular schedule. Prayer, he explains, "is sort of a deep introspection. It brings me closer to the divine presence."

For people like this, it is often especially important to nurture their spirituality in a way that encourages it to interlace with all aspects of their life. "The central way you should express your spirituality is in your way of living," Arthur asserts. "You can't get off with being nasty to your spouse and then going off and ladling soup at a kitchen and saying, 'I'm doing my religious duty this way or I'm fulfilling my spirituality,' like that. Serving is an important part of my spirituality, but it's not the only thing."

An Episcopalian woman illustrates another way of combining spiritual practice and service. For the past five years she has been working full-time with people who are dying of AIDS. Studying the story of the Good Samaritan was partly what prompted her to become involved in this activity. But she found so little support from the clergy at her church for what she was doing that she left in disgust. Her spirituality has deepened more outside the church than it ever did previously. She explains, "If it hadn't been for the AIDS ministry, I wouldn't have known what spirituality was. It has given me that sense that I'm a spiritual being— that every day, every moment I am connected with the creator. Working with these people has broken my heart again and again. I have had to have my heart mended again and again. I've had to learn again and again how to love. I can't do that without a loving creator. It's a mystery." It was necessary for her to "get into the mud," she believes, in order to understand what it means to be Christ-like. As her spirituality has deepened and as she has begun to find support in a new congregation, she is also coming to a new appreciation of the church. "No matter how imperfect the organizational church is," she asserts, "we need it. We need community. Sure, I pray alone. It causes me to reflect on the creator. But I also need community."

THE VALUE OF SPIRITUAL PRACTICE

People can be spiritual in a generic way without being engaged in spiritual practice at any given moment (for example, simply taking for granted that all of life is spiritual). A focus on practice nevertheless emphasizes the importance of making a deliberate attempt to relate to the sacred. To suggest that people of faith can benefit by paying attention to spiritual practice is hardly a novel idea. But Americans are conditioned to believe in quick fixes, often believing it sufficient to mutter a self-interested prayer or to take solace in the fact that someone else has reported a dramatic encounter with an angel in the morning newspaper or to be part of a religious community.

An analogy may be instructive. Suppose it were discovered that most of the population suffered from ill health—perhaps from high blood pressure, poor nutrition, a lack of exercise, or chronic anemia. Suppose there were ample hospital wards, nursing homes, and rehabilitation centers. Imagine further that someone said; "Let's get all the sick people and put them together in these wards; they can talk to each other, and soon they'll be better. Get them together, perhaps they can experience a healing power in their midst and even be encouraged to help care for one another; in any case, they'll soon be better." Ludicrous as this idea may seem, it is the way many people talk about spirituality. What we know about physical health is that we have to take responsibility for it. Getting support from other sick people and visiting the doctor may be important, but basic health begins by practicing it from day to day. Throughout history, the saints have known this about spiritual health as well. The idea of spiritual practices encourages individuals to take responsibility for their own spiritual development by spending time working on it, deliberating on its meaning and how best to pursue it, seeking to understand the sacred through reading and from the counsel of others, and seeking to have contact with the sacred through personal reflection and prayer.

Practice-oriented spirituality is thus different from seeker-oriented spirituality chiefly in providing a more orderly, disciplined, and focused approach to the sacred. The people we talked to who were trying to practice their spirituality from day to day were not immune from having to choose what to do and where to focus their attention, but they tended to settle into a routine that permitted them to cultivate a deep spirituality rather than being influenced by their moods, circumstances, or exposure to constantly changing ideas.

One man provided a nice illustration of this difference in discussing why he tries to study the Bible for a significant amount of time every day. He realizes that he is a "hot-tempered and hasty person," so his Bible reading provides a stabilizing and moderating dimension to his life. "I figure that if you just keep to the same actions," he explains, "they become your habit eventually, [and they] lead to a certain kind of living pattern." As he reads, he also tries not to focus on each verse separately because that approach can be influenced too much by his needs at the moment. "We have to think about God's intent from a broad perspective," he says, "rather than just take a particular message only for our immediate needs."

Some religious leaders insist that people are incapable of practicing spirituality on their own and thus need to be encouraged to participate actively in their local congregations. The people we talked to who viewed spirituality as a practice were seldom isolated from others from whom they could receive (or to whom they could give) assistance. But they also insisted that spirituality had become meaningful to them mostly because they worked at it on their own. In fact, many observed that they had been unable to practice until spirituality ceased to be a feature of the familiar spaces in which they had been raised, and most said their religious communities took on meaning only when they began to practice spirituality in other ways.

Paradoxically, it is thus practice, rather than a spirituality of dwelling, that is most capable of generating a balanced perspective on the sacredness of the world. By engaging in spiritual practices, the practitioner retreats reflectively from the world in order to recognize how it is broken and in need of healing; then, in recognition that the world is also worthy of healing because of its sacral dimensions, the practitioner commits energy to the process of healing. In her book on contemplative prayer, Joan Chittister expresses this paradoxical relationship between spiritual practice and the world. "Contemplative prayer . . . is prayer that sees the whole world through incense—a holy place, a place where the sacred dwells, a place to be made different by those who pray, a place where God sweetens living with the beauty of all life. Contemplative prayer . . . unstops our ears to hear the poverty of widows, the loneliness of widowers, the cry of women, the vulnerability, the struggle of outcasts."[29]

The woman who works with AIDS patients elaborates this view of prayer. When asked about prayer, she says her understanding of it is best expressed in a story about one of her patients. "Her name was Valentina. Her husband had already died of AIDS. She had infected her little girl [in vitro] who was then about six years old. She herself was dying. She lay in the bed, swollen beyond belief. She was coughing up blood. She couldn't even lift the tissue to cover her mouth. She was suffering terribly. She looked up at me and said, 'Do you think God cares?' I told her, 'Yes, I [do], and I believe that what breaks our hearts also breaks the heart of God.' She said, 'Do you think God could take my life and spare my daughter's?' I said, 'Valentina, that is a very good prayer.'" Then, as the woman telling the story pauses to control her own tears, she whispers, "Is there a more holy prayer than that?"

Reinhold Niebuhr once observed that in the United States "our practice" is generally better than "our creed."[30] From what we have considered in previous chapters, we can extend this idea: the strength of U.S. culture at the end of the twentieth century is what many of its detractors dislike the most: its messiness. The ways families and personal lives are organized inevitably require many to negotiate and to live with confusion. People of different faiths are forced to interact with each other, to band together, to form alliances and coalitions, to compromise, and to bargain with other groups to get what they want. The outcome of this process is always uncertain. In many ways, a spirituality of seeking may be well suited to a system of this kind. Spiritual seekers do not have a corner on the truth but are forced to gain insight and support from a variety of sources; and they need to exercise personal responsibility, even though they are embedded in webs of social relationships.

Spiritual practice takes this kind of seeking a step further, adding the vital element of sustained commitment, without which no life can have coherence. Practices may be messier than the commanders of large-scale institutions would like, but they ultimately sustain these institutions by giving individuals the moral fortitude to participate in them without expecting to receive too much from them. If Americans' practices were, indeed, better than their creeds, there would be much about which to be optimistic.

Traditionally, the spiritual ideal has been to live a consistent, fully integrated life of piety, such that one's practice of spirituality becomes indistinguishable from the rest of one's life. The Benedictine David Steindl-Rast expresses this view when he writes, "We must avoid putting too much emphasis on practices, which are a means to an end. The end is practice, our whole lives as practice."[31] The shift that has taken place in U.S. culture over the past half century, however, means that attention again needs to be given to specific spiritual practices by those who desire to live their whole lives as practice. This heightened level of attention has been necessitated by the fact that fewer people live within spiritual enclaves that they can take for granted and because more options are available from which to piece together a spiritual life. Nevertheless, the point of spiritual practice is not to elevate an isolated set of activities over the rest of life but to electrify the spiritual impulse that animates all of life.

Notes

1. FROM DWELLING TO SEEKING

1. George H. Gallup, Jr., *Religion in America: 1996 Report* (Princeton, N.J.: Princeton Religion Research Center, 1996).

2. Tarrance Group Report on Religion in America, a survey of one thousand registered voters conducted in March 1994; I wish to thank Jeff Scheler of *U.S. News & World Report* for making this report available.

3. As shown in Jon Butler, *Awash in a Sea of Faith: Christianizing the American People* (Cambridge, Mass.: Harvard University Press, 1992), and in Catherine L. Albanese, *Nature Religion in America: From the Algonquin Indians to the New Age* (Chicago: University of Chicago Press, 1991), there were also undercurrents of folk religion, superstition, and spiritualism that were not fully compatible with organized expressions of Christianity and Judaism. For more on the tensions between organized religion and other forms of spirituality, see Chapter 2.

4. Song of Solomon 1:16–17; 3:2.

5. Aristotle, *Politics*, I, ii-v; Emile Durkheim, *The Elementary Forms of the Religious Life* (New York: Free Press, 1915), p. 62; Plato, *Republic*, II, 367E–372A; Max Weber, *The Sociology of Religion* (1922; reprint, Boston: Beacon Press, 1993).

6. Max Lerner, *Wrestling with the Angel* (New York: Norton, 1990), p. 191.

7. Ann Truitt, *Daybook* (New York: Pantheon Books, 1982), p. 22.

8. Thomas Merton, "Elias—Variations on a Theme," in *The Strange Islands* (New York: New Directions, 1959), p. 233. The relationship between freedom and dwelling is also emphasized in Martin Heidegger, "Bauen Wohnen Denken," *Vorträge und Aufsätze* (Pfullingen: Neske, 1954).

9. *The Rule of Saint Benedict,* ed. by Timothy Fry (Collegeville, Minn.: Liturgical Press, 1982); Brian C. Taylor, *Spirituality for Everyday Living: An Adaptation of the Rule of St. Benedict* (Collegeville, Minn.: Liturgical Press, 1989),

esp. ch. 1; Joan Chittister, *Wisdom Distilled from the Daily: Living the Rule of St. Benedict Today* (New York: HarperCollins, 1991); and, for a sociological interpretation, Eviatar Zerubavel, *Hidden Rhythms: Schedules and Calendars in Social Life* (Berkeley: University of California Press, 1981), esp. ch. 2.

10. Quoted in Witold Rybczynski, *The Most Beautiful House in the World* (New York: Penguin Books, 1989), p. 171.

11. Alan Gussow, "A Sense of Place," in *The Earth Speaks*, ed. Steve Van Matre and Bill Weiler (Greenville, W.Va.: Institute for Earth Education, 1983), p. 45.

12. John Patrick Diggins, *The Promise of Pragmatism: Modernism and the Crisis of Knowledge and Authority* (Chicago: University of Chicago Press, 1994), p. 2.

13. Paul J. DiMaggio and Walter W. Powell, "Introduction," in *The New Institutionalism in Organizational Analysis*, ed. Walter W. Powell and Paul J. DiMaggio (Chicago: University of Chicago Press, 1991), pp. 1–38.

14. Kenneth L. Woodward, "A Time to Seek," *Newsweek*, 17 December 1990, p. 50. "What counts . . . if a church or synagogue is to attract its share of the . . . market," writes Woodward, "are the programs inside."

15. Douglas Davies, "Christianity," in *Sacred Place*, ed. Jean Holm with John Bowker (London: Pinter, 1994), p. 40; in an unsystematic analysis of hymn books, Davies suggests that images of heaven as a place became more common during the nineteenth century and remained so until the middle of the twentieth century, but by the 1980s these images had virtually disappeared.

16. Oscar Handlin, *The Uprooted* (New York: Little, Brown, 1951), p. 3.

17. Michael Walzer, *Thick and Thin: Moral Argument at Home and Abroad* (Notre Dame, Ind.: University of Notre Dame Press, 1994).

18. Jay B. McDaniel, *With Roots and Wings: Christianity in an Age of Ecology and Dialogue* (Maryknoll, N.Y.: Orbis Books, 1995).

2.   IN THE HOUSE OF THE LORD

1. Richard J. Foster, *Prayer: Finding the Heart's True Home* (San Francisco: Harper San Francisco, 1992), p. 1.

2. Themes of home and homesickness figure prominently in contemporary devotional and study guides; see Kent Ira Groff, *Active Spirituality: A Guide for Seekers and Ministers* (Washington, D.C.: Alban Institute, 1993).

3. Ned Stewart is a pseudonym. Like other interviewees mentioned in the text, his name has been altered and a few other distinguishing personal characteristics have been changed or withheld in order to protect his anonymity. As mentioned in the Preface, approximately two hundred people were interviewed. They are not a representative sample of a prespecified population. Rather, they were selected using a purposive quota design to ensure relatively equal numbers of men and women, younger and older people, and people from different socioeconomic strata, and to maximize diversity of religious backgrounds, current religious orientations, and racial or ethnic composition. They were interviewed using a semistructured interview guide (several different versions were used) that asked for a general account of the person's spiritual journey and then probed for specific responses to personal and public events and for involvement in various

religious and devotional activities. The themes around which the chapters of the book are organized (such as dwelling and seeking) were identified from analyzing the interviews rather than being preconceived and specifically addressed in the interviews. Each interview lasted approximately two hours. The interviews were taped and transcribed. Quotes from interviews have been edited slightly for grammar and clarity.

4. Davies, "Christianity." In the years immediately following World War II, Christians seemed particularly vulnerable to creating sacred spaces, prompting Heschel to warn that "God is not and cannot be localized" in the Christian manner—even as American Jews were constructing their own houses of worship in record numbers; Abraham Joshua Heschel, *Man's Quest for God: Studies in Prayer and Symbolism* (New York: Scribner's, 1954), p. 121.

5. James Bryce, *Reflections on American Institutions* (1888, reprint, Gloucester, Mass.: Peter Smith, 1970), p. 31.

6. David Freeman Hawke, *Everyday Life in Early America* (New York: Harper & Row, 1988), ch. 12.

7. Richard Tuck, "Rights and Pluralism," in *Philosophy in an Age of Pluralism: The Philosophy of Charles Taylor in Question,* ed. James Tully (Cambridge: Cambridge University Press, 1994), pp. 159–170.

8. Only later would many Americans learn of the intense devotion to the land that also characterized its earlier inhabitants. As one example, the Cherokee word *Eloheh* means both land and religion because a people's place on earth cannot be separated from their vision and meaning; Joseph Bruchec and Diana Landau, *Singing of Earth* (San Francisco: Walking Stick Press, 1993), p. 57.

9. Daniel J. Boorstin, *The Americans: The Colonial Experience* (New York: Vintage Books, 1958), p. 4.

10. Timothy L. Smith, "Congregation, State, and Denomination: The Forming of the American Religious Structure," *William and Mary Quarterly* 25 (1968): 155–162; Kai T. Erikson, *Wayward Puritans: A Study in the Sociology of Deviance* (New York: Wiley, 1966).

11. Harry S. Stout, "Ethnicity: The Vital Center of Religion in America," *Ethnicity* 2 (1975): 204–224.

12. Oscar Handlin and Mary F. Handlin, *Facing Life: Youth and the Family in American History* (Boston: Little, Brown, 1971), pp. 5–6.

13. From an interview with Marianne Brace, "Indian Tales and a Nickel for the Birds," *Independent,* 4 June 1994, 30.

14. Robert C. Ostergren, "The Immigrant Church as a Symbol of Community and Place in the Upper Midwest," *Great Plains Quarterly* 1 (1981): 225–238.

15. Robert F. Harney, "Religion and Ethnocultural Communities," *Polyphony* 1 (1978): 1.

16. Reprinted in Sidney E. Mead, *The Lively Experiment: The Shaping of Christianity in America* (New York: Harper, 1963), p. 15. Also: "He who would understand America must understand that through all the formative years, space has overshadowed time" (p. 11).

17. Jay P. Dolan, "The Immigrants and Their Gods: A New Perspective in American Religious History," *Church History* 57 (1988): 61–72.

18. For example, see Bruce M. Stave and John F. Sutherland, *From the Old Country: An Oral History of European Migration to America* (New York: Twayne, 1994).

19. Will Herberg, *Protestant, Catholic, Jew* (New York: Doubleday, 1955), p. 11.

20. How closely spirituality, church, and home were connected was evident in a survey conducted among women in Muncie, Indiana, in 1924: 69 percent said their mothers had taught them loyalty to the church while they were children living at home, and 50 percent said they were teaching this value to their own children. Another study, more than a half century later, helped put these findings in perspective. In that study (conducted in 1978), only 35 percent of mothers said they had been taught loyalty to the church, and only 22 percent said they were teaching it to their children. Anne Remley, "From Obedience to Independence," *Psychology Today*, October 1988, 56–59; Duane F. Alwin, "From Obedience to Autonomy: Changes in Traits Desired in Children, 1924–1978," *Public Opinion Quarterly* 52 (1988): 33–52.

21. James H. S. Bossard and Eleanor S. Boll, *Ritual in Family Living: A Contemporary Study* (Philadelphia: University of Pennsylvania Press, 1950). The study included one hundred autobiographies written between 1880 and 1950.

22. Ray Stannard Baker, *Native American* (New York: Scribner's, 1941), p. 31.

23. Mary P. Ryan, *Cradle of the Middle-Class: The Family in Oneida County, New York, 1790–1865* (New York: Cambridge University Press, 1981); Ruth Bloch, "American Feminine Ideals in Transition: The Rise of the Moral Mother, 1785–1815," *Feminist Studies* 4 (1978): 101–126; Rosemarie Zagarri, "Morals, Manners, and the Republican Mother," *American Quarterly* 44 (1992): 192–215; Janet Fishburn, *The Fatherhood of God and the Victorian Family: The Social Gospel in America* (Philadelphia: Fortress Press, 1981); Karen Halttunen, *Confidence Men and Painted Women: A Study of Middle-Class Culture in America, 1830–1870* (New Haven, Conn.: Yale University Press, 1982); Janet H. Hunter, "Inscribing the Self in the Heart of the Family: Diaries and Girlhood in Late-Victorian America," *American Quarterly* 44 (1992): 51–81.

24. Jack Larkin, *The Reshaping of Everyday Life, 1790–1840* (New York: Harper & Row, 1988), ch. 3; Colleen McDannell, *The Christian Home in Victorian America, 1840–1900* (Bloomington: Indiana University Press, 1986).

25. Henry Seidel Canby, *The Age of Confidence* (New York: Farrar & Reinhart, 1939), pp. 51–53.

26. This interlacing of spirituality with home, church, and community sometimes ran counter to the progressive, industrial culture in which Americans lived. Merchants and industrialists had urged individualism, a willingness to move on when prosperity beckoned, to abandon the familiar settlements of one's youth whenever the need arose. But Americans were also ambivalent about the machinations of railroad magnates, industrialists, and bankers. See Michael Paul Rogin, *Ronald Reagan, the Movie and Other Episodes in Political Demonology* (Berkeley: University of California Press, 1987), pp. 184–185; Michael Zuckerman, "Holy Wars, Civil Wars: Religion and Economics in Nineteenth-Century

America," *Prospects* 16 (1991): 205–240. Americans valued the stability and homogeneity of their communities. Their faith undergirded these values, sanctifying neighborliness, attachment to local churches, cooperation, and even a pastoral ideal—all of which conflicted with notions of market competition. Indeed, these local attachments—more than rampant individualism—figured prominently in the intermittent call of religious revivalists. One of their favorite invitational hymns intoned, "I've wandered far away from God, now I'm coming home." It continues, "I'm coming home, coming home, never more to roam." But those who favored the progressive mood of the early twentieth century also relied on spatial imagery, inscribing themselves within a sacred abode. Having abandoned the sterner, judgmental deity of their immigrant forebears, they felt at home with God and sometimes imagined themselves to be building God's kingdom in North America. Looking back over the past century at the close of the First World War, Santayana observed that the dominant thrust of nineteenth-century Americans had been to make themselves at home, both spiritually and materially. "The world, they felt, was a safe place, watched over by a kindly God, who exacted nothing but cheerfulness and good-will from his children; and the American flag was a sort of rainbow in the sky, promising that all storms were over." George Santayana, *Character and Opinion in the United States* (1920; reprint, New Brunswick, N.J.: Transaction, 1991), p. 14.

27. Ann Taves, *The Household of Faith: Roman Catholic Devotions in Mid-Nineteenth-Century America* (Notre Dame, Ind.: University of Notre Dame Press, 1986), p. 48. See also Robert A. Orsi, *Thank You, St. Jude: Women's Devotion to the Patron Saint of Hopeless Causes* (New Haven, Conn.: Yale University Press, 1996).

28. The familiar understanding of spirituality also emphasized *habit*. To dwell with God was not only to know God but to live in a space characterized by habits. *Habit* is derived from the same root as habitat and habitation. It connotes routine behavior that a person automatically possesses and that, in turn, possesses the person. It was, Hobbes wrote, "motion made more easy and ready by custom." Thomas Hobbes, *English Works* (Aalen, Germany: Scientia, 1966), p. 348. Thus, just as one creates a certain appearance or denotes a condition of life by wearing a habit, so one clothes oneself in customary behavior by acquiring habits. As the social psychologist Emory Bogardus explained, "Habit means to have. Habit gives possession. Nothing is well done until it is done by habit. Reliability and thoroughness depend on habit." Emory S. Bogardus, *Essentials of Social Psychology*, 4th ed. (Los Angeles: Jesse Ray Miller Press, 1923), pp. 45–46. Bogardus and other educators of his era urged parents to instill habits in their children. The family had this responsibility because habits needed to be acquired early in life. Habits were also most easily expressed and maintained at home—one's habitation. Home was familiar territory; its daily rituals of sleeping and eating, rising, working, and interacting reinforced the implicit norms that defined who one was. Not surprisingly, many parents emphasized that spirituality could also become familiar by cultivating regular habits of prayer and devotion. A spirituality of dwelling was thus habitual, embedded in the routines and rituals of domestic space. It defined the core of one's being so basically that

little thought needed to be given to these routines and rituals. Spirituality could therefore be taken for granted much of the time. Except when periodic reminders were required, it could function simply as an implicit part of one's outlook on the world.

29. Os Guiness, *The American Hour: A Time of Reckoning and the Once and Future Role of Faith* (New York: Free Press, 1993), p. 82.

30. Of course there had always been tension in U.S. Christianity concerning how broadly the Lord's house was to be conceived and, therefore, what the proper focus of individual spiritual practice should be. Those who considered themselves fundamentalists, evangelicals, pentecostalists, or pietists generally emphasized the sanctity of the individual soul, its need for regeneration, and the value of regular rites of spiritual cleansing, while those who emphasized the building of God's kingdom on earth favored spiritual activities deemed to be of some social as well as personal benefit. Fundamentalists often regarded the world as a dangerous place; accordingly, the role of prayer and Bible reading was to fend off temptation, and the house of God was quite literally a safe haven from the world. Those who considered social action beneficial often considered such devotion to one's personal needs a selfish form of retreat from the world; spirituality was better expressed on one's feet than on one's knees. Yet the tension between these different orientations was seldom taken to extremes. Mainline Protestant and Catholic church leaders who advocated social redemption also encouraged believers to pray regularly and to cultivate personal piety through daily rituals of religious observance.

31. Michael R. Weisser, *A Brotherhood of Memory: Jewish Landsmanshaftn in the New World* (New York: Basic Books, 1985).

32. David Halberstam, *The Fifties* (New York: Villard Books, 1993), p. 5.

33. For example, Whittaker Chambers, whose confession of communist sympathies before the House Un-American Activities Committee drew widespread attention in 1948, wrote in his personal memoir that his family had been social outcasts with "no friends, no social ties, no church, [and] no community." Quoted in Halberstam, *The Fifties,* p. 13.

34. For example, see Deborah Dash Moore, *To the Golden Cities: Pursuing the American Jewish Dream in Miami and L.A.* (New York: Free Press, 1994).

35. Premillennial theology takes various forms, but it generally emphasizes that Christ will return to earth and establish a thousand-year reign in which the righteous will be rewarded; in contrast, in postmillennial theology the second coming of Christ is assumed to follow a gradual emergence of human progress.

36. Theodore Caplow et al., *Recent Social Trends in the United States, 1960–1990* (Montreal: McGill-Queen's University Press, 1991), p. 289.

37. Gallup Poll (October 1956).

38. One leader, in a widely read interpretation of the current mood, explained that postwar Americans were "groping for a spiritual home." A. Roy Eckardt, *The Surge of Piety in America: An Appraisal* (New York: Association Press, 1958), p. 26; see also Herbert W. Schneider, *Religion in 20th Century America* (Cambridge, Mass.: Harvard University Press, 1952), p. 189.

39. David Riesman, *The Lonely Crowd: A Study of the Changing American Character* (1950; reprint, New Haven, Conn.: Yale University Press, 1961).

40. Denise Levertov, "Mass for the Day of St. Thomas Didymus," excerpted in *Cries of the Spirit: A Celebration of Women's Spirituality,* ed. Marilyn Sewell (Boston: Beacon Press, 1991), pp. 225–226.

41. Throughout much of its history, organized religion had actively fought noninstitutionalized forms of popular piety, branding them as heresy and attempting to assert itself as mediator rather than encouraging believers to interact directly with God or to define spirituality in their own way. In Spain, France, and Russia, for instance, traditional folk beliefs, magic, witchcraft, and devotion to local saints were long prevalent in rural areas, despite efforts by clergy to combat them. See Marie-Hélène Froeschlé-Chopard, "Les dévotions populaires d'après les visites pastorales: Un example: le diocèse de Vence au début du XVIIIe siècle," *Revue d'histoire de l'église de France* 60 (1974): 85–99; William A. Christian, Jr., *Person and God in a Spanish Valley* (New York: Seminar Press, 1972). In the United States, these traditional practices had never been as strong as in countries with long histories of feudal and peasant-landlord relationships. During the early nineteenth century, churchly religion had also become democratized, extending into the frontier regions and drawing new settlers into the new denominations through revivalism. See Nathan O. Hatch, *The Democratization of American Christianity* (New Haven, Conn.: Yale University Press, 1989). During the remainder of the century, immigrant churches monopolized popular piety by providing a focal point for immigrant communities. In Catholic circles, devotionalism was also carefully regulated by the church. Prayers printed in devotional guidebooks were officially approved, and many were associated with congregational worship. See Taves, *Household of Faith,* p. 29.

42. James Turner, *Without God, without Creed: The Origins of Unbelief in America* (Baltimore: Johns Hopkins University Press, 1985).

43. As if evidence of the intensity of these struggles were needed, in 1958 one of the first systematic surveys focusing on religious beliefs and practices was conducted in Detroit, and its author concluded that white Protestants, black Protestants, Catholics, and Jews were extensively involved with their own religious communities and expressed their faith largely within these communities. Examining the geographic patterns in Detroit, he concluded that the different faiths lived mostly in different parts of the city and associated their faith with the spaces in which they lived. There were also strong pressures to keep things that way. See Gerhard Lenski, *The Religious Factor: A Sociological Study of Religion's Impact on Politics, Economics, and Family Life* (Garden City, N.Y.: Doubleday, 1961), p. 41. Church builders worried that people would be lured away by alternate amusements if church buildings themselves did not keep up to date and if programs did not draw people into church activities: as one authority observed in 1957, "The first requirement of a church or temple today is that it be of today, contemporary, a structure embracing the total life of the parishioner." Otto Spaeth, founder of the Liturgical Arts Society, quoted in Edwin Scott Gaustad, *A Religious History of America* (New York: Harper & Row, 1966), p. 307. And religious construction did expand enormously, rising from $500 million in 1950 to more than $1.2 billion in 1965 (adjusted for inflation). Robert Wuthnow, *Experimentation in American Religion* (Berkeley: University of California Press, 1978), pp. 120–121. A church planner for one mainline Protestant

denomination recalled that five times as many new churches were built each year during the 1950s than during any year after 1965; Robert S. Hoyt, "The End of the Christian Century" (paper presented at the Symposium on Ending the Christian Century, Northwestern Pennsylvania Synod of the Evangelical Lutheran Church in America, Thiel College, 1994). Church construction significantly shaped understandings of spirituality itself, providing encouragement for the idea that spirituality and the construction of houses of worship were synonymous. "There was so much money," a church consultant told me, "that we got the idea of thinking about spirituality in terms of larger organizations." Not only were local churches built, but denominations were able to buy buildings to house national offices and to develop a cadre of bureaucrats to staff these offices. The successful administrator was the one who could hire more staff and create a more elaborate organizational chart.

44. For example, a woman who was a child when her mother became interested in spiritualism remembers how hard it was for her mother to cultivate this interest. None of the established churches in town, Protestant or Catholic, would have anything to do with it nor would the sectarian churches. Her mother was reduced to borrowing books about spiritualism from the library and reading them in private until she eventually lost enthusiasm for the project.

45. Among other illustrative works, see Jim Lilliefors, *Highway 50: Ain't That America* (Golden, Colo.: Fulcrum, 1993).

46. Arthur R. Vidich and Joseph Bensman, *Small Town in Mass Society: Class, Power, and Religion in a Rural Community* (Princeton, N.J.: Princeton University Press, 1958), p. 231.

47. Herbert Gans, "Progress of a Suburban Jewish Community," *Commentary*, February 1957, 120. Among Catholics in Chicago, similar changes were evident; see Orsi, *Thank You, St. Jude*.

48. Irving Howe, *World of Our Fathers* (New York: Harcourt Brace Jovanovich, 1976), p. 615.

49. As descendants of immigrants, Americans held distinctive notions of what homes—temporal or spiritual—should be. Through their stories of pilgrims and their biblical traditions, U.S. Christians and Jews had always identified with Abram's journey from the Caldees to the Promised Land. Home was not just any place but a special location that had been divinely appointed. It was less a place of nostalgia, defined by the *nostos*, or journey of return, that characterized Odysseus, for example, than a place of hope that was given literally by the indwelling of the sacred. "It is as if the 'abstract' home we carried with us in our wanderings could possess and inhere in the actual houses we built, as if they were thereby somehow ensouled"; John Hollander, "It All Depends," in *Home: A Place in the World*, ed. Arien Mack (New York: New York University Press, 1993), pp. 36–37.

50. The word *home* is sometimes thought to have originated in the Indo-European root *kei*, meaning to lie or settle, from which comes the Greek word *khomi*, implying a settlement, a commune, or a neighborly mode of dwelling.

51. For more than a century, clergy had championed the home as a sacred place where weary believers could withdraw from the dangers of the world, especially the city with its debauchery, crime, and moral laxity, so it was scarcely

out of character for clergy in the 1950s to draw on homes for imagery about how best to dwell with God. Within the home, husbands could find refreshment from their day's work, children could learn Bible verses and good behavior, and wives could fulfill the high calling of mother and household manager. One pastor expressed the common view, writing that the home was "a safe and alluring shelter for yourselves amid the vicissitudes of life, becoming more and more the abode of peace and love as the world grows dark without." William M. Thayer, *Pastor's Wedding Gift* (Boston, 1854), p. 36; quoted in Kirk Jeffrey, "The Family as a Utopian Retreat from the City: The Nineteenth Century Contribution," *Soundings: An Interdisciplinary Journal* 55 (1972): 26.

52. The familiar line in Robert Frost's poem "The Death of the Hired Man" asserts that "home is the place where, when you have to go there, they have to take you in." It is uttered by a man. Less familiar, but more insightful, is his wife's reply: "I should have called it something you somehow haven't to deserve." The husband's statement, Frost himself explained on one occasion, was meant to suggest the rights and responsibilities normally expected of family members. The wife's was less conditional. "The mother way. You don't have to deserve your mother's love. You have to deserve your father's. He's more particular." Quoted in Richard Poirier, *Robert Frost: The Work of Knowing* (New York: Oxford University Press, 1977), pp. 254–255.

53. My analysis of data collected in 1992 as part of research on religion and economic values; the questions and methods are described in Robert Wuthnow, *God and Mammon in America* (New York: Free Press, 1994).

54. Quoted in Jenna Weissman Joselit, *The Wonders of America: Reinventing Jewish Culture, 1880–1950* (New York: Hill & Wang, 1994), p. 6.

55. Margaret M. Poloma and George H. Gallup, Jr., *Varieties of Prayer* (Philadelphia: Trinity Press International, 1991), p. 3.

56. Many of these guides emphasized devotion to Mary, who in turn symbolized the church. Thus, one writer suggests that "the worship of Mary . . . transformed [the church] from the *place* of worship to the *object* of worship"; Gerhard Ebeling, *The Word of God and Tradition: Historical Studies Interpreting the Divisions of Christianity* (London: William Collins Sons, 1968), p. 187.

57. Quoted in Gaustad, *Religious History of America*, p. 286.

58. The spirituality of homes and congregations was also reinforced by the mass media. Popular evangelist Billy Graham, for example, publicized a brand of spirituality that stressed dwelling with God as much as it did individual salvation. His revivals encouraged Americans to make a personal commitment to Jesus and to a life based on obedience to the Bible. Critics accused him of encouraging a privatized, otherworldly concern with eternal life to the point that believers were no longer interested in the great social reforms that had animated liberal Christianity during the preceding half century and evangelicals during the century before that. Some church leaders also predicted that his revivals would diminish the public's interest in playing an active role in their institutions. But Graham's theology and his popular appeal were consistent with the broader orientations in U.S. religion. Like seven-year-old Ned Stewart, Graham emphasized a spirituality of dwelling, telling his audiences that heaven was a place "as real as Los Angeles, London, Algiers, or Boston" and describing it in homey terms:

"we are going to sit around the fireplace and have parties and the angels will wait on us." Quoted in William Martin, *A Prophet with Honor: The Billy Graham Story* (New York: Morrow, 1991), pp. 125–126. Graham's success, moreover, came from working with church leaders, Protestants and Catholics alike, rather than against them. If his brand of spirituality was private and personal, it nevertheless encouraged converts to find God on Sunday mornings in their preferred houses of worship. See William G. McLoughlin, Jr., *Billy Graham: Revivalist in a Secular Age* (New York: Ronald Press, 1960). In comparison with spirituality in more recent decades, when it is defined in the wider culture by poets, popular writers, and other figures outside organized religion, popular spirituality in the 1950s was closely identified with prominent religious figures: Norman Vincent Peale was the pastor of Marble Collegiate Church in New York City; Fulton Sheen was a Catholic bishop; Reinhold Niebuhr taught at Union Theological Seminary in New York City and spent his weekends traveling to speak at local churches; Charles E. Fuller's popular radio broadcasts reminded listeners that Fuller was also the name of a theological seminary. Even in the social sciences, leading students of U.S. religion such as Joseph Fichter, Thomas O'Dea, and Peter Berger were church members or priests interested chiefly in the well-being of religious institutions. If the public took its cues about spirituality from prominent figures, therefore, it had little reason to look any further than organized religion.

59. Paul C. Glick, "A Demographer Looks at American Families," *Journal of Marriage and the Family* 37 (1975): 15–26.

60. U.S. Bureau of the Census, *Statistical Abstract of the United States: 1980* (Washington, D.C.: Government Printing Office, 1980), p. 62.

61. Charles Y. Glock, Benjamin B. Ringer, and Earl R. Babbie, *To Comfort and to Challenge: A Dilemma of the Contemporary Church* (Berkeley: University of California Press, 1967), ch. 3.

62. Bert N. Adams, *Kinship in an Urban Setting* (Chicago: Markham, 1968), a report of research conducted in 1963; Claude S. Fischer, "The Dispersion of Kinship Ties in Modern Society: Contemporary Data and Historical Speculation," *Journal of Family History* 7 (1982): 353–375.

63. Ethel Shanas, "Social Myth as Hypothesis: The Case of the Family Relations of Old People," *Gerontologist* 19 (1979): 3–9.

64. Magazine articles encouraged the father to be a family man, to devote more time to his children, and to spend more time at home; for some examples, see Donald Katz, *Home Fires: An Intimate Portrait of One Middle-Class Family in Postwar America* (New York: HarperCollins, 1992), p. 75.

65. Halberstam, *The Fifties*, p. 509.

66. Herberg, *Protestant, Catholic, Jew*, p. 59.

67. Brett Harvey, *The Fifties: A Women's Oral History* (New York: Harper Collins, 1993), esp. ch. 6.

68. Mary Douglas, "The Idea of a Home: A Kind of Space," in *Home: A Place in the World*, ed. Arien Mack (New York: New York University Press, 1993), p. 263. She observes that an important way homes bring space under control is by storing. Odds and ends can be placed in storerooms—pantries, milk houses, wine cellars, and potato sheds—to meet future needs. Householders'

preparations in the home became a tale of good and bad. Had enough fuel been laid in for a harsh winter? Was food sufficient when visitors arrived unexpectedly? There was an implicit bargain with nature: good, responsible behavior could be counted on to bring favorable outcomes in the future.

69. In a notable study of the Catholic family, Jesuit sociologist John Thomas observed that habits alone could not withstand the pressures of external social forces. The family, buttressed by the parish and parochial schools, he argued, needed to "encompass the individual with strong emotional bonds" and thus become the social basis for conformity to Catholic norms; John L. Thomas, *The American Catholic Family* (Englewood Cliffs, N.J.: Prentice-Hall, 1956), p. 350.

70. Gallup Poll (November 16, 1954). Although the fear of communism was clearly its principal cause, interest in the nation as a spiritual entity was becoming a notable feature of U.S. culture in a variety of ways. In his survey of U.S. literature, Kazin observed that the decades prior to World War II had witnessed a growing obsession with the national identity. "Whole divisions of writers now fell upon the face of America with a devotion that was baffled rather than shrill, and an insistence to know and to love what it knew that seemed unprecedented"; Alfred Kazin, *On Native Grounds: An Interpretation of Modern American Prose Literature* (1942; reprint, New York: Harcourt Brace, 1982), p. 486. Among them were Van Wyck Brooks, whose *Flowering of New England* represented an elegiac piety toward the past, the Work Projects Administration writers and documentary reporters who sought to detail the land and its people, and such widely read authors as Erskine Caldwell, James Agee, and Walker Evans. Favorite themes included prosaic descriptions of ordinary people and of the land, the scenic glory of the West, small towns, the plight of Dust Bowl farmers, and forgotten heroes such as Abraham Lincoln, Benjamin Franklin, Davy Crockett, Paul Bunyan, Mike Fink, and Johnny Appleseed. The 1950s inherited this legacy. Adults had been reared on classroom renditions of thirties' literature. Their understandings of spirituality were influenced not only by their experiences at worship services but also by the stories of pioneers and lumberjacks who combined simple faith and occasional prayers with hard work, devotion to family, and deep pride in their native land.

71. Reinhold Niebuhr, *The Irony of American History* (New York: Scribner's, 1952), p. 3.

72. These were ways to "cosmicize" the world, as Eliade observed. "Religious man's profound nostalgia," he wrote, "is to inhabit a 'divine world' [and to believe] that his house shall be like the house of the gods." To live without a "pure and holy cosmos," Eliade warned, is to live with chaos and to experience the "terror of nothingness." In a desacralized world, where a sacred cosmos could no longer be taken for granted, it was thus imperative that people should "imitate the work of the gods" by situating themselves in sacred space. In this way, Eliade suggested, modern man "not only cosmicizes chaos but also sanctifies his little cosmos by making it like the world of the gods"; Mircea Eliade, *The Sacred and the Profane: The Nature of Religion,* trans. Willard Trask (1957; reprint, New York: Harcourt Brace, 1989, p. 65).

73. Herberg, *Protestant, Catholic, Jew,* p. 260.

74. Georg Lukacs, *The Theory of the Novel,* trans. Anna Bostock (1920; reprint, Cambridge, Mass.: MIT Press, 1971), p. 30.

75. The 1950s were widely regarded as a time of religious revival; see Reinhold Niebuhr, "Is There a Revival of Religion?" *New York Times Magazine*, 10 November 1950; W. H. Hudson, "Are Churches Really Booming?" *Christian Century* 77 (December 21, 1955): 1494–1496; Seymour Martin Lipset, "Religion in America: What Religious Revival?" *Columbia University Forum* 2 (winter 1959): 1–5.

76. Writing of the "religious establishment" that had grown so powerful during the preceding decade, Berger observed in 1961 that "the main approach [of religious leaders] to the social world is one of affirming the *status quo* and of seeking to harmonize whatever forces tend to disturb it." He added, "It would require a good satirical pen indeed to describe the embarrassment that would be caused . . . by the appearance of anyone claiming to have had a genuine encounter with the supernatural"; Peter L. Berger, *The Noise of Solemn Assemblies: Christian Commitment and the Religious Establishment in America* (Garden City, N.Y.: Doubleday, 1961), pp. 45–47.

77. U.S. Bureau of the Census, *Statistical Abstract . . . 1960* and *1980*. U.S. Bureau of the Census, *U.S. City and County Databook* (Washington, D.C.: U.S. Government Printing Office, 1949 and 1986).

78. As congregations became larger, commitment did not diminish numerically, but it did become qualitatively different. A national sample of nearly three hundred thousand congregations (Catholic and Protestant) in 1987 showed that 22 percent of those founded between 1951 and 1970 could be classified as "large," compared with only 11 percent of those founded between 1931 and 1950; mixing of Protestant congregations and Catholic parishes makes it difficult, however, to know how reliable these figures are. Virginia A. Hodgkinson, Murray S. Weitzman, and Arthur D. Kirsch, *From Belief to Commitment: The Activities and Finances of Religious Congregations in the United States* (Washington, D.C.: Independent Sector, 1988), p. 9.

Data from one national study showed that Protestants who attended larger churches were different from Protestants who attended smaller ones in many ways. They attached less importance to their communities; although they had changed jobs more often, they knew their co-workers better than their neighbors; they were less likely to view their church as a refuge from the world and less likely to say that people in their congregation cared about them; and even though they attended services just as often, they were less likely to have talked to a member of the clergy about stress and more likely to have joined a support group to deal with stress. They were also more likely to have sought professional help for financial troubles than to have taken these problems to their pastor; indeed, members of large congregations were just as likely to have taken financial problems to a therapist as to a member of the clergy, whereas members of small or medium-sized congregations were three times more likely to have taken these concerns to the clergy than to therapists. These results are from my 1992 Economic Values Survey (Wuthnow, *God and Mammon in America*). Conclusions are drawn from an analysis of Protestant church members (Catholics were excluded because size of parish is a less meaningful measure than size of congregation); all persons in the study were working full- or part-time. In a comparison of members of congregations with one thousand or more members with those in congregations smaller than two hundred members, those in large congregations were 12 percent less likely than those in small congregations to say their community was very important to them, 8 percent more likely to have worked at six or more different jobs, 16 percent more likely to say they know their co-workers better than their neighbors, 12 percent less likely to say that escaping daily cares is an important reason why they go to church, 12 percent less likely to say that people caring about them at church is a reason for going, no different on likelihood of attending church weekly, 7 percent less likely to talk with clergy about stress, 3 percent more likely to attend a support group for stress (or, in relative terms, twice as likely to do this), 8 percent less likely to talk to clergy about finances, and 5 percent more likely to discuss finances with a therapist.

79. Robert Wuthnow, *The Restructuring of American Religion: Society and Faith since World War II* (Princeton, N.J.: Princeton University Press, 1988), ch. 2. Among other things, these changes made it increasingly difficult for Americans to settle into their congregations for a lifetime and to make friends who would maintain the plausibility of their world-view. In one national study, those who grew up before 1960 were significantly more likely than respondents in two younger cohorts to say that their best friends were members of their own faith and, indeed, of their own congregation. These results are from my analysis of the 1988 General Social Survey (Chicago: National Opinion Research Center, machine-readable data file). In the cohort born before 1946, for example, 30 percent of Protestants said their best friend was a member of their own congregation (70 percent identified this friend as a Protestant), whereas among those born between 1946 and 1958, only 22 percent did so (60 percent said this friend was a Protestant), and, in the cohort born after 1958, 17 percent said their best friend was from their congregation (and 52 percent said he or she was a fellow Protestant). Patterns for second and third friends and among Catholics and Jews were similar. The same study revealed the social factors most responsible for this loosening of friendship ties: people who had attained college degrees were significantly less likely to say their friends were from their congregation than people who had not attended college (graduate degrees contributed further loosening), and people (a majority) who had ever lapsed in religious membership were much less likely to have a friend in their congregation.

80. If congregational friendship can be interpreted as an indication that one's spirituality is anchored in a particular place, the ways a spirituality of this kind differs from a more free-floating spirituality can be observed in the same study: people with a friend in their congregation were significantly more likely than those whose best friend did not belong to their congregation to say that it was very important to follow the church's teachings, to attach high value to attending church regularly, to say they paid attention to church teachings in making personal decisions, and to regard God as a judgmental figure. In short, they were more likely to grant the church a monopoly over their spirituality. But the less churched did not lack spirituality altogether. Indeed, they were as likely to believe in an afterlife or to have had a powerful religious experience, and they were only modestly less likely to feel close to God and to pray regularly. Exact percentages for those whose best friend was in their congregation and those whose best friend was not in their congregation, respectively, were: said it was important to follow the church's teachings, 48 and 30; said these teachings were important in their own decisions, 49 and 26; said it was important to attend church

regularly, 47 and 26; regarded God as a judge, 44 and 34; believed in an after-life, 78 and 78; had had a powerful religious experience, 34 and 33; felt at least somewhat close to God, 92 and 85; and prayed at least several times a week, 84 and 72. Data from my analysis of a 1988 Gallup survey.

Another study demonstrates the impact of socially broadening experiences on conventional congregational commitments: by the late 1980s, 76 percent of the respondents said it is possible to be a good Christian or Jew without attending religious services—itself evidence of how pervasive the idea that spirituality can be practiced apart from congregations had become. But further analysis shows only a 51 percent positive response among persons whose social characteristics most closely emulated those of the 1950s (members of an older birth cohort who had no college education and whose religious membership had never lapsed), while it rose to 91 percent among those most influenced by social trends after the 1950s (younger birth cohort, college graduates, and those whose membership had lapsed temporarily). There is also reason to sus-pect that the connection between spirituality and place may be weakening even for those who do stay put. Older Americans who have lived in their present neighborhoods for at least ten years are likely to have been members of their present religious congregations for at least ten years, whereas younger cohorts who have also been stable residents of their neighborhoods are much less likely to have remained members of the same congregation. Older people who are in-tegrated into their communities—have more friends in their neighborhoods—are likely to have been long-time members of their present congregation, whereas younger people who are equally integrated into their communities are less likely to have remained in the same congregation. This is my analysis of data collected in 1991 for a study of small groups; Robert Wuthnow, *Sharing the Journey: Support Groups and America's New Quest for Community* (New York: Free Press, 1994). Results are for persons who were members of some kind of small group. Of course cohort differences may not imply historical trends. But the evidence suggests a tendency for people to dislocate themselves from particular religious communities even if they do not do so for geographic reasons.

The results of a study that projected the future of new congregations are also revealing. Based on more than fifteen hundred computer-generated "imagine areas," each with a radius of fifteen miles, the study concluded that regional churches will increasingly replace neighborhood churches because of the grow-ing diversity of local areas. Rather than participating in a tight-knit membership community, the average parishioner will commute considerable distances to so-called magnet ministries that attract people because of specialized programs. Whether such congregations can dominate spirituality the way local neighbor-hood churches and synagogues did in the 1950s is questionable. Summarized in Hoyt, "The End of the Christian Century," p. 9.

81. Arlene Skolnick, *Embattled Paradise: The American Family in an Age of Uncertainty* (New York: Basic Books, 1991), pp. 49–50.

82. Whereas a third had young children in 1960, for instance, fewer than one fifth did by 1980. U.S. Bureau of the Census, *Statistical Abstract . . . 1980*, p. 41.

83. That spirituality was no longer as tightly connected with family as it once was is suggested by a study conducted in 1982 that asked a national sample of respondents about various sources of self-esteem. Older birth cohorts did not differ from younger ones much in the extent to which they said "family" was an important source of self-esteem or in the extent to which they said self-esteem is about "your relation to God." Yet these two sources of self-esteem were more strongly associated with each other among the older cohorts than among the younger ones, an indication that older people were more likely to think of God and home as being connected than were younger people. From the Self-Esteem Survey, conducted by the Gallup Organization in 1982; my analysis. (Using gamma as a measure of association, the two items were related at the .615 level among persons age fifty or over, .534 among persons age thirty to forty-nine, and .435 among persons age eighteen to twenty-nine.)

Another indication of how changing family patterns may have contributed to the decline of institutional religion relative to personalized spirituality is evident in data that compare the proportions of people with various life-styles who attend religious services regularly with the proportions who say they have thought a lot about their relationship with God during the past year. The ratio provides a rough sense of how well institutional religion may monopolize the urge to think about God among various segments of the population. Ratios of one or higher indicate that institutional religion is doing relatively well, whereas scores of less than one suggest an interest in spirituality that extends beyond institutional religion. For married people, parents with two children living at home, and women who are employed only part-time, institutional religion has relatively high scores, while scores are lower for single, widowed, divorced, and separated people; people with no children or with only one child living at home; and women working full-time—categories that have all grown substantially since the 1950s. The data are my own calculations from the Economic Values Survey I conducted in 1992; Wuthnow, *God and Mammon in America.*

84. Robert N. Bellah, "No Direction Home—Religious Aspects of the American Crisis," in *Search for the Sacred: The New Spiritual Quest,* ed. Myron B. Bloy, Jr. (New York: Seabury, 1972), p. 64. See also Peter L. Berger, Brigitte Berger, and Hansfried Kellner, *The Homeless Mind: Modernization and Consciousness* (New York: Random House, 1973), pp. 184–185. Speaking as much for his readers as for himself, Berger wrote that "homelessness . . . has become metaphysical"—a development that "is very difficult to bear." Berger had formulated a widely read vision of religion as a "sacred canopy." Peter L. Berger, *The Sacred Canopy: Elements of a Sociological Theory of Religion* (Garden City, N.Y.: Doubleday, 1967). The imagery was that of a place, a secure dwelling in which to commune with God, but it was more abstract and inclusive than the spiritual homes in which Americans had lived in the 1950s. Indeed, one way of understanding Berger's interest in the sacred canopy is as an effort to conceive of spirituality in a way that would retain the appeal of a sacred place but without the constraints of the religious establishment. In this effort, Berger revealed more clearly than any writer in the fifties how a spirituality of place was maintained—and thus how changing social conditions would undermine the sacred canopy's foundations. A sacred canopy is an intellectual shield against

harm, especially the terror of meaninglessness. Although the angel of death cannot literally be kept out, one's home is impregnable if an interpretation can be found to make sense of all evil. A sacred canopy is also a place where chaos is kept at bay. Order means having a place for everything and having everything in its place. It is a unitary place that operates according to rules pertaining universally to those within it. It is threatened by uncertainty about the rules and by multiple conceptions of ultimate value. A sacred canopy must also be maintained, which means interacting with others who share the same conception of the world. Spiritual practice must be communal, so congregations, homes, and communities also help maintain the plausibility of one's universe. Above all, spirituality is a tent over daily life. When the social space in which a sacred canopy has been maintained starts to change, questions invariably arise about its adequacy. Not only the mind, but the soul as well, senses that it is homeless.

85. Kai T. Erikson, *Everything in Its Path: Destruction of Community in the Buffalo Creek Flood* (New York: Simon & Schuster, 1976).

86. William Paulson, "Hearth and Homelessness: Place, Story, and Novel in Flaubert's Sentimental Educations," in *Home and Its Dislocations in Nineteenth-Century France,* ed. Suzanne Nash (Albany: State University of New York Press, 1993), p. 87.

87. Kathleen Norris, *Dakota: A Spiritual Geography* (New York: Ticknor and Fields, 1993), pp. 92–93.

88. The examples given in the text are drawn from my own visit to Iona and from Gordon Legge, "Celtic Revival," *Calgary Herald,* 11 June 1994, 1–2.

89. Joseph Campbell with Bill Moyers, *The Power of Myth,* ed. Betty Sue Flowers (New York: Doubleday, 1988).

90. Thomas Bender, "Making Places Sacred," in *The Power of Place: Sacred Ground in Natural and Human Environments,* ed. James A. Swan (Wheaton, Ill.: Quest Books, 1991), p. 323.

91. Ibid., p. 332.

92. Wendell Berry, *What Are People For?* (San Francisco: North Point Press, 1990), p. 155.

93. Richard Feather Anderson, "Geomancy," in *The Power of Place: Sacred Ground in Natural and Human Enviroments,* ed. James A. Swan (Wheaton, Ill.: Quest Books, 1991), p. 195.

3. THE NEW SPIRITUAL FREEDOM

1. The Second Vatican Council was favorably received among American Catholics, more than two-thirds of whom said they approved of the changes effected by the Council. Andrew M. Greeley, *The American Catholic: A Social Portrait* (New York: Basic Books, 1976), p. 130.

2. Charles Y. Glock and Robert N. Bellah, eds., *The New Religious Consciousness* (Berkeley: University of California Press, 1976).

3. Research on changing religious patterns during the 1960s is presented in Robert Wuthnow, *The Consciousness Reformation* (Berkeley: University of California Press, 1976), and in Robert Wuthnow, *Experimentation in American Religion* (Berkeley: University of California Press, 1978). For a narrative

overview, see Robert S. Ellwood, *The Sixties Spiritual Awakening: American Religion Moving from Modern to Postmodern* (New Brunswick, N.J.: Rutgers University Press, 1994).

4. On baby-boomer religion, see Dean R. Hoge, Benton Johnson, and Donald A. Luidens, *Vanishing Boundaries: The Religion of Mainline Protestant Baby Boomers* (Louisville, Ky.: Westminster/John Knox, 1994), and Wade Clark Roof, *A Generation of Seekers: The Spiritual Journeys of the Baby Boom Generation* (San Francisco: Harper San Francisco, 1993).

5. For the most part, middle-class Americans seemed less intent on practicing a deep personal piety than did members of working-class communities, as did third-generation Americans compared with first- or second-generation immigrants. See Lenski, *The Religious Factor,* pp. 57–60. Movement into the middle class and the erosion of ethnic ties were thus expected to result in increased secularity—not necessarily associated with absolute declines in church membership but with the movement toward the bland, comfortable, conformist faith that Herberg (*Protestant, Catholic, Jew*) found among third-generation Americans.

6. Heschel, *Man's Quest for God,* p. xi. Some observers thought that personal spirituality would increase, perhaps especially among Catholics, as a result of growing emphasis on the contemplative life within the church itself. See John Tracy Ellis, *American Catholicism* (Chicago: University of Chicago Press, 1956), pp. 133–136. Their predictions, however, were drawn from modest increases in membership in the contemplative orders and from the popularity of Thomas Merton's writings. It was not clear how these influences might translate into devotional activities within the wider population.

7. Thomas Jefferson, *Revisal of the Laws: Drafts of Legislation, A Bill for Establishing Religious Freedom,* 1776, Section I.

8. For example, Winter likened the new religious movements to the mendicant experiments of the Middle Ages; Gibson Winter, *Being Free: Reflections on America's Cultural Revolution* (New York: Macmillan, 1970), pp. 93–96. Cox noted the similarity between youth rock festivals and earlier "feasts of fools"; Harvey Cox, *The Feast of Fools: A Theological Essay on Festivity and Fantasy* (New York: Harper & Row, 1969).

9. Edward E. Plowman, *The Underground Church* (Elgin, Ill.: David C. Cook, 1971).

10. Durkheim, *Elementary Forms of the Religious Life.*

11. Friedman, whose widely read *Capitalism and Freedom* was published just prior to the upheaval of the late 1960s, explained the connection between conscience and freedom when he wrote that free people are "proud of a common heritage and loyal to common traditions" and when he warned that the chief threat to the "rare and delicate plant" of freedom is "the concentration of power"; Milton Friedman, *Capitalism and Freedom* (Chicago: University of Chicago Press, 1962), p. 2.

12. Norman Mailer, "The White Negro: Superficial Reflections on the Hipster," in *Legacy of Dissent,* ed. Nicolaus Mills (1957; reprint, New York: Touchstone, 1994), esp. pp. 168–171.

13. Martin Luther King, Jr., *Stride toward Freedom: The Montgomery Story* (New York: Harper & Row, 1958).

14. Martin Luther King, Jr., "I Have a Dream," August 28, 1963; electronic text prepared by National Public Telecomputing Network (NPTN).

15. Joseph R. Washington, Jr., *Black Religion: The Negro and Christianity in the United States* (Boston: Beacon Press, 1964), p. 257.

16. Ibid., p. 266.

17. Jack Kerouac, *On the Road* (New York: Viking Press, 1957), p. 6.

18. "All of a sudden church took on a whole different meaning for me," Jim explains. "I was doing things because *I* wanted to do them. I started seeing myself in a different light. I guess that's the best way to say it. In other words, at that time I accepted the fact that I had a divine purpose for existing, that the Lord was actively involved in my life, that I mattered. It was just a spiritual consciousness. I felt a relationship with the Lord, an ongoing, close relationship."

19. Among the many studies that have described these influences, two that provide especially revealing information from interviews and firsthand observation are Mary Jo Weaver, *New Catholic Women* (Bloomington: Indiana University Press, 1995), and Cynthia Eller, *Living in the Lap of the Goddess: The Feminist Spirituality Movement in America* (New York: Crossroad, 1993).

20. Carol Gilligan, *In a Different Voice: Psychological Theory and Women's Development* (Cambridge, Mass.: Harvard University Press, 1982); Mary Field Belenky et al., *Women's Ways of Knowing: The Development of Self, Voice, and Mind* (New York: Basic Books, 1986).

21. Elizabeth A. Johnson, *She Who Is: The Mystery of God in Feminist Theological Discourse* (New York: Crossroad, 1993); Christie Cozad Neuger, ed., *The Arts of Ministry: Feminist-Womanist Approaches* (Louisville, Ky.: Westminster/John Knox, 1996); Sara Maitland, *A Big-Enough God: A Feminist's Search for Joyful Theology* (New York: Holt, Rinehart & Winston, 1995); Elisabeth Schussler Fiorenza, *Bread Not Stone: The Challenge of Feminist Biblical Interpretation* (Boston: Beacon Press, 1995).

22. It is important not to exaggerate the impact of feminist spirituality at the grass-roots level however. Among our interviewees, a majority claimed to have been influenced in some way by feminist thinking, but its impact was much more in reinforcing convictions about equal opportunities for women, rights, and freedom of choice than about concepts of God, theology, or religious practice. Women who said they had been particularly influenced by it also emphasized how it had empowered them to become stronger individuals and thus to feel more confident about their own decisions. Wilma Nichols's comments were, in this respect, typical. "I was very much moved by the feminist movement. I was very inspired by the feminist movement. However, I didn't like some of the earlier leaders. I, at this point, can't really think of names, but I felt that striving for equality for women is necessary and should be! It's a given, it should be. It made me feel somewhat stronger to know that women's rights were a major concern of my culture, my society, and my era. When I was younger, I felt that my problems were not really societal, but then that was because I was too caught up in my own difficulties. As I got older I said yes, my problems are societal." A Catholic woman, age forty-five, offered this comment: "I believe especially the Catholic church is still bound in their old thoughts with that, but I think it helped at least for myself as a woman to realize I'm just as important and can be a ve-

hicle of God's love as [much as] any man can be. As much as people will gripe about it, I think it's raised the awareness and consciousness. Bob and I get into it because he's not real fond of the really strong feminist, and I think I'm a feminist." A Jewish man, age fifty, also provided an illustrative comment. "It has to do with being married to a woman who's interested in those issues. One of the things I've come to see is that I've come to have an appreciation for that kind of strength. One of the things I like about Judaism is that there seems to be, at least in the strains of Judaism that I find interesting, a real support for that position—women who take important roles and are themselves strong people and make their own lives. There's a real tradition of that in Judaism that perhaps is less common in some other religious groups."

23. Michael Novak, *The Experience of Nothingness* (New York: Harper & Row, 1970), p. 4.

24. These shifts are evident in popular interpretations of the writings of Peter Berger and Thomas Luckmann; in Bellah, "No Direction Home"; and in the works of scholars such as Norman O. Brown, R. D. Laing, Theodore Roszak, and Herbert Marcuse.

25. U.S. Bureau of the Census, *Statistical Abstract . . . 1992*, p. 559.

26. In 1958, there were approximately twenty-seven hundred bookstores across the country, and more than half reported only modest sales; by 1977, more than ten thousand bookstores were in operation, those with modest sales made up less than a third of the total, and chain stores were rapidly taking a large share of the market. Paul D. Doebler, "Growth and Development of Consumer Bookstores since 1954—An Update through 1977," in *Book Industry Trends: 1980*, ed. John P. Dessauer et al. (Darien, Conn.: Book Industry Study Group, 1980), pp. 43–56.

27. David Kennedy, *Birth Control in America* (New Haven, Conn.: Yale University Press, 1970).

28. Hoge, Johnson, and Luidens, *Vanishing Boundaries*, p. 74.

29. Personal communication from Paul DiMaggio at Princeton University and Timothy Dowd at Emory University.

30. Paul C. Glick, "A Demographer Looks at American Families," *Journal of Marriage and the Family* 37 (1975): 15–26.

31. Wuthnow, *Restructuring*, p. 155.

32. U.S. Bureau of the Census, *Statistical Abstract . . . 1992*, p. 143.

33. In addition to exposing people to new ideas and broadening their horizons, schooling also significantly increased the likelihood that people would continue to be influenced by a wide variety of cultural sources.

34. U.S. Bureau of the Census, *Statistical Abstract . . . 1989*, p. 424. If baby boomers were the direct beneficiaries of this prosperity, they were not the only segment of the population to gain new freedom. The decline in poverty levels lifted millions of families to a point where they could maintain homes, purchase televisions, and think about educating their children. This was also the period in which older people came to expect that retirement would provide opportunities to explore new horizons. Between 1960 and 1975, for instance, average life expectancy for older men increased by about a year and for older women by more than two years; over the same period, the proportion of men working past

age sixty-five declined from about a third to only a fifth, and fewer than one in ten older women was gainfully employed. The fact that older Americans had more disposable income and lived increasingly in their own homes or in retirement communities also offered their children greater freedom to adopt new lifestyles and new styles of consumption. Even if, as some research suggests, intergenerational interaction remained strong in terms of paying visits and giving gifts, the pattern of interacting with significant others was shifting in a manner similar to the shift in in spirituality—from association rooted in a single geographic place to more intentional, sporadic contact within a more dispersed social space.

35. One survey found that four people in ten thought a lot about "why there is suffering in the world"—as many as who thought this much about personal happiness and more than those who thought about purpose in life or life after death. Bay Area Survey, in Charles Y. Glock, *Perspectives on Life in America Today, 1973* [machine-readable data file] (Berkeley: Survey Research Center, 1975); my analysis.

36. Norris, *Dakota*, p. 122.

37. Maya Angelou, *Wouldn't Take Nothing for My Journey Now* (New York: Random House, 1993), p. 76.

38. Dietrich Bonhoeffer, *Letters and Papers from Prison* (1953; reprint, New York: Macmillan, 1962).

39. Bellah, "No Direction Home," p. 74.

40. Norman O. Brown, *Love's Body* (New York: Vintage Books, 1968), p. 262.

41. Harvey Cox, *The Secular City: Secularization and Urbanization in Theological Perspective*, 2d ed. (New York: Collier Books, 1990), p. 9.

42. The city was an especially attractive metaphor. For white, middle-class Americans, it connoted not squalor but opportunity. It was a place not of degradation but of affluence. The city was style more than substance. It meant freedom from tradition, impersonality—even anonymity—in the sense that one could escape the watchful eye of parents and neighbors. It was less a place than a flow of communication and ideas and people. Its diversity forced people to think and to know their own minds more fully. Advocates of spiritual seeking did not describe the city as a sacred abode, certainly not as a city of God. It was, rather, a place to visit, as on a weekend trip from the suburbs, or to read about and to be amused by. The city as metaphor was everywhere; one did not have to be there to participate in it.

43. Harold E. Quinley, *The Prophetic Clergy: Social Activism among Protestant Ministers* (New York: Wiley, 1974), p. 61.

44. Hoge, Johnson, and Luidens, *Vanishing Boundaries*, pp. 73–87.

45. People who valued the freedom to explore spirituality in their own way had no trouble doing so. For example, by 1982 the American public was spending more than $700 million on religious books—a market that would more than double during the next decade and that was largely in the hands of commercial and independent publishers rather than denominational presses. In addition, the market for self-help, inspiration, psychology, and recovery books was growing even more rapidly. U.S. Bureau of the Census, *Statistical Abstract . . . 1992*, p. 235. The more eclectic style in reading habits was already becoming evident

in the 1960s and 1970s, when only two top-selling books (other than the Bible) dealt with spirituality from what might be considered an orthodox perspective (both were by C. S. Lewis—*Mere Christianity* and *The Screwtape Letters* and both sold approximately 1.5 million copies in this period). In comparison, at least ten bestsellers during these years focused on issues that might have been considered "spiritual" in a broader sense and specifically challenged or offered alternatives to conventional theology—among them, William Golding's *Lord of the Flies* (7 million copies), Kahlil Gibran's *The Prophet* (5 million), Alex Comfort's *Joy of Sex* (4 million), Albert Camus's *The Stranger* (3 million), Richard Bach's *Jonathan Livingston Seagull* (3 million), Hal Lindsey's *Late Great Planet Earth* (2.3 million), Elisabeth Kübler-Ross's *On Death and Dying* (2.1 million), and Eldridge Cleaver's *Soul on Ice* (1.3 million).

46. George H. Gallup, Jr., *Religion in America: 1978* (Princeton, N.J.: Gallup Organization, 1978), p. 52. The larger impact of Eastern spirituality was to popularize practices that could be pursued piecemeal and on one's own. Unlike the emphasis in Judaism and in Christianity on "householders," for example, Buddhism has traditionally stressed withdrawal from household duties as a means of attaining spiritual insight; indeed, the term *monk* is often synonymous in Asian languages with "home leaver." "No one can do zazen easily in a room full of children," observes Hawaiian Zen master Robert Aitken Roshi. Usually Zen practice involves "a degree of physical separation from the household." Quoted in Robert Aitken and David Steindl-Rast, *The Ground We Share: Everyday Practice, Buddhist and Christian,* ed. Nelson Foster (Liguori, Mo.: Triumph Books, 1994), p. 68. In the United States, those who became most attracted to Zen, Transcendental Meditation, and other Asian spiritual practices were in fact separated from traditional households by virtue of being young, single or divorced, relatively well educated, and in many cases living in urban areas at some distance from their extended families. A 1973 study in California that asked metropolitan residents about a dozen new religious movements found that half were familiar with at least four of them and 83 percent were familiar with at least one of them. Familiarity was highest among respondents with higher levels of education and among younger persons. When these two factors were examined simultaneously, education had the stronger effect and was much of the reason why younger people were more familiar with new religious movements than older people. Other factors, such as parents' education, gender, and how often respondents had changed residences were not associated with greater familiarity. Bay Area Survey, in Glock, *Perspectives on Life in America Today* [machine-readable data file]; my analysis. In multiple regression models, education and age were both significant predictors of familiarity with a larger number of new religious movements at the .001 level (betas of .356 and .187 respectively); mother's education, father's education, sex, childhood church attendance, and changing residences in the past two years were not statistically significant.

47. Organized religion showed some of the effects of these wider explorations. For example, despite the relative affluence of these years, organized religion did not experience the financial growth it had during the 1950s and early 1960s; indeed, in per capita and inflation-adjusted dollars, the amount given in 1968 was higher than in any subsequent year for the next decade and a half. Caplow et al., *Recent Social Trends,* p. 289. Also, in comparison with the growth

in numbers of clergy that had occurred in the 1950s, the 1960s showed virtually no net growth, and only toward the end of the 1970s, when women gained entry to seminaries, did these numbers begin to increase again. At this point, however, most of the growth in seminary enrollments was occurring in specialized ministry programs rather than in training for traditional pastoral duties in congregations. Thus, by 1980, when approximately five hundred thousand ordained clergy were counted in the U.S. Census, only about half were serving in parishes.

48. Gallup Unchurched American Study (Gallup, *Religion in America: 1978*), my analysis of persons age eighteen through thirty-four; 36 percent were single, and 9 percent were divorced or separated; 52 percent had lived in their present community fewer than five years, 40 percent fewer than three years; 69 percent had moved in the past five years, 30 percent had moved more than twice. Like other studies, this one confirmed the impact that both new attitudes toward religion and spirituality, and new life-styles were having on the churches. Young people were significantly less likely to be active in a church or synagogue if they held any of the following attitudes: thought a person should arrive at his or her religious beliefs independent of a church or synagogue, felt that he or she was still searching for goals and a purpose in life, felt the churches had lost touch with spirituality, felt religious organizations were too restrictive on moral issues, thought churches and synagogues were too concerned with organizational matters, thought sexual freedom was a good thing, deemphasized traditional family ties, or deemphasized respect for authority. The 1973 Bay Area Survey (Glock, *Perspectives on Life in America Today* [machine-readable data file]) showed similar results: among eighteen- to thirty-year-olds, 65 percent had attended religious services nearly every week while they were growing up, but only 15 percent were still attending this often. The same study, however, showed continuing interest in spirituality: 40 percent still prayed at least once a week, 64 percent still thought about the existence of God, 71 percent said they believed in God, 63 percent believed in life after death, 33 percent thought it was possible to communicate with the dead, 66 percent spent time meditating about their lives, and 48 percent felt they had been in touch with the holy or sacred.

49. Among semiskilled workers, only 3 percent attended church weekly, compared with 24 percent of managers and executives, 8 percent of sales workers, 2 percent of service workers, 4 percent of divorced persons, 2 percent of black males, 8 percent of persons who had moved three times in the past five years, 7 percent of those earning less than $10,000 annually.

50. Winter, *Being Free*.

51. Theodore Roszak, *The Making of a Counter Culture: Reflections on the Technocratic Society and Its Youthful Opposition* (Garden City, N.Y.: Doubleday, 1969); Charles A. Reich, *The Greening of America* (New York: Random House, 1970).

4. DESIRE FOR DISCIPLINE

1. Riesman, *Lonely Crowd*; C. Wright Mills, *White Collar: The American Middle Classes* (New York: Oxford University Press, 1951); C. Wright Mills, *Power Elite,* (New York: Oxford University Press, 1959).

2. Rollo May, "The Significance of Symbols," in *Symbolism in Religion and Literature,* ed. Rollo May (New York: Braziller, 1959), p. 23.

3. Jacques Ellul, *The Technological Society* (New York: Knopf, 1964).

4. For example, a woman who grew up in Mississippi recalls the meaning of racial integration to her. "We were going to have to go to school with black kids, which terrified us. None of us liked the idea of it." Although she eventually adjusted to integration, she turned increasingly to religion as a way of coping with uncertainty. Another woman was more sympathetic to the civil rights movement but says "the lid had been opened" by it and the result was a great deal of chaos. She found the changes "unnerving." A man who had been a teenager during the sixties reflects that "the rejection of sexual morality as taught by the Bible was wrong"; he was "uncomfortable with people who were junking all their parents' values." His involvement in a conservative Protestant church was a way to preserve these values. Similarly, a Catholic woman, commenting on the Vietnam war, chooses her words carefully, describing it as a "confusing" issue, an event that seemed "senseless" and that in retrospect symbolized some of the chaos in her own life at the time. For many Americans, there was thus a growing desire to believe that moral and spiritual discipline was sorely needed if the frightening chaos of the 1960s was to be overcome.

5. James Dobson, *Dare to Discipline* (Chicago: Gospel Light, 1972). Dobson's focus on discipline was increasingly the emphasis of a much wider religiopolitical movement that included such figures as Tim and Beverly LaHaye, Bill Gaither, Josh McDowell, and Elizabeth Elliott, as well as Jerry Falwell and Pat Robertson. Increasingly, concern focused on the declining quality of the public schools, as study after study showed that test scores of U.S. schoolchildren were lower than those in countries such as Japan and Germany with whom the United States was in economic competition and that performance appeared to be declining year by year. The widely publicized report *A Nation at Risk* argued that drastic measures had to be taken if the United States was to remain educationally competitive; U.S. National Commission on Excellence in Education, *A Nation at Risk* (Cambridge, Mass.: USA Research, 1984). Those who searched for solutions that could be effected without increases in school budgets found character development to be an attractive target. If children were not performing adequately, the problem was faulty teaching of strong personal values, such as hard work, determination, sustained effort, and practice. The proof lay in private schools, where these values seemed to be upheld, and the further proof— by negative example—was the trouble in urban, mainly nonwhite schools, where minority children seemed guilty of laziness, sexual misconduct, and even bad taste in music. See William A. Donohue, "Why the Schools Fail: Reclaiming the Moral Dimension in Education," *Heritage Foundation Reports,* 23 June 1988.

6. Jimmy Carter's successful bid for the presidency was a triumph in part because of the concern generated by Watergate (and by other scandals of the period) that moral decency and ethical rigor were somehow losing ground. Carter exemplified both the homespun wisdom of the rural South and the technical competence of a nuclear physicist. "He talks about management, goals, planning, and efficiency, . . . a hardheaded business approach starting at the top, and he was much influenced on the need for it by his farmer orientation," counseled a

widely read biography published during his campaign. David Kucharsky, *The Man from Plains: The Mind and Spirit of Jimmy Carter* (New York: Harper & Row, 1976), pp. 27–28.

7. William Bennett, from a speech delivered to the Heritage Foundation; reprinted in "Getting Used to Decadence: The Spirit of Democracy in Modern America," *Heritage Foundation Reports*, 7 December 1993.

8. See Dean M. Kelley, *Why Conservative Churches Are Growing: A Study in Sociology of Religion*, rev. ed. (Macon, Ga.: Mercer University Press, 1986; originally published in 1972). Kelley's thesis was that churches needed to move beyond the laxity of the 1960s, giving the public a clear sense of meaning and purpose through strong preaching and social engagement. Although Kelley himself favored an inclusive emphasis on individual meaning and religious liberty, many of his interpreters were to derive lessons about a more restrictive sense of religious commitment.

9. Evangelicalism had grown quietly during the 1950s and 1960s and became increasingly visible to the wider public after the Carter campaign in 1975. Televised religion expanded to include evangelical programs by Falwell and Jimmy Swaggart as well as Billy Graham's periodic crusades and Oral Roberts's healing ministries. Falwell, chief architect in 1979 of the Moral Majority movement, was especially instrumental in drawing public atttention to such moral concerns as pornography, abortion, and violence on television. Known primarily for his efforts to address these issues through political means, Falwell also cautioned listeners during his weekly telecasts to pray regularly and to guard against moral temptation in their personal lives. See Gerald Strober and Ruth Tomczak, *Jerry Falwell: Aflame for God* (Nashville, Tenn.: Nelson, 1979).

Spiritual discipline was also prominently touted by television evangelist Pat Robertson, the Yale-educated son of upper-middle-class Baptists; he eventually ran for President and organized the influential conservative movement known as the Christian Coalition. As a sixth grader, Robertson had felt inadequate as he prayed, sensing that God was calling him to work harder, study more, and achieve great things; college and law school honed his desire to lead a disciplined, God-centered life. During the 1960s, the counterculture repulsed Robertson, who was already achieving prominence as a preacher, and by the late 1970s Robertson's television ministry was becoming a notable voice in favor of moral and spiritual renewal as a way of saving the United States from the anarchy he perceived to be undermining its Christian foundations. Unless such a renewal took place, Robertson warned, the country would go into a dramatic moral tailspin in which "honor, decency, honesty, self-control, sexual restraint, family values, and sacrifice [would be] replaced by gluttony, sensuality, delinquency, drunkenness, drug-induced euphoria, fraud, waste, debauched currency, and rampant inflation." Pat Robertson, *The Secret Kingdom* (Nashville, Tenn.: Nelson, 1982), p. 29.

On a local level, what Robertson, Falwell, and other national leaders were advocating was also being championed in pulpits and in countless prayer meetings and support groups. The freewheeling Jesus People groups of the 1960s were gradually replaced by charismatic Catholics, by Campus Crusade chapters, and by conservative Bible-study groups. "Discipline is the path to godliness," counseled one popular Bible-study guide. "You must learn to discipline yourself for the purpose of godliness." Jay E. Adams, *Godliness through Discipline* (Nutley, N.J.: Presbyterian and Reformed Publishing Co., 1977), p. 2. In a perceptive study, sociologist Steven Tipton argued that many of the religious movements of the mid-to-late 1970s were providing ways for Americans who had been exposed to the trauma of the 1960s (or who had just missed it) to regain a sense of order in their personal lives. Steven M. Tipton, *Getting Saved from the Sixties: Moral Meaning in Conversion and Cultural Change* (Berkeley: University of California Press, 1982).

10. General Social Survey (Chicago: National Opinion Research Center, machine-readable data file, 1990).

11. Reagan's speechwriter Peggy Noonan, a Brooklyn-born Irish Catholic whose working-class sensibilities had been offended by the countercultural laxity she observed in college, heartily endorsed these efforts to promote a traditional and wholesome way of life. Peggy Noonan, *What I Saw at the Revolution: A Political Life in the Reagan Era* (New York: Random House, 1990).

12. U.S. Bureau of the Census, *Statistical Abstract . . . 1992*, p. 530; business failures shot up from 43 per 10,000 firms in 1975 to 102 per 10,000 firms in 1987, with total liabilities rising from $4.3 billion to more than $36 billion. The economic growth that did take place during the Reagan era occurred mainly in the largest firms: for instance, revenues of corporations with receipts of $1 million or more grew from $5.7 trillion in 1980 to more than $9.1 trillion in 1988, while annual receipts of companies with revenues of less than $100,000 remained constant. On the whole, large corporations also fared significantly better than business partnerships; the number of such partnerships remained stagnant while they incurred net losses during several successive years. If discipline was becoming a more heartily endorsed culural motif, one source of its rising popularity can thus be attributed to the changing climate of business. With expansion in many sectors threatened and with competition both stiffer and embedded in larger networks of economic exchange, it was not surprising that employees felt pressure to regulate their own lives for increased efficiency and effectiveness. Indeed, studies showed that the average American was working more hours per year and that a growing share of married women had joined the work force, all in the context of increased financial burdens and credit-card debt. After the heightened expectations of the 1960s, consumer confidence fell dramatically: one index was 44 percent lower for 1974 through 1980 than for 1969 through 1973. Calculated from Philip E. Converse et al., *American Social Attitudes Data Sourcebook* (Cambridge: Harvard University Press, 1980), p. 235.

13. U.S. Bureau of the Census, *Statistical Abstract . . . 1989*, p. 435.

14. Frank Levy, *Dollars and Dreams* (New York: Russell Sage Foundation, 1987), p. 56.

15. Todd Brentwood (Chapter 3) was one person who found "how-to" books about spirituality of interest in his pursuit of economic success.

16. Richard J. Foster, *Celebration of Discipline: The Path to Spiritual Growth* (New York: Harper & Row, 1978), p. 97.

17. Anne Ortlund, *Disciplines of the Beautiful Woman* (Waco, Tex.: Word Books, 1977), p. 11.

18. In my research on support groups I found that 40 percent of Americans were currently involved in some kind of small group that met regularly and that provided caring and support for its members, and, of these members, 42 percent said they had joined their group because they wanted to become more disciplined in their spiritual lives. Comparing these people with the 58 percent who did not list spiritual discipline as a reason for joining offers some empirical evidence of the characteristics that may have led people to become interested in spiritual discipline and some clues to the meaning of this interest. Spiritual discipline was indeed closely associated with an increased interest in spiritual matters in general and prayer in particular. This interest was expressed more commonly by conservative Christians than by religious liberals or by spiritual nomads, but it was not uncommon among nomads either. Women were more likely to be interested in spiritual discipline than men, and younger women were somewhat more interested in it than older women (or than men of their own age). For men and women alike, spiritual discipline sparked more interest among those who had experienced emotional crises than among those who had not. However, people interested in spiritual discipline seemed to be motivated mainly by a desire for personal growth rather than by a desire to resolve personal difficulties. They were on a quest not to abandon the good life but to enrich their commitments to family, careers, and material pleasures. Indeed, they were just as likely as anyone else to describe themselves as ambitious and free-spirited. But they saw the Bible as a book of rules, if not of specific answers, that they could apply to their lives. And they saw their support groups as places to receive advice, encouragement, and a warm embrace from their fellow members. My analysis of the Small Groups Survey data; see Wuthnow, *Sharing the Journey.*

19. Ronald Reagan, *In God I Trust,* compiled by David R. Shepherd (Wheaton, Ill.: Tyndale House, 1984), pp. 46–47.

20. Rogin, *Ronald Reagan, the Movie,* p. 36.

21. John Calvin, *Institutes of the Christian Religion,* ed. Hugh T. Kerr (1559; reprint, Louisville, Ky.: Westminster/John Knox, 1989), p. 112.

22. Weber, *Protestant Ethic,* p. 181.

23. Quoted in Frances FitzGerald, *Cities on a Hill: A Journey through Contemporary American Cultures* (New York: Simon & Schuster, 1986), p. 164.

24. George Gilder, "Wealth and Poverty Revisited," *American Spectator,* July 1993, 4.

25. Jerry Falwell, interviewed by Judy Woodruff, *Inside Politics,* CNN, June 16, 1994.

26. Norris, *Dakota,* p. 23.

27. "Premarital Sex," *Gallup Report* 263 (August 1987): 20–22; by 1987, the public was still divided as to whether premarital sex was wrong, 46 percent saying it was, and 48 percent saying it was not—virtually the same division as in 1973, when 48 percent said it was wrong; 43 percent, not wrong. See Tom W. Smith, "Attitudes towards Sexual Permissiveness: Trends and Correlates," *GSS News,* September 1992, 1–8; "Morality," *U.S. News & World Report,* December 9, 1985, 52; Sandy Banisky, "Spanking: Discipline or Abuse?" *St. Louis Post-Dispatch,* 3 August 1994, 3F; "Sign of the Times," *Washington Times,* 24 June

1994, C15; Kathryn Dore Perkins, "Parents' Dilemma—To Spank or Not," *Sacramento Bee,* 5 June 1994, A1; Michael Elliott, "Crime and Punishment," *Newsweek,* April 18, 1994, 18.

28. Despite the attention being given to cracking down on children and teenagers, statistics showed little change in patterns of misconduct; for example, the high school dropout rate remained constant between 1980 and 1986, as did the number of high school students who damaged school property or who had fights with their parents or who were arrested for running away from home. Caplow et al., *Recent Social Trends,* pp. 228–230. A national study in 1989 found that Americans were still stretching the boundaries of traditional morality and concluded that the more conservative political climate of the 1980s was not producing adherence to strict moral codes—for example, a quarter admitted dishonesty on tax returns; more younger people than older people took a relativistic attitude toward lying and stealing; and, among high school seniors, 67 percent said they would inflate an expense account, 66 percent would lie to achieve a business objective, 50 percent would pad an insurance claim, and 36 percent would plagiarize to pass an exam. Rushworth M. Kidder, "Public Concern for Ethics Rises," *Christian Science Monitor,* 2 January 1990, 13.

29. Some research also shows the complexity of Americans' views toward moral and spiritual discipline. Although many people favor the strict morality that was championed in the 1980s, for example, this support does not indicate a willingness to sacrifice personal freedom. In one study, 59 percent of those surveyed said having "moral standards" was absolutely essential—a higher percentage than for virtually any other type of value, such as family, community, or work—and there was a strong relationship between this value and respondents' saying that their relationship to God was absolutely essential and their claiming that they tried to be guided by what they "thought was morally right" when faced with a tough ethical decision. Yet those who valued moral standards more highly were also more likely to value their personal freedom and to say it was very important to pay attention to their own feelings. That this emphasis was not a repudiation of the values of the 1960s and 1970s was also suggested by the fact that younger people were still less likely to emphasize moral standards than older people who had matured before the 1960s. Taking age differences into account, this value was nevertheless more likely to be emphasized by married people and by people with children than by those who were single or childless (consistent with arguments about maturation encouraging a return to traditional values). Further understanding of what it means to emphasize strict moral standards comes from the fact that people in professional occupations were more likely to attach high importance to such standards than people in semiskilled jobs, as were people with higher levels of education and those who had more control over their own decisions at work. In short, discretion—the result of the very freedom that came into vogue during the 1960s—is also the condition that encourages people to recognize their need for moral standards. In addition, moral standards were more highly valued by people who said they experienced a lot of pressure in their work, who said their work was very competitive, and who were subjected to stress on a regular basis. For them, the

complexity of life and the need to make daily decisions were sufficiently taxing that they regarded moral discipline as a virtue. There is also some evidence that valuing moral standards goes along with actively trying to control one's life; for instance, those who emphasized moral standards were also more likely to say they prayed or meditated to relieve stress and that they exercised to reduce stress, but that they did not simply "keep it in" or engage in addictive behaviors when they experienced stress. The relationship between this emphasis on moral discipline and spirituality is evident from the fact that people in the same study who placed high value on moral standards were also more likely to pray, to value their relationship with God, and to be interested in developing their spirituality. There was also a tendency for valuing moral standards to go hand in hand with more active involvement in conventional religious activities, such as attending worship services. That such structured activities help to provide spiritual discipline is suggested by the fact that people who participated in them and who valued strict moral standards were also more likely to say they received divine guidance when they participated. Yet finding simple answers to difficult personal situations is only part of the story. These people also said they attended religious services because they gained a sense of comfort from doing so. Perhaps it is the reassurance that one is living right, even more than specific advice, that people are seeking. New analysis of data from the Economic Values Survey, 1992 (Wuthnow, *God and Mammon in America*).

Reanalyzing data obtained in another national survey, I found that people who were committed to their spiritual development and who prayed on a regular basis were no less likely than those who prayed infrequently to value self-expression; they were, however, more likely to say that duty comes before pleasure, and they were significantly more likely to favor strict morality, especially in sexual matters. (From my analysis of data collected in 1988 by the Gallup Organization as part of the Study of Unchurched Americans. Questions were included on welcoming or not welcoming more emphasis on self-expression, sexual freedom, and working hard.)

Other evidence suggests far less personal resolve to live according to strict moral standards or spiritual absolutes and deeper unwillingness to appear intolerant or to impose one's views on someone else than concern about moral decay, scandals, corruption, and the breakdown of society. In a 1992 study of the American electorate, 51 percent agreed that "the world is always changing and we should adjust our view of moral behavior to those changes," whereas 40 percent disagreed (among people age thirty or younger, 63 percent agreed). With another statement, "we should be more tolerant of people who choose to live according to their own moral standards even if they are very different from our own," 60 percent agreed, and 38 percent disagreed. But if a majority opted for tolerance and openness, there was also sentiment that the innovations being tolerated might be contrary to the public good; for instance, 69 percent agreed that "the newer lifestyles are contributing to the breakdown of our society," while only 18 percent disagreed (National Election Study, Institute for Social Research, University of Michigan, Ann Arbor, 1992). Fearing what may come of the commitment to tolerance and diversity but reluctant to abandon this commitment, many turn to television preachers and conservative politicians to do their work for them; rather than appearing personally intolerant, they pin their hopes on some religiopolitical movement to clean up the streets and put moral offenders out of sight.

30. Caplow et al., *Recent Social Trends,* p. 289. After fifteen years of decline, religious book publishing leveled off at about 6 percent of total publishing, meaning that the number of new titles each year was gradually increasing; and religious bookstores started making a comeback, with an increase from approximately fourteen hundred in 1975 to more than thirty-eight hundred in 1987. Religious television programming also rose, becoming a billion dollar industry before it was rocked by sexual and financial scandals at the end of the decade.

31. Ibid., pp. 312–318. For instance, between 1980 and 1988 the portion of households subscribing to cable television grew from 20 percent to 51 percent; videocassette recorders were available in only 1 percent of households at the start of the decade, but in two-thirds by the end; the number of commercial radio and television stations grew steadily; Sunday newspaper circulation edged up by some six million readers; approximately one billion people attended movie theaters each year; and, perhaps most important, television, radio, and newspaper advertising grew by more than $50 billion in only seven years.

32. U.S. Bureau of the Census, *Statistical Abstract . . . 1992.*

33. Caplow et al., *Recent Social Trends,* p. 346, summarizing data from Harris Polls; Gallup surveys showed a decline from 68 percent in 1975 to 52 percent in 1989 for "great deal" and "quite a lot" of confidence in organized religion combined. Surprisingly, the public thought religion was becoming more important: whereas only 14 percent said so in a 1970 poll, 49 percent did so in 1985. Yet most of the data gleaned from opinion polls about personal religious commitment showed little evidence of an across-the-board revival. The percentage of those saying religion was very important in their lives, for instance, remained about the same each year, as did figures for belief in God. Although the evangelical movement gained public attention as a result of Carter's claim to have been "born again" and because of the political muscle of Falwell and Robertson, there was little evidence that evangelicalism was attracting a substantially greater share of the public. In 1976, 34 percent said they were "born again"; a decade later, exactly the same percentage did so. Over the same period, no change occurred in the numbers who said they tried to convert their friends to Jesus. Nor was there any increase in numbers of Americans who took the Bible as literal truth. Caplow et al., *Recent Social Trends,* p. 379. Had Americans' quest for spiritual discipline in the 1980s been a serious one, many of these indicators of religious commitment would have risen. That they did not is, again, evidence that discipline was a matter more of style than of substance.

34. Harry Crews, *Body* (New York: Poseidon Press, 1990), is a satirical look at body building that evokes many of the popular criticisms of self-discipline.

35. Hugh T. Kerr, "Spiritual Discipline," *Theology Today* 49 (1993): 452.

5. ANGEL AWAKENINGS

1. Sandi Dolbee, "A Look Inside: The Me Generation Searches for Its Soul," *San Diego Union-Tribune,* 20 May 1994, E1.

2. Quoted in Mead, *The Lively Experiment*, p. 89.

3. Statistics from Sebastian Smith, "Angel Mania Takes Flight in U.S.," *Agence France Presse*, 13 January 1994, 1. Sophy Burnham, *A Book of Angels* (New York: Ballantine, 1990); Sophy Burnham, ed., *Angel Letters* (New York: Ballantine, 1991); Sophy Burnham, *The President's Angel* (New York: Ballantine, 1993); Alma Daniel, Timothy Wyllie, and Andrew Ramer, *Ask Your Angels* (New York: Ballantine, 1992); John Randolph Price, *Angels within Us* (New York: Ballantine, 1993); Joan Wester Anderson, *Where Angels Walk: True Stories of Heavenly Visitors* (New York: Barton & Brett, 1992); Maria Parisen, *Angels & Mortals: Their Co-creative Power* (New York: Quest, 1990); Eileen Elias Freeman, *Touched by Angels* (New York: Warner Books, 1993); Terry Lynn Taylor, *Messengers of Light: The Angels Guide to Spiritual Growth* (New York: Kramer, 1990); Terry Lynn Taylor, *Guardians of Hope: The Angels Guide to Personal Growth* (New York: Kramer, 1991); Terry Lynn Taylor, *Answers from Angels: A Book of Angel Letters* (New York: Kramer, 1992); Terry Lynn Taylor, *Creating with the Angels* (New York: Kramer, 1993); John Ronner, *Do You Have a Guardian Angel?* (Murfreesboro, Tenn.: Mamre Press, 1985); Frank Peretti, *This Present Darkness* (New York: Crossway Books, 1986); Frank Peretti, *Piercing the Darkness* (New York: Crossway Books, 1989); Roger Elwood, *Angelwalk* (New York: Crossway Books, 1988).

4. Smith, "Angel Mania Takes Flight in U.S.," 1.

5. Linda Mack, "Angelic Twin Cities," *Star Tribune*, 12 June 1994, 6F.

6. CBS News Poll, October 1993. Similar results were obtained in a Yankelovich Partners survey on January 22, 1993, which showed that seven adults in ten believed in the existence of angels; about half the public thought they themselves were protected by a guardian angel, and about one in three had felt the presence of an angel (reported in "Angels," *Emerging Trends*, January 1994, 1). According to another national poll conducted that same year, 69 percent of Americans "personally believe[d] in the existence of angels," 46 percent believed they had their "own personal guardian angel," and 32 percent said they had personally "felt an angelic presence" in their life. Another poll found that 80 percent of Americans believed they had a guardian angel, and 22 percent had communicated with their angel. Still another poll found that 77 percent of the public believed in angels, up from only 56 percent fifteen years earlier. In another poll, conducted in October 1993, 71 percent said they believed in the existence of angels, and 31 percent reported they had seen an angel. Roper Center, "Public Opinion Online," December 2, 1993.

7. Mary Peterson Kauffold, "All the Angles on Angels," *Chicago Tribune*, 6 June 1993, 1; Southern Focus Poll, Survey Research Center, University of North Carolina, Chapel Hill, February 1994.

8. *USA Today*, 9 September 1986, 1.

9. Reported in Bruce Greyson and Anne Longley, "A Glimpse Beyond," *People*, 1 August 1994, 43.

10. Roper Center, "Public Opinion Online," August 4, 1992, a Times-Mirror Survey; surveys in 1987, 1988, 1989, and 1990 showed similar results. The 68 percent figure is from the General Social Survey (Chicago: National Opinion Research Center, machine-readable data file, 1991).

11. General Social Survey (Chicago: National Opinion Research Center, machine-readable data file, 1991); my analysis. The percentages who definitely believed in miracles among each group were: women, 51, men, 37; high school graduates, 48, college graduates, 41; Protestants, 51, Catholics, 43, Jews, 7, no religious preference, 17; people age fifty or older, 52, people age thirty-one through forty-nine, 44, people age eighteen through thirty, 40.

12. For an extended discussion of channeling, see Michael F. Brown, *The Channeling Zone: American Spirituality in an Anxious Age* (Cambridge, Mass.: Harvard University Press, 1997).

13. Gallup Poll, August 5, 1990.

14. For an overview, see Paul Heelas, *The New Age Movement: The Celebration of the Self and the Sacralization of Modernity* (London: Blackwell, 1996).

15. Gallup Poll, September 1990.

16. Poll results reported in *USA Today*, 9 September 1986, 1.

17. Dolbee, "A Look Inside," E1.

18. Quoted in F. Lynne Bachleda, "Angels in America," *Publishers Weekly*, 12 July 1993, 31.

19. Randall Balmer, "Some of Us Need Angels in Our Lives," *Phoenix Gazette*, 2 April 1994, D6.

20. Quoted in Lance Morrow, "The Bishop of Our Possibilities," *Time*, 10 May 1982, 124.

21. Jack Kerouac, *On the Road;* quoted in John Tytell, *Naked Angels: The Lives and Literature of the Beat Generation* (New York: McGraw-Hill, 1976), p. 140.

22. Eugene Taylor, "Desperately Seeking Spirituality," *Psychology Today*, November/December 1994, 54–68; italics added.

23. Betty J. Eadie, *Embraced by the Light* (Placerville, Calif.: Gold Leaf Press, 1992).

24. Freeman, *Touched by Angels*.

25. Gallup Survey, 1990; my analysis. For instance, those who believe in spiritual or psychic healing are twice as likely as those who do not believe in this kind of healing to say they have also experienced contact with the dead, to believe that spirit beings can temporarily assume control of human bodies during a trance, and to believe in extrasensory perception.

26. One of the earliest contributions to the debate on the privatization of modern religion is that of Thomas Luckmann, *The Invisible Religion: The Transformation of Symbols in Industrial Society* (London: Macmillan, 1967), and one of the more recent, José Casanova, *Public Religions in the Modern World* (Chicago: University of Chicago Press, 1994).

27. Among others, see Landrum P. Leavell, *Angels, Angels, Angels* (Nashville, Tenn.: Broadman Press, 1973), and Max von Moos, *Angels and Men* (New York: Seabury, 1977). Anticipating the more popular, firsthand-experience format of writing about angels were Hope Macdonald, *When Angels Appear* (Grand Rapids, Mich.: Zondervan, 1982), and F. Forrester Church, *Entertaining Angels: A Guide to Heaven for Atheists and True Believers* (New York: Harper & Row, 1987).

28. "What (and What Not) to Pray For," *Emerging Trends*, April 1994, 1; "Grading Biblical Knowledge on a Curve," *Emerging Trends*, June 1994, 2;

"Modern Teens View Religion Differently," *Emerging Trends,* June 1994, 1–2; Lydia Saad and Leslie McAneny, "Most Americans Think Religion Losing Clout in the 1990s," *The Gallup Poll,* 14 April 1994, 1–2.

29. U.S. Bureau of the Census, *Statistical Abstract . . . 1989,* p. 229; John P. Robinson, "Where's the Boom?" *American Demographics* 9 (March 19, 1987), 34–37. The trade-off between broader experiences of mystery and organized religion is evident in statistical studies too. Unlike studies focusing on belief in miracles (which show a correspondence with organized religious involvement), research on other kinds of mysterious experiences shows that these are more likely among people who are less likely to be involved in organized religion at present. For example, one national study showed that members of younger birth cohorts are significantly more likely than members of older cohorts to believe they have had experiences such as déjà vu or clairvoyance, but they are significantly less likely to participate in organized religion. According to the 1988 General Social Survey (Chicago: National Opinion Research Center, machine-readable data file), 27 percent of respondents age forty-three and over had experienced déjà vu at least several times, compared with 42 percent of respondents age thirty-one to forty-two and 42 percent of respondents age eighteen through thirty; 46 percent of the older group had never experienced it, compared with only 20 and 22 percent of the younger groups. About 10 percent more of the younger cohorts than of the older group had experienced clairvoyance.

Despite the fact that women may be targeted more by authors of books about mysterious experiences, such experiences are reported about equally by women and by men. Also, people who have lower levels of confidence in the clergy are more likely to report such experiences, and these experiences go together with individualistic attitudes toward religion and morality—for instance, with agreeing that morality is a personal matter, with denying that one tries to follow the Bible in making decisions, with saying that church teachings are unimportant in making decisions, with denying that it is important to attend church regularly, and with saying that it is not important to believe in God without doubts. Similar patterns emerge in comparisons of people who believe in or who have experienced such phenomena as astrology, psychic healing, communication with the dead, and channeling. My analysis of the 1990 Gallup Survey (GNS7521).

30. That such experiences go hand in hand with feeling that the forces governing the universe are benign was evident in a significant correlation between people who claim to have had mysterious experiences and those who believe that both the world and human nature are mostly good. My analysis of the 1990 Gallup Survey (GNS7521).

31. Quoted in Greyson and Longley, "A Glimpse Beyond," p. 5.

32. Norman Lear, speech to the National Press Club, Washington, D.C., December 9, 1993.

33. Harris Poll, September 12, 1994; asked whether they believe in ghosts, 36 percent of a national sample of 1,249 adults said yes. A Gallup Poll (October 1991) found 28 percent who said they believed "in ghosts or that spirits of dead people can come back in certain places and situations." A 1989 survey conducted by Kane, Parsons and Associates for *Parents Magazine* found that 33 percent thought it true that "there are spirits or ghosts in the world that make their presence known to living people."

34. Bigelow Holding Company, "Unusual Personal Experiences," September 1991; 11 percent of more than five thousand respondents said they had seen a ghost. A Gallup Poll (August 5, 1990) found 9 percent who said they had seen or been in the presence of a ghost.

35. Freeman, *Touched by Angels*.

36. Cristina Garcia, "Thousands Seek Spiritual Guidance," *Time*, 15 December 1986, 36.

37. Quoted in Lee Krenis More, "Dawning of the Age of Acquiring Credibility," *Gannett News Service*, 23 May 1994, 1.

38. Quoted in Marci McDonald, "The New Spirituality," *Maclean's*, 10 October 1994, 44.

39. Quoted in Clark Morphew, "Cuddly Angels Fly in the Face of Tradition," *Austin American-Statesman*, 22 April 1995, E9.

40. Quoted in ibid., p. E9.

41. Veronique de Turenne, "Guardian Angels," *Chicago Tribune*, 23 December 1992, 5.

42. Taylor, "Desperately Seeking Spirituality," 54.

43. Quoted in Susan Ketchin, *The Christ-Haunted Landscape: Faith and Doubt in Southern Fiction* (Jackson: University Press of Mississippi), p. 48.

44. Gallup Survey, 1990; my analysis.

45. Larry Witham, "A 'Spirited' Enthusiasm for Angels," *Washington Times*, 16 April 1995, D2.

46. The comparison is usually with Western Europe, where participation in organized religion is generally lower than in the United States and where academic culture and journalism are often more willing to embrace secularity.

47. Hannah Arendt, *The Human Condition* (Chicago: University of Chicago Press, 1958), p. 209.

48. McDonald, "The New Spirituality," 44.

6.   SPIRITUALITY OF THE INNER SELF

1. Thomas Moore, *Care of the Soul: A Guide for Cultivating Depth and Sacredness in Everyday Life* (New York: Harper Collins, 1992).

2. John Bradshaw, *Homecoming: Reclaiming and Championing Your Inner Child* (New York: Bantam Books, 1990); Gerald G. May, *Addiction and Grace: Love and Spirituality in the Healing of Addictions* (New York: HarperCollins, 1988); J. Keith Miller, *A Hunger for Healing: The Twelve Steps as a Classic Model for Christian Spiritual Growth* (San Francisco: Harper San Francisco, 1991); M. Scott Peck, *The Road Less Traveled: A New Psychology of Love, Traditional Values and Spiritual Growth* (New York: Simon & Schuster, 1978).

3. Carol Ochs, "The Presence in the Desert," *Cross Currents* 43 (1993): 293–294.

4. On the complexity of these ideas of individual responsibility, see especially John Steadman Rice, *A Disease of One's Own: Psychotherapy, Addiction, and the Emergence of Co-dependency* (New Brunswick, N.J.: Transaction, 1995).

5. These conceptions of the self emphasized predispositions, which were laid down early in life as a result of nature and nurture and then guided the

individual's behavior in daily life. Harvard's Gordon Allport wrote that personality consisted essentially of "broad intentional dispositions," which in most
cases included what he described as a "religious sentiment" or "comprehensive
attitude" shaped by familism, dependence, and authority. Gordon W. Allport,
Becoming: Basic Considerations for a Psychology of Personality (New Haven,
Conn.: Yale University Press, 1955), pp. 92–95. Parsons wrote that personality
was a "system of need-dispositions," the most important of which were "internalized social values" and "role expectations." Talcott Parsons, "Personality as
a Social System," in *Toward a General Theory of Action: Theoretical Foundations for the Social Sciences,* ed. Talcott Parsons and Edward A. Shils (New York:
Harper & Row, 1951), p. 115. Adorno and his associates fashioned similar arguments in their influential research on the authoritarian personality. Fascism
and other forms of extremist behavior could be explained, they argued, as the
result of deviant parental practices that created inconsistent need dispositions in
children. T. W. Adorno et al., *The Authoritarian Personality* (New York: Harper
& Row, 1950).

6. Describing this kind of self as the "sociable self, which engages easily in
social interaction and focuses on the expectations of significant others," Luhmann argues that it often engages in "superficial conversation" and that "its
essence is to take the role of the other and to avoid bothering others with one's
own problems or peculiarities." Niklas Luhmann, "The Individuality of the Individual," in *Reconstructing Individualism: Autonomy, Individuality, and the
Self in Western Thought,* ed. Thomas C. Heller, Morton Sosna, and David E.
Wellbery (Stanford, Calif.: Stanford University Press, 1986), p. 316.

7. Howard S. Becker and Anselm L. Strauss, "Careers, Personality, and Adult
Socialization," *American Journal of Sociology* 62 (1956): 263.

8. Conformity to the norms of familiar places, moreover, functioned ipso
facto to sacralize these places. As Berger noted in his later criticisms of the religious establishment, "Since one ought fundamentally to adjust to society, this
means that society is fundamentally good—our society, that is" (*Noise of Solemn
Assemblies,* p. 46). Common-sense understandings of the self in churches, synagogues, and seminaries were congruent with social scientists' emphasis on personality, attitudes, and values. The extent to which these communities emphasized adherence to strict doctrinal formulas varied, and some theologians
inveighed against the conformity to mass culture they saw being encouraged in
congregations. But, at a deeper level, congregations were understood to be agents
of socialization, helping families instill good values in their children. Sunday
schools flourished, preaching offered practical advice for daily living, and Americans turned to their clergy for help with emotional problems. The self was a mal-
leable entity, needing to be instructed and nurtured; it was, nevertheless, a repository of values that would guide behavior largely without effort once it had been
effectively trained. As an inhabitant of social space, the self was thus subject to
the discipline of prevailing institutions whose power was, in Davis's words, "productive, not just repressive" in their encouragement of "patterns of behaviour,
ways of thought, forms of desires and interests." Charles Davis, *Religion and
the Making of Society: Essays in Social Theology* (Cambridge: Cambridge University Press, 1994), p. 163. The closest links between psychological conceptions

of the self and spirituality were forged by pastoral counselors. See E. Brooks Holifield, *A History of Pastoral Care in America: From Salvation to Self-Realization* (Nashville, Tenn.: Abingdon Press, 1983), pp. 259–306.

9. Some of the leading therapeutic models from which pastoral counselors drew laid the groundwork for a looser, more liberated conception of the self that was to become prominent in the next decade. Carl Rogers, whose writings became influential among mainstream Protestant counselors, argued that therapy should be directed chiefly toward releasing the individual's own "drive to health" and that acceptance, especially of the client's feelings, was key to this process. See Carl R. Rogers, *On Becoming a Person* (Boston: Houghton Mifflin, 1961), p. 26. In practice, Rogerian counselors bridled at impositions on the autonomous self. They argued that individuals had possibilities greater than they were capable of expressing within institutional contexts.

10. Freudian psychology was also beginning to filter into popular conceptions of the self, but its impact in the 1950s was considerably different from what it would be by the late 1960s. Karen Horney, Alfred Adler, Rollo May, and Harry Stack Sullivan incorporated Freudian concepts into their particular methods of treating mental illness. See Calvin S. Hall and Gardner Lindzey, *Theories of Personality* (New York: Wiley, 1957), pp. 114–156. Fromm's popular *Escape from Freedom* and *Man for Himself* drew from Freud, as did Erikson's work on childhood development. Erich Fromm, *Escape from Freedom* (New York: Farrar and Rinehart, 1941); Erich Fromm, *Man for Himself* (New York: Rinehart, 1947); Erik H. Erikson, *Childhood and Society* (New York: Norton, 1950). Words such as *neurosis* and *psychotic* filtered into public vocabularies, and magazines carried stories about sexual repression and dreams. However, in the United States psychoanalysts paid less attention to the inward depths of personal disorders and focused more on techniques of managing these disorders, including medication, than did psychoanalysts in Europe. See Edith Kurzweil, *The Freudians: A Comparative Perspective* (New Haven, Conn.: Yale University Press, 1989). Freud's negative views of religion caused his work to be severely criticized by such prominent religious leaders as E. Stanley Jones and Bishop Fulton Sheen, and to be dismissed by much of the church-going public. E. Stanley Jones, *The Way to Power and Poise* (New York: Abingdon-Cokesbury Press, 1949); Fulton J. Sheen, *Life Is Worth Living* (New York: McGraw-Hill, 1953). Only later, with the rise of countercultural protests, did Freudian views of sexual repression and of the deeper layers of the subconscious mind gain acceptance, and even then they were often considered less important than Marxist analyses of the economic and political conditions of society.

11. Expressivity harked back to William Blake and Johann Wolfgang von Goethe and to Ralph Waldo Emerson and William Wordsworth. See Charles Taylor, *Sources of the Self: The Making of the Modern Identity* (Cambridge, Mass.: Harvard University Press, 1989), esp. pp. 368–390, 456–497. It was, however, understood in contemporary rather than in historic terms. The expressions that were valued were the opposite of everything critics had emphasized about the 1950s. If the uniform of the Cold War bureaucrat was the gray flannel suit, then brightly colored clothes of one's own making or choosing were a symbol of self-expression. If having a good disposition meant learning to

handle one's emotions, then self-expression was ebullient exaltation of one's feelings. If the workplace had defined Organization Man, play was now the means of liberating the self. And if rationality, science, technique, and planning were key to the success of advanced industrial society, fantasy, poetry, and spontaneity were the means of self-expression. As he had done in anticipating the broader turmoil of the 1960s, Mailer captured the essential relationship between self-expression and spirituality in his essay "The White Negro." The new thinking, Mailer observed, viewed the self as an endless and uncharted territory to be discovered through new experiences. Once it was regarded as a vast, mysterious sea, the self could also be imagined as a powerful source of sacred energy. To be in touch with the self, Mailer wrote, "is to have grace, is to be closer to the secrets of that inner unconscious life which will nourish you if you can hear it, for you are then nearer to that God which . . . is located in the senses of [the] body, that trapped, mutilated and nonetheless megalomaniacal God who is It, who is energy, life, sex, force, the Yoga's *prana,* the Reichian's orgone, Lawrence's 'blood,' Hemingway's 'good,' the Shavian life-force; 'It'; God; not the God of the churches but the unachievable whisper of mystery, . . . the paradise of limitless energy and perception" (p. 12).

12. Rogers, *On Becoming a Person,* p. 24.

13. Aitken and Steindl-Rast, *The Ground We Share,* p. 24.

14. Rogers himself was an early example of these influences, having shed his conservative Protestant upbringing during a six-month tour of China in the 1920s. For many others, groundwork for rediscovering the inner self was laid during the 1950s, especially in the encounter between Christianity and Buddhism in the wake of World War II, which was an unanticipated offshoot of American missionary efforts in South and East Asia.

15. These included: Thomas J. J. Altizer, *Oriental Mysticism and Biblical Eschatology* (Philadelphia: Westminster Press, 1961); George Appleton, *On the Eight-Fold Path: Christian Presence amid Buddhism* (New York: Oxford University Press, 1961); Tucker N. Callaway, *Japanese Buddhism and Christianity: A Comparison of the Christian Doctrine of Salvation with That of Some Major Sects of Japanese Buddhism* (Tokyo: Shinkyo Shuppansha Protestant Publishing, 1957); Bryan de Kretser, *Man in Buddhism and Christianity* (Calcutta: Y.M.C.A. Publishing House, 1954); Lynn A. De Silva, *Reincarnation in Buddhist and Christian Thought* (Colombo, Sri Lanka: Christian Study Centre, 1968); Aelred Graham, *Zen Catholicism: A Suggestion* (New York: Harcourt, Brace & World, 1963); Winston L. King, *Buddhism and Christianity: Some Bridges of Understanding* (Philadelphia: Westminster Press, 1962); Thomas Merton, *Zen and the Birds of Appetite* (New York: New Directions, 1968); Daisetz Teitaro Suzuki, *Mysticism: Christian and Buddhist* (New York: Macmillan, 1957); Daniel Berrigan and Thich Nhat Hanh, *The Raft Is Not the Shore: Conversations toward a Christian-Buddhist Awareness* (Boston: Beacon Press, 1975); and Hans Küng and Julia Ching, *Christianity and Chinese Religions* (New York: Doubleday, 1989).

16. Yankelovich, Skelly and White, Inc., *The 1978 Consumer Research Study on Reading and Book Purchasing* (Darien, Conn.: Book Industry Study Group, 1978), p. 150.

17. The literature criticizing self-expression is too extensive to discuss here. Many of the criticisms voiced during the 1970s and 1980s were presaged in Philip Rieff's influential *Triumph of the Therapeutic: Uses of Faith after Freud* (New York: Harper & Row, 1966). Drawing broadly on sociological insights, Rieff expressed concern that moral constraints based on religious teachings were being replaced by an "expressive-impulsive" orientation.

The trade-off that Rieff sensed between self-oriented spirituality and community-focused religion was prominent in the work of a number of his contemporaries. Berger and Luckmann wrote of religion becoming privatized as people turned inward to explore their inner selves. Berger emphasized that the very notion of the inner self was a cultural construct, promulgated most forcefully by psychoanalysis, and that it was an attempt to relocate, if not redefine, the sacred. "The other world, which religion located in a transcendental reality, is now introjected within human consciousness itself." Peter L. Berger, "Toward a Sociological Understanding of Psychoanalysis," *Social Research* 32 (spring 1965): 41. For Luckmann, the chief problem was that individuals were intent on demonstrating their autonomy and thus cutting themselves off from religious tradition and community. He associated autonomy with a lack of social restraint, an overemphasis on self-expression, and an inexhaustible quest to understand the inner self. "Since the inner man is, in effect, an undefinable entity, its presumed discovery involves a lifelong quest." Luckmann, *The Invisible Religion*, p. 110. This quest, Luckmann feared, encouraged people to withdraw from public life and to become alienated from social institutions because these institutions were perceived as threats to possibilities for self-exploration. *Inner* thus meant something too subjective to be understood except through an interminable succession of experiences involving intimacy, sexuality, and emotion.

A decade later, similar concerns about the self were articulated by sociologist Richard Sennett and historian Christopher Lasch, both of whom wrote about narcissism as a contemporary malady. Richard Sennett, *The Fall of Public Man* (New York: Random House, 1976), and Christopher Lasch, *The Culture of Narcissism: American Life in an Age of Diminishing Expectations* (New York: Norton, 1979). See also Daniel Bell, "Beyond Modernism, beyond Self," in *Art, Politics, and Will: Essays in Honor of Lionel Trilling*, ed. by Quentin Anderson, Stephen Donadio, and Steven Marcus (New York: Basic Books, 1977), p. 249, and Robert N. Bellah et al., *Habits of the Heart: Individualism and Commitment in American Life* (Berkeley: University of California Press, 1985).

18. See, for example, Robert N. Bellah, "Individualism and the Crisis of Civic Membership," *Christian Century*, 8 May 1996, 514–515.

19. Clifford Geertz, *Local Knowledge: Further Essays in Interpretive Anthropology* (New York: Basic Books, 1983).

20. Sandra Harding, *Whose Science? Whose Knowledge? Thinking from Women's Lives* (Ithaca, N.Y.: Cornell University Press, 1991); Joan Scott, *Gender and the Politics of History* (New York: Columbia University Press, 1988).

21. Research shows that an emphasis on the self in matters of faith and morality is associated with having a somewhat more lax attitude about participating in religious organizations as a matter of duty and with having doubts about the existence of God; in short, self-reliance appears to go with living in a somewhat

more relativistic world. Yet self-reliance is a tenet to which most church-going people subscribe as well. In the 1988 General Social Survey (Chicago: National Opinion Research Center, machine-readable data file), 60 percent of those who attend religious services every week agreed that morality is a personal matter, and 55 percent said it is very important to follow their own conscience. Or, viewed differently, 42 percent of those who agree strongly that morality is a personal matter still attend religious services at least once a month, as do 42 percent of those who say it is very important to follow their own conscience.

22. Research has consistently shown the great extent to which Americans are committed to self-improvement and the large numbers of people who express doubts about their identities. A national study conducted in 1982, for example, showed that 94 percent felt attempts "to fulfill your potential as a person" were important (60 percent said they were very important), yet only 33 percent said they were "very satisfied" with their own attempts to fulfill their potential. Self Esteem Study, conducted by the Gallup Organization; my analysis. The same study, using a more sophisticated set of questions to measure self-esteem, found that 24 percent of the respondents scored high on self-esteem, 32 percent scored relatively low, and the remainder (44 percent) scored in the middle. The principal dependent variable in the study was the Rosenberg Self-Esteem Scale, developed by Morris Rosenberg for a previous study of self-esteem among adolescents. The scale consists of ten items to which respondents are asked to register strong or weak degrees of agreement or disagreement. Each item reflects a self-assessment of the respondent, such as "on the whole, I am satisfied with myself" or "at times I think I am no good at all." Half the items are worded positively and half are worded negatively. For present purposes, a single scale was created, giving respondents a point for each positively worded item that was given a "strongly agree" response and a point for each negatively worded item receiving a "strongly disagree" response. This scale was then collapsed into a three-point index, where scores of 0 or 1 were assigned to the "low" category, scores of 2 through 6 to the "medium" category, and scores of 7 through 10 to the "high" category. (This procedure differs somewhat from Rosenberg's method, which assigned more complex weights to the items; a comparison of results, however, shows no significant differences.) Another study found that 7 percent of working Americans said they had been bothered a lot in the past year by not feeling good about themselves, and another 34 percent said that not feeling good about themselves had bothered them a little. Economic Values Study, 1992 (Wuthnow, *God and Mammon in America*); new analysis.

These studies also demonstrate that problems with self-identity reflect people's social circumstances. The more acute type of self-doubt (being bothered a lot) is aggravated by living in circumstances that are beyond one's control and beneath the life expectations of average Americans, such as not having enough money to pay one's bills, having been laid off from work, having taken a cut in pay, being educationally disadvantaged, or working at a low-paying job. Being troubled by moderate self-doubt stems from a wider and less easily characterized array of sources. For instance, feeling guilty about how one handles money is a stronger predictor of moderate self-doubt than is worrying about being able to pay one's bills. Working at a job that one considers meaningless is also more strongly associated with moderate self-doubt than is feeling that one is working too hard and wanting to work less. Feeling pressured, wanting more out of life, and wondering whether one's priorities are somehow askew also contribute to this kind of self-doubt.

Such feelings are widespread among Americans, occurring in virtually everyone some of the time and in a sizable minority in relatively serious magnitude. Social conditions magnify these concerns, both by giving us choices and by making it difficult to determine which choice may have the most desirable consequences. Self-doubt results because it is clear that we are not simply pawns of circumstance but feel responsible for creating our own happiness. An indication of the extent to which Americans accept responsibility for their own self-esteem is the fact that the strongest predictor of self-esteem in the 1982 study was how satisfied people were with their "efforts to fulfill [their] potential as a person." Of eleven activities, this one had the strongest effect of all (based on discriminant analysis of the Self-Esteem Survey, with the Rosenberg self-esteem scale as the dependent variable and items about satisfaction with various activities as predictor variables). Also indicative of the degree to which personal responsibility is at stake is the fact that the next highest predictors of self-esteem were also activities largely under the control of the individual and ones that imply an expenditure of effort to maintain or live up to: one's moral standards, one's interpersonal relationships, and one's work. In comparison, how satisfied people were with their relationship to God came in next to last among the eleven items included in the study.

23. Ellen Kurtz, *Not-God: A History of Alcoholics Anonymous* (Center City, Minn.: Hazelden, 1979).

24. Margaret Jones, "Getting Away from the 'R' Word," *Publishers Weekly,* 5 July 1993, 42–44.

25. Wuthnow, *Sharing the Journey*, p. 65.

26. Terence T. Gorski, *Understanding the Twelve Steps: An Interpretation and Guide for Recovering People* (New York: Simon & Schuster, 1989), p. 187.

27. Although it encourages introspection, AA parts company with critics who believe that Americans are already too focused on themselves, suggesting instead that people may be selfish because they have never taken an honest look at themselves. "Taking a Fourth Step inventory is a lot like shining a bright light into a cave," writes therapist Terence Gorski. "When you turn on the light, you can see all sorts of scary things crawling around inside" (ibid., p. 187). In this perspective, the self is quite different from the repressed self of the 1960s, which needed only to shake off social inhibitions and express itself. The self of AA is more akin to that of New England Puritans in their emphasis on fallibility and ignoble desires, even though these desires are described as an illness rather than sin. See Linda Mercandante, "Victims and Sinners in an Age of Addiction" (paper presented at the Center of Theological Inquiry, Princeton, N.J., February 1994). The personal inventory it encourages is, in Freudian terms, a quest to deflate the ego that fancies itself to be in control and to confront the passions associated with the id. AA language provides both a set of techniques for exploring the inner self and a guide to what may be found in that exploration. The techniques consist of various checklists and questions designed to prompt

personal reflection; the guide points to character defects, personal problems, mistaken beliefs, harmful ways of behaving toward others, painful and self-defeating habits, and irrational anxieties. Because candid introspection is likely to raise one's awareness of aspects of the self that are difficult to face, AA encourages people to select a personal sponsor or advisor to assist them in the inventory process.

28. May, *Addiction and Grace*, p. 1.

29. Ibid., p. 120.

30. Melody Beattie, *Codependent No More: How to Stop Controlling Others and Start Caring for Yourself* (San Francisco: Harper San Francisco, 1987); Melody Beattie, *Codependents' Guide to the Twelve Steps* (New York: Simon & Schuster, 1990), p. 75.

31. Beattie, *Codependents' Guide to the Twelve Steps*, p. 75.

32. Beattie, *Codependent No More*, p. 125.

33. Research suggests that many people turn to spiritual sources for help in dealing with self-doubts and that this quest reinforces the increasing diversity of religion in the United States. The resources that make a difference are ones that bolster the self's capacity to act as decisionmaker and that help perform repair work on the self when it receives bruises in the process of making its decisions. These resources are still provided primarily and to the widest number of people by religious organizations: the activities that help people feel better about themselves are generally formal activities, performed in the company of others, rather than informal activities performed alone. Yet these activities are quite diverse, revealing the diversity of programs that effective religious organizations feel compelled to supply. Evidence shows that people who hear inspirational sermons feel better about themselves, but so do people who attend support groups (that may or may not be under religious auspices), as do those who participate in religious counseling programs, attend spiritual retreats, or take part in prayer or religious discussion groups at their places of employment. These conclusions are drawn from examining multiple correlations between self-doubt and a variety of religious and quasi-religious activities in the Economic Values Survey (Wuthnow, *God and Mammon in America*). But if self-doubt provides a continuing reason for the existence of religious organizations, catering to this need puts organized religion on an equal—if not slippery—footing with other ways of alleviating self-doubt. Some evidence, for instance, suggests that physical exercise and talking over problems with one's spouse may be more effective in warding off moderate self-doubt than talking with the clergy, and for acute self-doubt the same evidence indicates that visiting a therapist is probably more effective than talking with the clergy.

34. Erich Fromm, *Psychoanalysis and Religion* (New Haven, Conn.: Yale University Press, 1950), p. 74, distinguished "adjustment therapy" from "soul therapy," explaining that adjustment therapy would help an individual conform with social demands, while soul therapy would help provide "optimal development of a person's potentialities and the realization of his individuality."

35. Moore's reluctance to define the soul is similar to that of Mary Oliver, "Some Questions You Might Ask," in *New and Selected Poems* (Boston: Beacon Press, 1992), who writes, "Is the soul solid, like iron? Or is it tender and breakable, like the wings of a moth in the beak of the owl?" (p. 65).

36. Moore, *Care of the Soul,* p. xi. Psychologist James Hillman, *A Blue Fire: Selected Writings* (New York: Harper & Row, 1989), from whom Moore borrows extensively, states that soul is a perspective or quality, rather than a substance, and that it can be used almost interchangeably with words as varied as spirit, heart, life, warmth, humanness, essence, emotion, quality, and virtue (p. 19).

37. Moore, *Care of the Soul,* p. 5.

38. Ibid., p. xvii.

39. Uma Silbey, *Enlightenment on the Run: Everyday Life as Spiritual Path* (San Rafael, Calif.: Airo Press, 1993), pp. 9–10.

40. Ibid., p. 19.

41. Moore, *Care of the Soul,* p. xiii.

42. Peck, *The Road Less Traveled,* p. 185.

43. Moore, *Care of the Soul,* p. 49.

44. Hillman, *A Blue Fire,* pp. 20–21.

45. Robert Sardello, *Love and the Soul* (New York: HarperCollins, 1995), p. xvi.

46. Moore, *Care of the Soul,* p. 68.

47. Taylor, *Sources of the Self,* argues that Romantic ideas of a unitary self are difficult to sustain under present complex conditions (p. 462).

48. Moore, *Care of the Soul,* p. 271.

49. R. Laurence Moore, *Religious Outsiders and the Making of Americans* (New York: Oxford University Press, 1986).

50. Moore, *Care of the Soul,* pp. 66–67; Hillman, *A Blue Fire,* pp. 38–45.

51. Hillman, *A Blue Fire,* p. 41.

52. Anthropologists have long observed that religious polytheism occurs in societies that honor places or positions by associating specialized deities with them (gods of particular city-states, clans, or occupations). Among other studies, see Guy E. Swanson, *The Birth of the Gods: The Origin of Primitive Beliefs* (Ann Arbor: University of Michigan Press, 1960); Ralph Underhill, "Economic and Political Antecedents of Monotheism: A Cross-Cultural Study," *American Journal of Sociology* 80 (1975): 841–861. In his classic work on Australian religions, French sociologist Emile Durkheim (*Elementary Forms of the Religious Life*) argued that generally human societies associate sacredness with those people or experiences that we deem superior to ourselves and on whom we depend.

53. Lynda Sexson, *Ordinarily Sacred* (New York: Crossroad, 1982), cited in Moore, *Care of the Soul,* p. 215.

54. Sardello, *Love and the Soul,* p. 21.

55. On dispersion, see Michel Foucault, *The Archaeology of Knowledge* (New York: Harper & Row, 1972), pp. 3–39.

56. On the social construction of the modern individual, see George M. Thomas et al., *Institutional Structure: Constituting State, Society, and the Individual* (Beverly Hills, Calif.: Sage, 1987), esp. chs. 10, 11, and 12.

57. Some of these arguments are reviewed and defended in Derek Parfit, *Reasons and Persons* (Oxford: Clarendon Press, 1984).

58. Robert S. McPherson, *Sacred Land, Sacred View: Navajo Perceptions of the Four Corners Region* (Salt Lake City: Signature Books, 1992).

59. William Barrett, *Death of the Soul: From Descartes to the Computer* (New York: Doubleday, 1986), pp. 115–116.

60. Larry Dossey, *Recovering the Soul: A Scientific and Spiritual Search* (New York: Bantam Books, 1989), p. 2.

61. Silbey, *Enlightenment on the Run*. This view of the self differs from—and sometimes explicitly rejects—earlier psychological theories that emphasized personality as a kind of solidified, preexisting entity that determined how a person would respond to new situations. "The whole idea of personality types," observes one critic, "is based upon a faintly nineteenth-century notion that a human personality is a discrete and enduring entity, a hard stone in the river bed of culture." Thomas G. Long, "Myers-Briggs and Other Modern Astrologies," *Theology Today* 49 (1992): 295. The dispersed self also contrasts with the self of personal-identity theorists, which is assumed to develop through a specified sequence of stages. "It is quite possible," wrote Lifton, that "the image of personal identity, in so far as it suggests inner stability and sameness, is derived from a vision of a traditional culture in which man's relationship to his institutions and symbols [is] still relatively intact, [which] is hardly the case." Robert Jay Lifton, "Protean Man," *Partisan Review*, winter 1968, 13; Lifton emphasized the "continuous psychic recreation" of the self; however, Protean Man has greater continuity and coherence than the dispersed self.

62. Lifton, "Protean Man," p. 17, notes that it is probably "one of the functional patterns of our day."

63. The person fashions the soul out of the stuff of momentary experiences; the soul is a story one tells about the journey one has been experiencing. As such, the soul is largely mental, consisting, as philosopher Richard Swinburne argues, of "apparent memory," which is the basis for assuming that personal identity exists at all and yet is something that can be said to have been created by God or to have a mysterious sacred existence beyond conscious thought itself. Richard Swinburne, *The Evolution of the Soul* (Oxford: Clarendon Press, 1986), esp. ch. 9.

64. "Starved for ideas and feelings that can give coherence," Lifton warned, the new self would turn to images that were "limited and often fleeting" ("Protean Man," p. 21).

65. Kenneth J. Gergen, *The Saturated Self: Dilemmas of Identity in Contemporary Life* (New York: Basic Books, 1991), coined the term *multiphrenia* to describe "the splitting of the individual into a multiplicity of self-investments." He observes, "It would be a mistake to view this multiphrenic condition as a form of illness, for it is often suffused with a sense of expansiveness and adventure. Someday there may indeed be nothing to distinguish multiphrenia from simply 'normal living'" (p. 74).

66. Philosopher George Kateb expresses a related idea when he observes that a fully developed self involves not only "thinking one's own thoughts" but also "thinking one's own thoughts *through*." Such a process, he warns, is "arduous, intermittent, expressed in and defeated by moods," yet it is also the route to "self-recovery." George Kateb, "Exile, Alienation, and Estrangement: Introduction," in *Home: A Place in the World,* ed. Arien Mack (New York: New York University Press, 1993), pp. 135–138.

67. Anthony Giddens, *Modernity and Self-Identity: Self and Society in the Late Modern Age* (Stanford, Calif.: Stanford University Press, 1991), p. 18.

68. Jean Bethke Elshtain, *Public Man, Private Woman: Women in Social and Political Thought* (Princeton, N.J.: Princeton University Press, 1981), writes of "the redemption of everyday life" as a broader intellectual current. In a more recent essay she remarks on the contrast between this orientation and a focus on self-expression: "this vision of self-celebrating self-expression . . . disdains 'mere life,' the life of labour, householdery, maternity and paternity"; Jean Bethke Elshtain, "The Risks and Responsibilities of Affirming Ordinary Life," in *Philosophy in an Age of Pluralism: The Philosophy of Charles Taylor in Question*, ed. James Tully (Cambridge: Cambridge University Press, 1994), p. 68.

69. C. G. Jung, *Letters*, vol. 2: *1951–61,* ed. Gerhard Adler and Aniela Jaffe (Princeton, N.J.: Princeton University Press, 1975), p. 171.

7.   THE PRACTICE OF SPIRITUALITY

1. These views go together, so that writers such as Bellah et al. in *Habits of the Heart* can identify someone who has her own private religion as a sign of the rank individualism of our times and argue that we must band together in congregations if we are to save ourselves. Or someone like Carter can decry the exclusion of organized, communal religion from American public life and implicitly assume that religion that is purely private cannot be good for anything; Stephen L. Carter, *The Culture of Disbelief: How American Law and Politics Trivialize Religious Devotion* (New York: Basic Books, 1993).

2. Valuable background on theological and historical understandings of devotional practices is found in Frank C. Senn, ed., *Protestant Spiritual Traditions* (New York: Paulist Press, 1986); Don E. Saliers, *Worship and Spirituality* (Philadelphia: Westminster, 1984); and John Macquarrie, *Paths in Spirituality,* 2d ed. (Harrisburg, Pa.: Morehouse Publishing, 1992).

3. William James, *The Varieties of Religious Experience: A Study in Human Nature* (1902; reprint, New York: New American Library, 1958), p. 352; see also James E. Dittes, "Beyond William James," in *Beyond the Classics: Essays in the Scientific Study of Religion,* ed. Charles Y. Glock and Phillip E. Hammond (New York: Harper & Row, 1973), ch. 7.

4. Teresa of Avila, *Autobiography,* ed. E. Allison Peters (New York: Image Books, 1991); John of the Cross, *Selected Writings,* ed. Kieran Kavanaugh (New York: Paulist Press, 1987); St. Francis de Sales, *Introduction to the Devout Life,* trans. and ed. John K. Ryan (New York, Image Books, 1989); on small groups, Wuthnow, *Sharing the Journey;* on meditation books, Gustav Niebuhr, "Seeking Solace and Support in Meditation Books," *New York Times,* 29 June 1994, A1, A17.

5. The main theoretical orientations toward religion in the social sciences have also paid some attention to spiritual practices, although it is often difficult to glean much from these works that is directly relevant to the present situation. Weber, for example, deals with prayer and Bible reading in only a few scattered passages in his extensive treatment of religion in *Economy and Society,* and Troeltsch's *Social Teaching of the Christian Churches* is valuable mostly in sug-

gesting the inherent tensions between institutional religion and those forms of private devotion that lead to a "purely spiritual religion." For Weber, the relevant portions are included in *Sociology of Religion;* and for Troeltsch, in Ernst Troeltsch, *The Social Teaching of the Christian Churches* (1931; reprint, New York: Harper & Row, 1960), esp. vol. 2, pp. 734–746.

6. My discussion of practice draws from Alasdair MacIntyre, *After Virtue: A Study in Moral Theory*, 2d ed. (Notre Dame, Ind.: University of Notre Dame Press, 1984); and Jeffrey Stout, *Ethics after Babel: The Languages of Morals and Their Discontents* (Boston: Beacon Press, 1988). MacIntyre (p. 187) writes, "By a 'practice' I am going to mean any coherent and complex form of socially established cooperative human activity through which goods internal to that form of activity are realized in the course of trying to achieve those standards of excellence which are appropriate to, and partially definitive of, that form of activity, with the result that human powers to achieve excellence, and human conceptions of the ends and goods involved, are systematically extended." The characteristics I discuss in the text differ somewhat in emphasis from MacIntyre's.

7. Quoted in William A. Barry, *Finding God in All Things: A Companion to the Spiritual Exercises of St. Ignatius* (Notre Dame, Ind.: Ave Maria Press, 1991), pp. 13–14.

8. Jean Comaroff, *Body of Power, Spirit of Resistance: The Culture and History of a South African People* (Chicago: University of Chicago Press, 1985), pp. 3–5, delineates two other meanings of practice: one that corresponds most closely with the phrase *lived experience* and one that emphasizes discourse. These, in my view, are too undifferentiated to be helpful in analyzing specific clusters of activity; they also draw the line too sharply between spoken action and other kinds of behavior and between the capacity for conscious reflection and taken-for-granted ways of behaving. Comaroff's discussion of "signifying practice" is more suggestive.

9. For instance, in emphasizing the connection between meditation and spirituality, Goldsmith writes that "meditation, if practiced faithfully, opens our consciousness to permit God to function in our life, to permit Christ to live our life— *but it must be practiced.*" Joel S. Goldsmith, *The Art of Meditation* (San Francisco: Harper San Francisco, 1956), p. 27.

10. Stout, *Ethics after Babel,* is a prominent example; see also the opening pages of Joseph Raz, "Multiculturalism: A Liberal Perspective," *Dissent,* winter 1994.

11. Standard references include Sherry B. Ortner, "Theory in Anthropology since the Sixties," *Comparative Studies in Society and History* 26 (1984): 126–166, which emphasizes "practice" in the work of Clifford Geertz; Pierre Bourdieu, *Outline of a Theory of Practice* (Cambridge: Cambridge University Press, 1977); and Pierre Bourdieu, *The Logic of Practice* (Cambridge: Polity Press, 1990).

12. This realization has been furthered by gender theory and by feminist methodology in the social sciences. See, for example, Bettina Aptheker, *Tapestries of Life: Women's Work, Women's Consciousness, and the Meaning of Daily Experience* (Amherst: University of Massachusetts Press, 1989); Deborah Tan-

nen, *You Just Don't Understand: Women and Men in Conversation* (New York: Ballantine, 1990); and Belenky et al., *Women's Ways of Knowing.*

13. Despite renewed scholarly interest in the idea of practice, interpreters of religion and society have, as I have indicated, often missed its significance. In their view, the alternative to participating in religious institutions is to retreat into a purely "privatized" form of spirituality. People are "churched," attending services and believing in the teachings of the church, or else they are "unchurched," perhaps still believing in God but doing nothing of consequence with their faith and perhaps harboring beliefs that are purely figments of their imaginations. Either they are in community, finding the sacred by collectively ascribing to what the leaders of religious institutions provide for them, or they are indifferent, apathetic, uninvolved, or at best seeking spirituality without effective guidance or serious engagement.

14. We need to be careful about how goal-oriented we assume deliberate behavior to be. Playing chess may have a clear, definable goal (winning) that dominates the players' minds and that governs their every move. Attending a worship service, I suspect, may be harder to understand in terms of goals. Deemphasizing goal attainment also helps to avoid thinking about practices in terms of strategy or calculation. People may calculate how to win at chess; the nature of the game encourages thinking ahead as many moves as possible. Gardening is a better case because it combines some planning with a great deal of improvisation.

15. Adams, *Godliness through Discipline,* p. 6.

16. Quoted in Ketchin, *The Christ-Haunted Landscape,* p. 90. Still, human practice is deliberate as long as one can choose to do otherwise. And deliberate actions are not only voluntary but are actions about which we deliberate. They are actions, Aristotle argued, "where the result is obscure and the right course not clearly defined," unlike simple activities that require little mastery at all. Aristotle, *Nicomachean Ethics,* trans. J. A. K. Thomson (Baltimore: Penguin Books, 1976), p. 119 (book 3, 112b5–26).

17. In the language of current moral philosophy, the primary rewards that come from participating in a particular practice are, by definition, internal to the practice itself. The joy of worship, for example, is an internal good that can be obtained only by worshiping. In contrast, external goods are the prestige, status, and money that may be the by-products of a practice but that have no specific connection with it. A worshiper may elevate his or her status in the community, for example, but could perhaps achieve the same results by playing golf at an exclusive country club; Stout, *Ethics after Babel,* p. 267.

18. James, *The Varieties of Religious Experience,* p. 42.

19. To say that internal goods can be attained only by engaging in a practice is not to suggest, however, that these goods are attainable only at the time one is fully devoted to a practice. A gardener knows what it is like to see plants growing, to sink one's hands into the warm soil, and to revel in a fresh blossom. Those experiences are likely to be most intense during the act of gardening itself. These goods, however, can extend into other situations as well: when a gardener paints a picture or writes in a journal and experiences the sensation again, when a gardener shares stories with another gardener or with an interested journalist, or

when a gardener wakes in the night with a new thought about gardening. The main difference between spiritual practice and gardening is that "spiritual goods" are much more difficult to measure than almost any other kind of good. Gardeners know they have made a mistake if their garden grows weeds; it is harder for spiritual practitioners to know whether they are truly in contact with God or just imagining it. Several other points follow: it is often difficult to distinguish between internal and external goods (for example, the joy of worship or the joy of simply feeling good); it may be hard to specify rules and to measure performance by using those rules (Aristotle's point about deliberation); and much of spiritual practice is likely to be concerned with defining the nature of its internal goods (that is, the sacred). For these reasons, writings on spiritual practice focus on describing what God is like, detailing manifestations of the sacred, and debunking false views of the sacred. Similarly, people who are regularly engaged in spiritual practices say they enjoy these activities not only because the activities help resolve their personal problems or give them good feelings but because they desire to know and experience the sacred.

20. Saying that practices are supported by an industry helps by sharpening the distinction between the two. A practice is not simply the norms of an institution writ small—the norms and assumptions that have been internalized by an individual. Rather, a practice is a set of activities that an individual or group of individuals engage in by drawing loosely from the resources available from one or more relevant industries.

21. Wendell Berry, *What Are People For?*, p. 96.

22. This does not mean that practitioners should conform blindly to the rules or that all the rules can be spelled out ahead of time or even that we can know for sure that a particular action will get us what we want. Thus it makes little sense to reduce practices to rational-choice models of behavior.

23. Stout, *Ethics after Babel*, p. 270, writes that the way to understand the language of a practice is to "listen in patiently as doctors and nurses talk about their lives, their patients, and each other, uninterrupted by Socratic questions. Probing that talk for foundational principles doesn't help much. Its significance is all on the surface, reflecting on goods to be sought, evils to be avoided, the do's and don't's of ends and means, the joys and sorrows of unintended consequences, good and bad traits of character, and agents who deserve praise or blame, each bit of discourse bearing some intelligible relation to other bits and to the practice as a whole, ordered toward its distinctive goods." Much of this language, I would add, remains unspoken in the course of pursuing a practice itself. Doctors and nurses do, for example, talk about some of these things, but they are frequently too busy with the tasks at hand and guided too much by shared assumptions to have the time or need to articulate what they are doing. For this reason, it is valuable to conduct interviews, asking people to reflect on their experience, to recount the stories they have heard, and to relate the stories they have used to make sense of their own lives.

24. Susanne Juhasz, "Towards a Theory of Form in Feminist Autobiography: Kate Millett's *Flying* and *Sita;* Maxine Hong Kingston's *The Woman Warrior*," in *Women's Autobiography: Essays in Criticism*, ed. Estelle C. Jelinek (Bloomington: Indiana University Press, 1980), pp. 223–224.

25. Stephen Turner, *The Social Theory of Practices: Tradition, Tacit Knowledge, and Presuppositions* (Chicago: University of Chicago Press, 1994), p. 11, writes, "It is our shared practices that enable us to be persuaded and persuade, to be explainers, or to justify and have the justifications accepted."

26. MacIntyre, *After Virtue*, p. 194.

27. Jack Kornfield, *A Path with Heart: A Guide through the Perils and Promises of Spiritual Life* (New York: Bantam Books, 1993), p. 34, emphasizes the value of practicing over a period of time (although not exclusively) within a single tradition: "If we do a little of one kind of practice and a little of another, the work we have done in one often doesn't continue to build as we change to the next. It is as if we were to dig many shallow wells instead of one deep one. In continually moving from one approach to another, we are never forced to face our own boredom, impatience, and fears."

28. I take it that the "practices" described in Dorothy C. Bass, ed., *Practicing Our Faith: A Way of Life for a Searching People* (San Francisco: Jossey-Bass, 1997), consist partly of the "interlacing" of specific devotional activities with other realms of human experience, such as being hospitable, making decisions, finding community, and dealing with illness and death.

29. Chittister, *Wisdom Distilled from the Daily*, p. 35.

30. Niebuhr, *The Irony of American History*, p. 10.

31. Aitken and Steindl-Rast, *The Ground We Share*, p. 68.

Selected Bibliography

Adams, Bert N. *Kinship in an Urban Setting.* Chicago: Markham, 1968.

Adams, Jay E. *Godliness through Discipline.* Nutley, N.J.: Presbyterian and Reformed Publishing, 1977.

Adelman, Ken. "True Believer." *Washingtonian,* December 1993, 1.

Adorno, T. W., E. Frenkel-Brunswick, D. J. Levinson, and R. N. Sanford. *The Authoritarian Personality.* New York: Harper & Row, 1950.

Aitken, Robert, and David Steindl-Rast. *The Ground We Share: Everyday Practice, Buddhist and Christian.* Edited by Nelson Foster. Liguori, Mo.: Triumph Books, 1994.

Albanese, Catherine L. *Nature Religion in America: From the Algonquin Indians to the New Age.* Chicago: University of Chicago Press, 1991.

Allport, Gordon W. *Becoming: Basic Considerations for a Psychology of Personality.* New Haven, Conn.: Yale University Press, 1955.

Altizer, Thomas J. J. *Oriental Mysticism and Biblical Eschatology.* Philadelphia: Westminster Press, 1961.

Alwin, Duane F. "From Obedience to Autonomy: Changes in Traits Desired in Children, 1924–1978." *Public Opinion Quarterly* 52 (1988): 33–52.

Anderson, Joan Wester. *Where Angels Walk: True Stories of Heavenly Visitors.* New York: Barton & Brett, 1992.

Anderson, Richard Feather. "Geomancy." In *The Power of Place: Sacred Ground in Natural and Human Enviroments,* edited by James A. Swan. Wheaton, Ill.: Quest Books, 1991.

Angelou, Maya. *Wouldn't Take Nothing for My Journey Now.* New York: Random House, 1993.

"Angels." *Emerging Trends,* January 1994, 1–2.

Appleton, George. *On the Eight-Fold Path: Christian Presence amid Buddhism.* New York: Oxford University Press, 1961.

Aptheker, Bettina. *Tapestries of Life: Women's Work, Women's Consciousness, and the Meaning of Daily Experience*. Amherst: University of Massachusetts Press, 1989.

Arendt, Hannah. *The Human Condition*. Chicago: University of Chicago Press, 1958.

Bachleda, F. Lynne. "Angels in America." *Publishers Weekly*, 12 July 1993, 31–35.

Baker, Ray Stannard. *Native American*. New York: Scribner's, 1941.

Barrett, William. *Death of the Soul: From Descartes to the Computer*. New York: Doubleday, 1986.

Barry, William A. *Finding God in All Things: A Companion to the Spiritual Exercises of St. Ignatius*. Notre Dame, Ind.: Ave Maria Press, 1991.

Bass, Dorothy C., ed. *Practicing Our Faith: A Way of Life for a Searching People*. San Francisco: Jossey-Bass, 1997.

Bau, Ignatius. *This Ground Is Holy: Church Sanctuary and Central American Refugees*. New York: Paulist Press, 1985.

Beattie, Melody. *Codependent No More: How to Stop Controlling Others and Start Caring for Yourself*. San Francisco: Harper San Francisco, 1987.

Beattie, Melody. *Codependents' Guide to the Twelve Steps*. New York: Simon & Schuster, 1990.

Becker, Howard S., and Anselm L. Strauss. "Careers, Personalty, and Adult Socialization." *American Journal of Sociology* 62 (1956): 253–263.

Belenky, Mary Field, Blythe McVicker Clinchy, Nancy Rule Goldberger, and Jill Mattuck Tarule. *Women's Ways of Knowing: The Development of Self, Voice, and Mind*. New York: Basic Books, 1986.

Bell, Daniel. "Beyond Modernism, beyond Self." In *Art, Politics, and Will: Essays in Honor of Lionel Trilling*, edited by Quentin Anderson, Stephen Donadio, and Steven Marcus. New York: Basic Books, 1977.

Bellah, Robert N. "Individualism and the Crisis of Civic Membership." *Christian Century*, 8 May 1996, 510–515,

Bellah, Robert N. "No Direction Home—Religious Aspects of the American Crisis." In *Search for the Sacred: The New Spiritual Quest*, edited by Myron B. Bloy, Jr. New York: Seabury, 1972.

Bellah, Robert N., Richard Madsen, William M. Sullivan, Ann Swidler, and Steven M. Tipton. *Habits of the Heart: Individualism and Commitment in American Life*. Berkeley: University of California Press, 1985.

Bender, Thomas. "Making Places Sacred." In *The Power of Place: Sacred Ground in Natural and Human Environments*, edited by James A. Swan. Wheaton, Ill.: Quest Books, 1991.

Berger, Peter L. *The Noise of Solemn Assemblies: Christian Commitment and the Religious Establishment*. Garden City, N.Y.: Doubleday, 1961.

Berger, Peter L. *The Sacred Canopy: Elements of a Sociological Theory of Religion*. Garden City, N.Y.: Doubleday, 1967.

Berger, Peter L. "Toward a Sociological Understanding of Psychoanalysis." *Social Research* 32 (spring 1965): 26–41. Reprinted in Peter L. Berger, *Facing Up to Modernity: Excursions in Society, Politics, and Religion* (New York: Basic Books, 1977).

Berger, Peter L., Brigitte Berger, and Hansfried Kellner. *The Homeless Mind: Modernization and Consciousness.* New York: Random House, 1973.

Berrigan, Daniel, and Thich Nhat Hanh. *The Raft Is Not the Shore: Conversations toward a Christian-Buddhist Awareness.* Boston: Beacon Press, 1975.

Berry, Wendell. *What Are People For?* San Francisco: North Point Press, 1990.

Bloch, Ruth. "American Feminine Ideals in Transition: The Rise of the Moral Mother, 1785–1815." *Feminist Studies* 4 (1978): 101–126.

Bly, Robert. *Iron John: A Book about Men.* Reading, Mass.: Addison-Wesley, 1990.

Bogardus, Emory S. *Essentials of Social Psychology.* 4th ed. Los Angeles: Jesse Ray Miller Press, 1923.

Bonhoeffer, Dietrich. *Letters and Papers from Prison.* 1953. Reprint, New York: Macmillan, 1962.

Boorstin, Daniel J. *The Americans: The Colonial Experience.* New York: Vintage Books, 1958.

Boorstin, Daniel J. *The Americans: The Democratic Experience.* New York: Vintage Books, 1973.

Bossard, James H. S., and Eleanor S. Boll. *Ritual in Family Living: A Contemporary Study.* Philadelphia: University of Pennsylvania Press, 1950.

Bourdieu, Pierre. *The Logic of Practice.* Cambridge: Polity Press, 1990.

Bourdieu, Pierre. *Outline of a Theory of Practice.* Cambridge: Cambridge University Press, 1977.

Brace, Marianne. "Indian Tales and a Nickel for the Birds." *Independent,* 4 June 1994, 30.

Bradshaw, John. *Homecoming: Reclaiming and Championing Your Inner Child.* New York: Bantam Books, 1990.

Brenneman, Betsy. "The Way It Happened." In *Search for the Sacred: The New Spiritual Quest,* edited by Myron B. Bloy, Jr. New York: Seabury, 1972.

Bronfenbrenner, Urie. "Socialization and Social Class through Time and Space." In *Readings in Social Psychology,* 3d ed., edited by E. E. Maccoby, T. M. Newcomb, and E. L. Hartley. New York: Holt, Rinehart & Winston, 1958.

Brown, Michael F. *The Channeling Zone: American Spirituality in an Anxious Age.* Cambridge, Mass.: Harvard University Press, 1997.

Brown, Norman O. *Love's Body.* New York: Vintage Books, 1968.

Bruchec, Joseph, and Diana Landau. *Singing of Earth.* San Francisco: Walking Stick Press, 1993.

Bryce, James. *Reflections on American Institutions.* 1888. Reprint, Gloucester, Mass.: Peter Smith, 1970.

Burnham, Sophy, ed. *Angel Letters.* New York: Ballantine, 1991.

Burnham, Sophy. *A Book of Angels.* New York: Ballantine, 1990.

Burnham, Sophy. *The President's Angel.* New York: Ballantine, 1993.

Butler, Jon. *Awash in a Sea of Faith: Christianizing the American People.* Cambridge, Mass.: Harvard University Press, 1992.

Callaway, Tucker N. *Japanese Buddhism and Christianity: A Comparison of the Christian Doctrine of Salvation with That of Some Major Sects of Japanese Buddhism.* Tokyo: Shinkyo Shuppansha Protestant Publishing, 1957.

Calvin, John. *Institutes of the Christian Religion*. Edited by Hugh T. Kerr. 1559. Reprint, Louisville, Ky.: Westminster/John Knox, 1989.

Campbell, Joseph, with Bill Moyers. *The Power of Myth*. Edited by Betty Sue Flowers. New York: Doubleday, 1988.

Canby, Henry Seidel. *The Age of Confidence*. New York: Farrar & Reinhart, 1939.

Caplow, Theodore, Howard M. Bahr, John Modell, and Bruce A. Chadwick. *Recent Social Trends in the United States, 1960–1990*. Montreal: McGill-Queen's University Press, 1991.

Carter, Stephen L. *The Culture of Disbelief: How American Law and Politics Trivialize Religious Devotion*. New York: Basic Books, 1993.

Casanova, José. *Public Religions in the Modern World*. Chicago: University of Chicago Press, 1994.

Chappell, Tom. *The Soul of a Business: Managing for Profit and the Common Good*. New York: Bantam Books, 1993.

Charry, Ellen T. "Raising Christian Children in a Pagan Culture." *Christian Century*, 16 February 1994, 166–169.

Chesterton, G. K. *What I Saw in America*. New York: Dodd, Mead, 1922.

Chittister, Joan. *Wisdom Distilled from the Daily: Living the Rule of St. Benedict Today*. New York: HarperCollins, 1991.

Christian, William A., Jr. *Person and God in a Spanish Valley*. New York: Seminar Press, 1972.

Church, F. Forrester. *Entertaining Angels: A Guide to Heaven for Atheists and True Believers*. New York: Harper & Row, 1987.

Ciardiello, Joe. "The Writer's Life: A Conversation between Alice Walker, Isabel Allende, and Jean Shinoda Bolen on Passion, Authenticity, and the Creative Fire." *New Age Journal*, November/December 1993, 85, 88.

Comaroff, Jean. *Body of Power, Spirit of Resistance: The Culture and History of a South African People*. Chicago: University of Chicago Press, 1985.

Conn, Joann Wolski. *The New Dictionary of Catholic Spirituality*. Collegeville, Minn.: Liturgical Press, 1992.

Converse, Philip E., Jean D. Dotson, Wendy J. Hoag, and William H. McGee III. *American Social Attitudes Data Sourcebook*. Cambridge: Harvard University Press, 1980.

Corless, Roger, and Paul F. Knotter. *Buddhist Emptiness and Christian Trinity: Essays and Explorations*. New York: Paulist Press, 1990.

Cox, Harvey. *The Feast of Fools. A Theological Essay on Festivity and Fantasy*. New York: Harper & Row, 1969.

Cox, Harvey. *The Secular City: Secularization and Urbanization in Theological Perspective*. 2d ed. New York: Collier Books, 1990.

Crews, Harry. *Body*. New York: Poseidon Press, 1990.

Daniel, Alma, Timothy Wyllie, and Andrew Ramer. *Ask Your Angels*. New York: Ballantine, 1992.

Davidman, Lynn. *Tradition in a Rootless World: Women Turn to Orthodox Judaism*. Berkeley: University of California Press, 1991.

Davie, Jody Shapiro. *Women in the Presence: Constructing Community and Seeking Spirituality in Mainline Protestantism*. Philadelphia: University of Pennsylvania Press, 1995.

Davies, Douglas. "Christianity." In *Sacred Place,* edited by Jean Holm with John Bowker. London: Pinter, 1994.

Davis, Charles. *Religion and the Making of Society: Essays in Social Theology.* Cambridge: Cambridge University Press, 1994.

de Kretser, Bryan. *Man in Buddhism and Christianity.* Calcutta: Y.M.C.A. Publishing House, 1954.

De Silva, Lynn A. *Reincarnation in Buddhist and Christian Thought.* Colombo, Sri Lanka: Christian Study Centre, 1968.

Dewey, John. *Theory of the Moral Life.* 1908. Reprint, New York: Holt, Rinehart & Winston, 1960.

Diggins, John Patrick. *The Promise of Pragmatism: Modernism and the Crisis of Knowledge and Authority.* Chicago: University of Chicago Press, 1994.

DiMaggio, Paul J., and Walter W. Powell. "Introduction." In *The New Institutionalism in Organizational Analysis,* edited by Walter W. Powell and Paul J. DiMaggio. Chicago: University of Chicago Press, 1991.

Dittes, James E. "Beyond William James." In *Beyond the Classics: Essays in the Scientific Study of Religion,* edited by Charles Y. Glock and Phillip E. Hammond. New York: Harper & Row, 1973.

Dobson, James. *Dare to Discipline.* Chicago: Gospel Light, 1972.

Doebler, Paul D. "Growth and Development of Consumer Books Stores since 1954—An Update through 1977." In *Book Industry Trends: 1980,* edited by John P. Dessauer, Paul D. Doebler, Peter H. Newman, J. Kendrick Noble, Jr., and E. Wayne Nordberg. Darien, Conn.: Book Industry Study Group, 1980.

Dolan, Jay P. "The Immigrants and Their Gods: A New Perspective in American Religious History." *Church History* 57 (1988): 61–72.

Donohue, William A. "Why the Schools Fail: Reclaiming the Moral Dimension in Education." *Heritage Foundation Reports,* 23 June 1988.

Donovan, John B. *Pat Robertson: The Authorized Biography.* New York: Macmillan, 1988.

Dossey, Larry. *Recovering the Soul: A Scientific and Spiritual Search.* New York: Bantam Books, 1989.

Douglas, Mary. "The Idea of a Home: A Kind of Space." In *Home: A Place in the World,* edited by Arien Mack. New York: New York University Press, 1993.

Durkheim, Emile. *The Elementary Forms of the Religious Life.* New York: Free Press, 1915.

Durkheim, Emile. *On Morality and Society.* Edited by Robert N. Bellah. Chicago: University of Chicago Press, 1973.

Eadie, Betty J. *Embraced by the Light.* Placerville, Calif.: Gold Leaf Press, 1992.

Ebeling, Gerhard. *The Word of God and Tradition: Historical Studies Interpreting the Divisions of Christianity.* London: William Collins Sons, 1968.

Eckardt, A. Roy. *The Surge of Piety in America: An Appraisal.* New York: Association Press, 1958.

Eliade, Mircea. *The Sacred and the Profane: The Nature of Religion.* Translated by Willard Trask. 1957. Reprint, New York: Harcourt Brace, 1989.

Eller, Cynthia. *Living in the Lap of the Goddess: The Feminist Spirituality Movement in America.* New York: Crossroad. 1993.

Ellis, John Tracy. *American Catholicism*. Chicago: University of Chicago Press, 1956.

Ellul, Jacques. *The Technological Society*. New York: Knopf, 1964.

Ellwood, Robert S. *The Sixties Spiritual Awakening: American Religion Moving from Modern to Postmodern*. New Brunswick, N.J.: Rutgers University Press, 1994.

Elshtain, Jean Bethke. *Public Man, Private Woman: Women in Social and Political Thought*. Princeton, N.J.: Princeton University Press, 1981.

Elshtain, Jean Bethke. "The Risks and Responsibilities of Affirming Ordinary Life." In *Philosophy in an Age of Pluralism: The Philosophy of Charles Taylor in Question*, edited by James Tully. Cambridge: Cambridge University Press, 1994.

Elwood, Roger. *Angelwalk*. New York: Crossway Books, 1988.

Erikson, Erik H. *Childhood and Society*. New York: Norton, 1950.

Erikson, Kai T. *Everything in Its Path: Destruction of Community in the Buffalo Creek Flood*. New York: Simon & Schuster, 1976.

Erikson, Kai T. *Wayward Puritans: A Study in the Sociology of Deviance*. New York: Wiley, 1966.

Fingarette, Herbert. *The Self in Transformation: Psychoanalysis, Philosophy and the Life of the Spirit*. New York: Harper & Row, 1963.

Fiorenza, Elisabeth Schussler. *Bread Not Stone: The Challenge of Feminist Biblical Interpretation*. Boston: Beacon Press, 1995.

Fischer, Claude S. "The Dispersion of Kinship Ties in Modern Society: Contemporary Data and Historical Speculation." *Journal of Family History* 7 (1982): 353–375.

Fishburn, Janet. *The Fatherhood of God and the Victorian Family: The Social Gospel in America*. Philadelphia: Fortress Press, 1981.

FitzGerald, Frances. *Cities on a Hill: A Journey through Contemporary American Cultures*. New York: Simon & Schuster, 1986.

Fleming, Robert. "'And All Things, Whatsoever Ye Shall Ask in Prayer, Believing Ye Shall Receive.'" *Omni*, May 1993, 27.

Fontinell, Eugene. "The Return of 'Selves.'" *Cross Currents* 43 (1993): 358–374.

Foster, Richard J. *Celebration of Discipline: The Path to Spiritual Growth*. New York: Harper & Row, 1978.

Foster, Richard J. *Prayer: Finding the Heart's True Home*. San Francisco: Harper San Francisco, 1992.

Foucault, Michel. *The Archaeology of Knowledge*. New York: Harper & Row, 1972.

Francis de Sales, St. *Introduction to the Devout Life*. Translated and edited by John K. Ryan. New York: Image Books, 1989.

Freeman, Eileen Elias. *Touched by Angels*. New York: Warner Books, 1993.

Friedan, Betty. *The Feminine Mystique*. New York: Norton, 1963.

Friedman, Milton. *Capitalism and Freedom*. Chicago: University of Chicago Press, 1962.

Froeschlé-Chopard, Marie-Hélène. "Les dévotions populaires d'après les visites pastorales: Un example: le diocèse de Vence au début du XVIIIe siècle." *Revue d'histoire de l'église de France* 60 (1974): 85–99.

Fromm, Erich. *Escape from Freedom.* New York: Farrar and Rinehart, 1941.

Fromm, Erich. *Man for Himself.* New York: Rinehart, 1947.

Fromm, Erich. *Psychoanalysis and Religion.* New Haven, Conn.: Yale University Press, 1950.

Furlong, Monica. *Zen Effects: The Life of Alan Watts.* Boston: Houghton Mifflin, 1986.

Gallup, George H., Jr. *Religion in America: 1978.* Princeton, N.J.: Gallup Organization, 1978.

Gallup, George H., Jr. *Religion in America: 1996 Report.* Princeton, N.J.: Princeton Religion Research Center, 1996.

Gans, Herbert. "Progress of a Suburban Jewish Community." *Commentary,* February 1957, 120–125.

Garcia, Christina. "Thousands Seek Spiritual Guidance." *Time,* 15 December 1986, 36.

Gaustad, Edwin Scott. *A Religious History of America.* New York: Harper & Row, 1966.

Geertz, Clifford. *The Interpretation of Cultures.* New York: Basic Books, 1973.

Geertz, Clifford. *Local Knowledge: Further Essays in Interpretive Anthropology.* New York: Basic Books, 1983.

George, Carl F. *The Coming Church Revolution: Empowering Leaders for the Future.* Old Tappan, N.J.: Fleming Revell, 1994.

Gergen, Kenneth J. *The Saturated Self: Dilemmas of Identity in Contemporary Life.* New York: Basic Books, 1991.

Giddens, Anthony. *Modernity and Self-Identity: Self and Society in the Late Modern Age.* Stanford, Calif.: Stanford University Press, 1991.

Gilder, George. "Wealth and Poverty Revisited." *American Spectator,* July 1993, 4.

Gilligan, Carol. *In a Different Voice: Psychological Theory and Women's Development.* Cambridge, Mass.: Harvard University Press, 1982.

Ginsburg, Faye D. *Contested Lives: The Abortion Debate in an American Community.* Berkeley: University of California Press, 1989.

Glick, Paul C. "A Demographer Looks at American Families." *Journal of Marriage and the Family* 37 (1975): 15–26.

Glock, Charles Y. *Perspectives on Life in America Today, 1973* [machine-readable data file]. Berkeley, Calif.: Survey Research Center, 1975.

Glock, Charles Y., and Robert N. Bellah, eds. *The New Religious Consciousness.* Berkeley: University of California Press, 1976.

Glock, Charles Y., Benjamin B. Ringer, and Earl R. Babbie. *To Comfort and to Challenge: A Dilemma of the Contemporary Church.* Berkeley: University of California Press, 1967.

Goldsmith, Joel S. *The Art of Meditation.* San Francisco: Harper San Francisco, 1956.

Gorski, Terence T. *Understanding the Twelve Steps: An Interpretation and Guide for Recovering People.* New York: Simon & Schuster, 1989.

"Grading Biblical Knowledge on a Curve." *Emerging Trends,* June 1994, 1–4.

Graham, Aelred. *Zen Catholicism: A Suggestion.* New York: Harcourt, Brace & World, 1963.

Greeley, Andrew M. *The American Catholic: A Social Portrait*. New York: Basic Books, 1976.

Greyson, Bruce, and Anne Longley. "A Glimpse Beyond." *People*, 1 August 1994.

Groff, Kent Ira. *Active Spirituality: A Guide for Seekers and Ministers*. Washington, D.C.: Alban Institute, 1993.

Guiness, Os. *The American Hour: A Time of Reckoning and the Once and Future Role of Faith*. New York: Free Press, 1993.

Gussow, Alan. "A Sense of Place." In *The Earth Speaks,* edited by Steve Van Matre and Bill Weiler. Greenville, W.Va.: Institute for Earth Education, 1983.

Halberstam, David. *The Fifties*. New York: Villard Books, 1993.

Hall, Calvin S., and Gardner Lindzey. *Theories of Personality*. New York: Wiley, 1957.

Halttunen, Karen. *Confidence Men and Painted Women: A Study of Middle-Class Culture in America, 1830–1870*. New Haven, Conn.: Yale University Press, 1982.

Handlin, Oscar. *The Uprooted*. New York: Little, Brown, 1951.

Handlin, Oscar, and Mary F. Handlin. *Facing Life: Youth and the Family in American History*. Boston: Little, Brown, 1971.

Harding, Sandra. *Whose Science? Whose Knowledge? Thinking from Women's Lives*. Ithaca, N.Y.: Cornell University Press, 1991.

Harney, Robert F. "Religion and Ethnocultural Communities." *Polyphony* 1 (1978): 1–10.

Harvey, Brett. *The Fifties: A Women's Oral History*. New York: HarperCollins, 1993.

Hatch, Nathan O. *The Democratization of American Christianity*. New Haven, Conn.: Yale University Press, 1989.

Hawke, David Freeman. *Everyday Life in Early America*. New York: Harper & Row, 1988.

Heelas, Paul. *The New Age Movement: The Celebration of the Self and the Sacralization of Modernity*. London: Blackwell, 1996.

Heelas, Paul. "The Sacralization of the Self and New Age Capitalism." In *Social Change in Contemporary Britain,* edited by Nicholas Abercrombie and Alan Warde. Cambridge: Polity Press, 1990.

Heidegger, Martin. *Vorträge und Aufsätze*. Pfullingen: Neske, 1954.

Herberg, Will. *Protestant, Catholic, Jew*. New York: Doubleday, 1955.

Heschel, Abraham Joshua. *Man's Quest for God: Studies in Prayer and Symbolism*. New York: Scribner's, 1954.

Hillman, James. *A Blue Fire: Selected Writings*. New York: Harper & Row, 1989.

Hobbes, Thomas. *English Works*. Aalen, Germany: Scientia, 1966.

Hodgkinson, Virginia A., Murray S. Weitzman, and Arthur D. Kirsch. *From Belief to Commitment: The Activities and Finances of Religious Congregations in the United States*. Washington, D.C.: Independent Sector, 1988.

Hoge, Dean R., Benton Johnson, and Donald A. Luidens. *Vanishing Boundaries: The Religion of Mainline Protestant Baby Boomers*. Louisville, Ky.: Westminster/John Knox, 1994.

Holifield, E. Brooks. *A History of Pastoral Care in America: From Salvation to Self-Realization*. Nashville, Tenn.: Abingdon Press, 1983.

Hollander, John. "It All Depends." In *Home: A Place in the World,* edited by Arien Mack. New York: New York University Press, 1993.

Howe, Irving. *World of Our Fathers.* New York: Harcourt Brace Jovanovich, 1976.

Hudson, W. H. "Are Churches Really Booming?" *Christian Century* 77 (December 21, 1955): 1494–1496.

Hunter, Janet H. "Inscribing the Self in the Heart of the Family: Diaries and Girlhood in Late-Victorian America." *American Quarterly* 44 (1992): 51–81.

James, William. *The Varieties of Religious Experience: A Study in Human Nature.* 1902. Reprint, New York: New American Library, 1958.

Jeffrey, Kirk. "The Family as a Utopian Retreat from the City: The Nineteenth Century Contribution." *Soundings: An Interdisciplinary Journal* 55 (1972): 24–36.

John of the Cross. *Selected Writings.* Edited by Kieran Kavanaugh. New York: Paulist Press, 1978.

Johnson, Elizabeth A. *She Who Is: The Mystery of God in Feminist Theological Discourse.* New York: Crossroad, 1993.

Jones, E. Stanley. *The Way to Power and Poise.* New York: Abingdon-Cokesbury Press, 1949.

Jones, Margaret. "Getting Away from the 'R' Word." *Publishers Weekly,* 5 July 1993, 42–44.

Joselit, Jenna Weissman. *The Wonders of America: Reinventing Jewish Culture, 1880–1950.* New York: Hill & Wang, 1994.

Juhasz, Susanne. "Towards a Theory of Form in Feminist Autobiography: Kate Millett's *Flying* and *Sita;* Maxine Hong Kingston's *The Woman Warrior.*" In *Women's Autobiography: Essays in Criticism,* edited by Estelle C. Jelinek. Bloomington: Indiana University Press, 1980.

Jung, C. G. *Letters.* Vol. 2: *1951–61,* edited by Gerhard Adler and Aniela Jaffé. Princeton, N.J.: Princeton University Press, 1975.

Kateb, George. "Exile, Alienation, and Estrangement: Introduction." In *Home: A Place in the World,* edited by Arien Mack. New York: New York University Press, 1993.

Katz, Donald. *Home Fires: An Intimate Portrait of One Middle-Class Family in Postwar America.* New York: HarperCollins, 1992.

Kazin, Alfred. *On Native Grounds: An Interpretation of Modern American Prose Literature.* 1942. Reprint, New York: Harcourt Brace, 1982.

Kelley, Dean M. *Why Conservative Churches Are Growing: A Study in Sociology of Religion.* Rev. ed. Macon, Ga.: Mercer University Press, 1986.

Kennedy, David. *Birth Control in America.* New Haven, Conn.: Yale University Press, 1970.

Kennedy, John F. *"Let the Word Go Forth": The Speeches, Statements, and Writings of John F. Kennedy, 1947–1963.* Edited by Theodore C. Sorensen. New York: Delacorte Press, 1988.

Kerouac, Jack. *On the Road.* New York: Viking Press, 1957.

Kerr, Hugh T. "Spiritual Discipline." *Theology Today* 49 (1993): 449–453.

Ketchin, Susan. *The Christ-Haunted Landscape: Faith and Doubt in Southern Fiction.* Jackson: University Press of Mississippi, 1994.

King, Martin Luther, Jr. *Stride toward Freedom: The Montgomery Story*. New York: Harper & Row, 1958.

King, Winston L. *Buddhism and Christianity: Some Bridges of Understanding*. Philadelphia: Westminster Press, 1962.

Kornfield, Jack. *A Path with Heart: A Guide through the Perils and Promises of Spiritual Life*. New York: Bantam Books, 1993.

Kucharsky, David. *The Man from Plains: The Mind and Spirit of Jimmy Carter*. New York: Harper & Row, 1976.

Kurtz, Ellen. *Not-God: A History of Alcoholics Anonymous*. Center City, Minn.: Hazelden, 1979.

Kurzweil, Edith. *The Freudians: A Comparative Perspective*. New Haven, Conn.: Yale University Press, 1989.

Lasch, Christopher. *The Culture of Narcissism: American Life in an Age of Diminishing Expectations*. New York: Norton, 1979.

Leavell, Landrum P. *Angels, Angels, Angels*. Nashville, Tenn.: Broadman Press, 1973.

Lenski, Gerhard. *The Religious Factor: A Sociological Study of Religion's Impact on Politics, Economics, and Family Life*. Garden City, N.Y.: Doubleday, 1961.

Lerner, Max. *Wrestling with the Angel*. New York: Norton, 1990.

Levertov, Denise. "Mass for the Day of St. Thomas Didymus." Excerpted in *Cries of the Spirit: A Celebration of Women's Spirituality*, edited by Marilyn Sewell. Boston: Beacon Press, 1991.

Levy, Frank. *Dollars and Dreams*. New York: Russell Sage Foundation, 1987.

Lifton, Robert Jay. "Protean Man." *Partisan Review*, winter 1968, 13–21.

Lilliefors, Jim. *Highway 50: Ain't That America*. Golden, Colo.: Fulcrum, 1993.

Linde, Charlotte. *Life Stories: The Creation of Coherence*. New York: Oxford University Press, 1993.

Lippmann, Walter. *A Preface to Morals*. New York: Macmillan, 1929.

Lipset, Seymour Martin. "Religion in America: What Religious Revival?" *Columbia University Forum* 2 (winter 1959): 1–5.

Long, Thomas G. "Myers-Briggs and Other Modern Astrologies." *Theology Today* 49 (1992): 290–295.

Luckmann, Thomas. *The Invisible Religion: The Transformation of Symbols in Industrial Society*. New York: Macmillan, 1967.

Luhmann, Niklas. "The Individuality of the Individual." In *Reconstructing Individualism: Autonomy, Individuality, and the Self in Western Thought*, edited by Thomas C. Heller, Morton Sosna, and David E. Wellbery. Stanford, Calif.: Stanford University Press, 1986.

Lukacs, Georg. *The Theory of the Novel*. Translated by Anna Bostock. 1920. Reprint, Cambridge, Mass.: MIT Press, 1971.

Luker, Kristin. *Abortion and the Politics of Motherhood*. Berkeley: University of California Press, 1984.

Lynd, Robert S., and Helen Merrel Lynd. *Middletown: A Study in Modern American Culture*. New York: Harcourt Brace, 1929.

Lyotard, Jean-Francois. *The Postmodern Condition: A Report on Knowledge*. Minneapolis: University of Minnesota Press, 1984.

Macdonald, Hope. *When Angels Appear*. Grand Rapids, Mich.: Zondervan, 1982.

MacIntyre, Alasdair. *After Virtue: A Study in Moral Theory*. 2d ed. Notre Dame, Ind.: University of Notre Dame Press, 1984.

Macquarrie, John. *Paths in Spirituality*. 2d ed. Harrisburg, Pa.: Morehouse Publishing, 1992.

Mailer, Norman. "The White Negro: Superficial Reflections on the Hipster." In *Legacy of Dissent*, edited by Nicolaus Mills. 1957. Reprint, New York: Touchstone, 1994.

Maitland, Sara. *A Big-Enough God: A Feminist's Search for Joyful Theology*. New York: Holt, Rinehart & Winston, 1995.

Marsden, George M. *Fundamentalism and American Culture: The Shaping of Twentieth-Century Evangelicalism, 1870–1925*. New York: Oxford University Press, 1980.

Martin, William. *A Prophet with Honor: The Billy Graham Story*. New York: Morrow, 1991.

Maslow, Abraham. *Motivation and Personality*. New York: Harper & Row, 1954.

Maslow, Abraham. *Toward a Psychology of Being*. Princeton, N.J.: Van Nostrand, 1962.

May, Gerald G. *Addiction and Grace: Love and Spirituality in the Healing of Addictions*. New York: HarperCollins, 1988.

May, Rollo. "The Significance of Symbols." In *Symbolism in Religion and Literature*, edited by Rollo May. New York: Braziller, 1959.

McCormick, Patrick. "Moral Theology 2000." *Catholic World*, September 1993, 212.

McDaniel, Jay B. *With Roots and Wings: Christianity in an Age of Ecology and Dialogue*. Maryknoll, N.Y.: Orbis Books, 1995.

McDannell, Colleen. *The Christian Home in Victorian America, 1840–1900*. Bloomington: Indiana University Press, 1986.

McDonald, Marci. "The New Spirituality." *Maclean's*, 10 October 1994.

McLoughlin, William G., Jr. *Billy Graham: Revivalist in a Secular Age*. New York: Ronald Press, 1960.

McPherson, Robert S. *Sacred Land, Sacred View: Navajo Perceptions of the Four Corners Region*. Salt Lake City: Signature Books, 1992.

Mead, Margaret. *Sex and Temperament in Three Primitive Societies*. 1935. Reprint, New York: Morrow Quill, 1980.

Mead, Sidney E. *The Lively Experiment: The Shaping of Christianity in America*. New York: Harper, 1963.

Mead, Sidney. E. *The Nation with the Soul of a Church*. 1967. Reprint, New York: Harper & Row, 1975.

Mercandante, Linda. "Victims and Sinners in an Age of Addiction." Paper presented at the Center of Theological Inquiry, Princeton, N.J., February 1994.

Merton, Thomas. *Collected Poems*. New York: New Directions, 1977.

Merton, Thomas. *The Strange Islands*. New York: New Directions, 1959.

Merton, Thomas. *Zen and the Birds of Appetite*. New York: New Directions, 1968.

Miller, J. Keith. *A Hunger for Healing: The Twelve Steps as a Classic Model for Christian Spiritual Growth*. San Francisco: Harper San Francisco, 1991.

Mills, C. Wright. *Power Elite*. New York: Oxford University Press, 1959.

Mills, C. Wright. *White Collar: The American Middle Classes*. New York: Oxford University Press, 1951.

"Modern Teens View Religion Differently." *Emerging Trends*, June 1994, 1–2.

Moore, Deborah Dash. *To the Golden Cities: Pursuing the American Jewish Dream in Miami and L.A.* New York: Free Press, 1994.

Moore, R. Laurence. *Religious Outsiders and the Making of Americans*. New York: Oxford University Press, 1986.

Moore, Thomas. *Care of the Soul: A Guide for Cultivating Depth and Sacredness in Everyday Life*. New York: HarperCollins, 1992.

Moos, Max von. *Angels and Men*. New York: Seabury, 1977.

Morrow, Lance. "The Bishop of Our Possibilities." *Time*, 10 May 1982, 124.

Neuger, Christie Cozad, ed. *The Arts of Ministry: Feminist-Womanist Approaches*. Louisville, Ky.: Westminster/John Knox, 1996.

Nichols, Martha. "Does New Age Business Have a Message for Managers?" *Harvard Business Review*, March 1994, 52.

Niebuhr, Reinhold. *The Irony of American History*. New York: Scribner's, 1952.

Niebuhr, Reinhold. "Is There a Revival of Religion?" *New York Times Magazine*, 10 November 1950, 1–12.

Nisbet, Robert A. *The Quest for Community*. New York: Oxford University Press, 1953.

Nixon, Richard. *Beyond Peace*. New York: Random House, 1994.

Noonan, Peggy. *What I Saw at the Revolution: A Political Life in the Reagan Era*. New York: Random House, 1990.

Norris, Kathleen. *Dakota: A Spiritual Geography*. New York: Ticknor and Fields, 1993.

Novak, Michael. *The Experience of Nothingness*. New York: Harper & Row, 1970.

Ochs, Carol. "The Presence in the Desert." *Cross Currents* 43 (1993): 293–306.

Oliver, Mary. *New and Selected Poems*. Boston: Beacon Press, 1992.

Orsi, Robert A. *Thank You, St. Jude: Women's Devotion to the Patron Saint of Hopeless Causes*. New Haven, Conn.: Yale University Press, 1996.

Ortlund, Anne. *Disciplines of the Beautiful Woman*. Waco, Tex.: Word Books, 1977.

Ortner, Sherry B. "Theory in Anthropology since the Sixties." *Comparative Studies in Society and History* 26 (1984): 126–166.

Ostergren, Robert C. "The Immigrant Church as a Symbol of Community and Place in the Upper Midwest." *Great Plains Quarterly* 1 (1981): 225–238.

Parfit, Derek. *Reasons and Persons*. Oxford: Clarendon Press, 1984.

Parisen, Maria. *Angels & Mortals: Their Co-creative Power*. New York: Quest, 1990.

Parsons, Talcott. "Personality as a Social System." In *Toward a General Theory of Action: Theoretical Foundations for the Social Sciences*, edited by Talcott Parsons and Edward A. Shils. New York: Harper & Row, 1951.

Parsons, Talcott. *The Social System*. New York: Free Press, 1951.

Parsons, Talcott. *The System of Modern Societies*. Englewood Cliffs, N.J.: Prentice-Hall, 1971.

Paulson, William. "Hearth and Homelessness: Place, Story, and Novel in Flaubert's *Sentimental Education*." In *Home and Its Dislocations in Nineteenth-Century France*, edited by Suzanne Nash. Albany: State University of New York Press, 1993.

Peale, Norman Vincent. *The Power of Positive Thinking*. Englewood Cliffs, N.J.: Prentice-Hall, 1952.

Peale, Norman Vincent. *Stay Alive All Your Life*. Englewood Cliffs, N.J.: Prentice-Hall, 1957.

Peck, M. Scott. *The Road Less Traveled: A New Psychology of Love, Traditional Values and Spiritual Growth*. New York: Simon & Schuster, 1978.

Peretti, Frank. *This Present Darkness*. New York: Crossway Books, 1989.

Plowman, Edward E. *The Underground Church*. Elgin, Ill.: David C. Cook, 1971.

Poirier, Richard. *Robert Frost: The Work of Knowing*. New York: Oxford University Press, 1977.

Poloma, Margaret M., and George H. Gallup, Jr. *Varieties of Prayer*. Philadelphia: Trinity Press International, 1991.

"Premarital Sex." *Gallup Report* 263 (August 1987): 1–4.

Price, John Randolph. *Angels within Us*. New York: Ballantine, 1993.

Quinley, Harold E. *The Prophetic Clergy: Social Activism among Protestant Ministers*. New York: Wiley, 1974.

Raz, Joseph. "Multiculturalism: A Liberal Perspective." *Dissent*, winter 1994, 67–79.

Reagan, Ronald. *In God I Trust*. Compiled by David R. Shepherd. Wheaton, Ill.: Tyndale House, 1984.

Reich, Charles A. *The Greening of America*. New York: Random House, 1970.

Remley, Anne. "From Obedience to Independence." *Psychology Today*, October 1988, 56–59.

Rice, John Steadman. *A Disease of One's Own: Psychotherapy, Addiction, and the Emergence of Co-dependency*. New Brunswick, N.J.: Transaction, 1995.

Rich, Adrienne. *What Is Found There: Notebooks on Poetry and Politics*. New York: Norton, 1994.

Rieff, Philip. *The Triumph of the Therapeutic: Uses of Faith after Freud*. New York: Harper & Row, 1966.

Riesman, David. *The Lonely Crowd: A Study of the Changing American Character*. 1950. Reprint, New Haven, Conn.: Yale University Press, 1961.

Robertson, Pat. *The Secret Kingdom*. Nashville, Tenn.: Nelson, 1982.

Rodderick, Anita. *Body and Soul: Profits with Principles—The Amazing Success Story of Anita Rodderick and The Body Shop*. New York: Crown, 1991.

Rogers, Carl R. *On Becoming a Person*. Boston: Houghton Mifflin, 1961.

Rogin, Michael Paul. *Ronald Reagan, the Movie and Other Episodes in Political Demonology*. Berkeley: University of California Press, 1987.

Ronner, John. *Do You Have a Guardian Angel?* Murfreesboro, Tenn.: Mamre Press, 1985.

Roof, Wade Clark. *A Generation of Seekers: The Spiritual Journeys of the Baby Boom Generation*. San Francisco: Harper San Francisco, 1993.

Rorty, Richard. *Objectivity, Relativism, and Truth: Philosophical Papers*, vol. 1. Cambridge: Cambridge University Press, 1991.

Rosenzweig, Bill, Mel Ziegler, and Patricia Ziegler. *The Republic of Tea: Letters to a Young Zentrepreneur*. New York: Doubleday, 1993.

Roszak, Theodore. *The Making of a Counter Culture: Reflections on the Technocratic Society and Its Youthful Opposition*. Garden City, N.Y.: Doubleday, 1969.

The Rule of Saint Benedict. Edited by Timothy Fry. Collegeville, Minn.: Liturgical Press, 1982.

Ryan, Mary P. *Cradle of the Middle-Class: The Family in Oneida County, New York, 1790–1865*. New York: Cambridge University Press, 1981.

Rybczynski, Witold. *The Most Beautiful House in the World*. New York: Penguin Books, 1989.

Saad, Lydia, and Leslie McAneny. "Most Americans Think Religion Losing Clout in the 1990s." *The Gallup Poll*, 14 April 1994, 1–2.

Saliers, Don E. *Worship and Spirituality*. Philadelphia: Westminster, 1984.

Sandel, Michael J. "Freedom of Conscience or Freedom of Choice." In *Articles of Faith, Articles of Peace: The Religious Liberty Clauses and the American Public Philosophy*, edited by James Davison Hunter and Os Guiness. Washington, D.C.: Brookings Institution, 1990.

Sandel, Michael J. *Liberalism and the Limits of Justice*. Cambridge: Cambridge University Press, 1982.

Santayana, George. *Character and Opinion in the United States*. 1920. Reprint, New Brunswick, N.J.: Transaction, 1991.

Sardello, Robert. *Love and the Soul*. New York: HarperCollins, 1995.

Schneider, Herbert W. *Religion in 20th Century America*. Cambridge, Mass.: Harvard University Press, 1952.

Schneider, Louis, and Sanford M. Dornbusch. *Popular Religion: Inspirational Books in America*. Chicago: University of Chicago Press, 1958.

Scott, Joan. *Gender and the Politics of History*. New York: Columbia University Press, 1988.

Senn, Frank C., ed. *Protestant Spiritual Traditions*. New York: Paulist Press, 1986.

Sennett, Richard. *The Fall of Public Man*. New York: Random House, 1976.

Sexson, Lynda. *Ordinarily Sacred*. New York: Crossroad, 1982.

Shanas, Ethel. "Social Myth as Hypothesis: The Case of the Family Relations of Old People." *Gerontologist* 19 (1979): 3–9.

Sheen, Fulton J. *Life Is Worth Living*. New York: McGraw-Hill, 1953.

Silbey, Uma. *Enlightenment on the Run: Everyday Life as a Spiritual Path*. San Rafael, Calif.: Airo Press, 1993.

Skolnick, Arlene. *Embattled Paradise: The American Family in an Age of Uncertainty*. New York: Basic Books, 1991.

Smelser, Neil J. *Theory of Collective Behavior*. New York: Free Press, 1962.

Smith, Timothy L. "Congregation, State, and Denomination: The Forming of the American Religious Structure." *William and Mary Quarterly* 25 (1968): 155–162.

Stave, Bruce M., and John F. Sutherland. *From the Old Country: An Oral History of European Migration to America*. New York: Twayne, 1994.

Steinem, Gloria. *Outrageous Acts and Everyday Rebellions*. New York: Holt, Rinehart & Winston, 1983.

Stout, Harry S. "Ethnicity: The Vital Center of Religion in America." *Ethnicity* 2 (1975): 204–224.

Stout, Jeffrey. *Ethics after Babel: The Languages of Morals and Their Discontents*. Boston: Beacon Press, 1988.

Streiker, Lowell. *New Age Comes to Main Street*. Nashville, Tenn.: Abingdon Press, 1990.

Strober, Gerald, and Ruth Tomczak. *Jerry Falwell: Aflame for God*. Nashville, Tenn.: Nelson, 1979.

Suzuki, Daisetz Teitaro. *Mysticism: Christian and Buddhist*. New York: Macmillan, 1957.

Swanson, Guy E. *The Birth of the Gods: The Origin of Primitive Beliefs*. Ann Arbor: University of Michigan Press, 1960.

Swinburne, Richard. *The Evolution of the Soul*. Oxford: Clarendon Press, 1986.

Tannen, Deborah. *You Just Don't Understand: Women and Men in Conversation*. New York: Ballantine, 1990.

Taves, Ann. *The Household of Faith: Roman Catholic Devotions in Mid-Nineteenth-Century America*. Notre Dame, Ind.: University of Notre Dame Press, 1986.

Taylor, Brian C. *Spirituality for Everyday Living: An Adaptation of the Rule of St. Benedict*. Collegeville, Minn.: Liturgical Press, 1989.

Taylor, Charles. *Human Agency and Language*. Cambridge: Cambridge University Press, 1985.

Taylor, Charles. *Sources of the Self: The Making of the Modern Identity*. Cambridge, Mass.: Harvard University Press, 1989.

Taylor, Eugene. "Desperately Seeking Spirituality." *Psychology Today*, November/December 1994, 54–68.

Taylor, Terry Lynn. *Answers from Angels: A Book of Angel Letters*. New York: Kramer, 1992.

Taylor, Terry Lynn. *Creating with the Angels*. New York: Kramer, 1993.

Taylor, Terry Lynn. *Guardians of Hope: The Angels Guide to Personal Growth*. New York: Kramer, 1991.

Taylor, Terry Lynn. *Messengers of Light: The Angels Guide to Spiritual Growth*. New York: Kramer, 1990.

Teresa of Avila. *Autobiography*. Edited by E. Allison Peters. New York: Image Books, 1991.

Teresa of Avila. *Interior Castle*. Edited by E. Allison Peters. New York: Image Books, 1961.

Thomas, George M., John W. Meyer, Francisco O. Ramirez, and John Boli. *Institutional Structure: Constituting State, Society, and the Individual*. Beverly Hills, Calif.: Sage, 1987.

Thomas, John L. *The American Catholic Family*. Englewood Cliffs, N.J.: Prentice-Hall, 1956.

Tillich, Paul. *The Protestant Era*. Chicago: University of Chicago Press, 1948.

Tipton, Steven M. *Getting Saved from the Sixties: Moral Meaning in Conversion and Cultural Change*. Berkeley: University of California Press, 1982.

Troeltsch, Ernst. *The Social Teaching of the Christian Churches*. 2 vols. 1931. Reprint, New York: Harper & Row, 1960.

Truitt, Ann. *Daybook*. New York: Pantheon Books, 1982.

Tuck, Richard. "Rights and Pluralism." In *Philosophy in an Age of Pluralism: The Philosophy of Charles Taylor in Question*, edited by James Tully. Cambridge: Cambridge University Press, 1994.

Turner, James. *Without God, without Creed: The Origins of Unbelief in America*. Baltimore: Johns Hopkins University Press, 1985.

Turner, Stephen. *The Social Theory of Practices: Tradition, Tacit Knowledge, and Presuppositions*. Chicago: University of Chicago Press, 1994.

Tytell, John. *Naked Angels: The Lives and Literature of the Beat Generation*. New York: McGraw-Hill, 1976.

Ulanov, Ann, and Barry Ulanov. *Primary Speech: A Psychology of Prayer*. Louisville, Ky.: Westminster/John Knox, 1982.

Underhill, Ralph. "Economic and Political Antecedents of Monotheism: A Cross-Cultural Study." *American Journal of Sociology* 80 (1975): 841–861.

U.S. National Commission on Excellence in Education. *A Nation at Risk*. Cambridge, Mass.: USA Research, 1984.

Van Dyne, Larry. "'How Do You Feel about That, Mr. President?'" *Washingtonian*, June 1994, 1–3.

Vidich, Arthur R., and Joseph Bensman. *Small Town in Mass Society: Class, Power, and Religion in a Rural Community*. Princeton, N.J.: Princeton University Press, 1958.

Walsh, John P. *Supermarkets Transformed: Understanding Organizational and Technological Innovations*. New Brunswick, N.J.: Rutgers University Press, 1994.

Walzer, Michael. *Thick and Thin: Moral Argument at Home and Abroad*. Notre Dame, Ind.: University of Notre Dame Press, 1994.

Washington, Joseph R., Jr. *Black Religion: The Negro and Christianity in the United States*. Boston: Beacon Press, 1964.

Watts, Alan. *The Spirit of Zen: A Way of Life*. New York: Grove Press, 1969.

Weaver, Mary Jo. *New Catholic Women*. Bloomington: Indiana University Press, 1995.

Weber, Max. *The Protestant Ethic and the Spirit of Capitalism*. 1904–1905. Reprint, New York: Scribner's, 1958.

Weber, Max. *The Sociology of Religion*. 1922. Reprint, Boston: Beacon Press, 1993.

Weisser, Michael R. *A Brotherhood of Memory: Jewish Landsmanshaftn in the New World*. New York: Basic Books, 1985.

"What (and What Not) to Pray For." *Emerging Trends*, April 1994, 1–4.

Whyte, William H., Jr. *The Organization Man*. Garden City, N.Y.: Doubleday, 1956.

Will, George F. *The Pursuit of Virtue and Other Tory Notions*. New York: Simon & Schuster, 1982.

Winter, Gibson. *Being Free: Reflections on America's Cultural Revolution.* New York: Macmillan, 1970.

Wood, Ralph C. "A River Runs Through It." *Christian Century,* 20 January 1993, 44.

Woodward, Bob. *The Agenda: Inside the Clinton White House.* New York: Simon & Schuster, 1994.

Woodward, Kenneth L. "A Time to Seek." *Newsweek,* 17 December 1990, 50.

Wrong, Dennis H. "The Oversocialized Conception of Man in Modern Sociology." *American Sociological Review* 26 (1961): 183–193.

Wuthnow, Robert. *Acts of Compassion: Caring for Others and Helping Ourselves.* Princeton, N.J.: Princeton University Press, 1991.

Wuthnow, Robert. *The Consciousness Reformation.* Berkeley: University of California Press, 1976.

Wuthnow, Robert. *Experimentation in American Religion.* Berkeley: University of California Press, 1978.

Wuthnow, Robert. *God and Mammon in America.* New York: Free Press, 1994.

Wuthnow, Robert. *The Restructuring of American Religion: Society and Faith since World War II.* Princeton, N.J.: Princeton University Press, 1988.

Wuthnow, Robert. *Sharing the Journey: Support Groups and America's New Quest for Community.* New York: Free Press, 1994.

Wyschogrod, Edith. *Saints and Postmodernism: Revisioning Moral Philosophy.* Chicago: University of Chicago Press, 1990.

Yankelovich, Skelly and White, Inc. *The 1978 Consumer Research Study on Reading and Book Purchasing.* Darien, Conn.: Book Industry Study Group, 1978.

York, Richard L. "Days after Block Island." In *Search for the Sacred: The New Spiritual Quest,* edited by Myron B. Bloy, Jr. New York: Seabury, 1972.

Zagarri, Rosemarie. "Morals, Manners, and the Republican Mother." *American Quarterly* 44 (1992): 192–215.

Zerubavel, Eviatar. *Hidden Rhythms: Schedules and Calendars in Social Life.* Berkeley: University of California Press, 1981.

Zuckerman, Michael. "Dr. Spock: The Confidence Man." In *The Family in History,* edited by Charles E. Rosenberg. Philadelphia: University of Pennsylvania Press, 1975.

Zuckerman, Michael. "Holy Wars, Civil Wars: Religion and Economics in Nineteenth-Century America." *Prospects* 16 (1991): 205–240.

Index

Compositor:	BookMasters, Inc.
Text:	10/13 Sabon
Display:	Sabon and Bickham Script
Printer and Binder:	Haddon Craftsmen, Inc.